International Political Economy Series

General Editor: Timothy M. Shaw, Professor and Director, Institute of International Relations, The University of the West Indies, Trinidad & Tobago

Titles include:

Leslie Elliott Armijo (*editor*)
FINANCIAL GLOBALIZATION AND DEMOCRACY IN EMERGING MARKETS

Robert Boardman
THE POLITICAL ECONOMY OF NATURE
Environmental Debates and the Social Sciences

Jörn Brömmelhörster and Wolf-Christian Paes *(editors)*
THE MILITARY AS AN ECONOMIC ACTOR
Soldiers in Business

Gerard Clarke and Michael Jennings *(editor)*
DEVELOPMENT, CIVIL SOCIETY AND FAITH-BASED ORGANIZATIONS
Bridging the Sacred and the Secular

Gordon Crawford
FOREIGN AID AND POLITICAL REFORM
A Comparative Analysis of Democracy Assistance and Political Conditionality

Matt Davies
INTERNATIONAL POLITICAL ECONOMY AND MASS COMMUNICATION IN CHILE
National Intellectuals and Transnational Hegemony

Martin Doornbos
INSTITUTIONALIZING DEVELOPMENT POLICIES AND RESOURCE STRATEGIES IN EASTERN AFRICA AND INDIA
Developing Winners and Losers

Fred P. Gale
THE TROPICAL TIMBER TRADE REGIME

Meric S. Gertler and David A. Wolfe
INNOVATION AND SOCIAL LEARNING
Institutional Adaptation in an Era of Technological Change

Anne Marie Goetz and Rob Jenkins
REINVENTING ACCOUNTABILITY
Making Democracy Work for the Poor

Andrea Goldstein
MULTINATIONAL COMPANIES FROM EMERGING ECONOMIES
Composition, Conceptualization and Direction in the Global Economy

Mary Ann Haley
FREEDOM AND FINANCE
Democratization and Institutional Investors in Developing Countries

Keith M. Henderson and O. P. Dwivedi (*editors*)
BUREAUCRACY AND THE ALTERNATIVES IN WORLD PERSPECTIVES

Jomo K.S. and Shyamala Nagaraj (*editors*)
GLOBALIZATION VERSUS DEVELOPMENT

Angela W. Little
LABOURING TO LEARN
Towards a Political Economy of Plantations, People and Education in Sri Lanka

John Loxley *(editor)*
INTERDEPENDENCE, DISEQUILIBRIUM AND GROWTH
Reflections on the Political Economy of North–South Relations at the Turn of the Century

Don D. Marshall
CARIBBEAN POLITICAL ECONOMY AT THE CROSSROADS
NAFTA and Regional Developmentalism

Susan M. McMillan
FOREIGN DIRECT INVESTMENT IN THREE REGIONS OF THE SOUTH AT THE END OF THE TWENTIETH CENTURY

S. Javed Maswood
THE SOUTH IN INTERNATIONAL ECONOMIC REGIMES
Whose Globalization?

John Minns
THE POLITICS OF DEVELOPMENTALISM
The Midas States of Mexico, South Korea and Taiwan

Philip Nel
THE POLITICS OF ECONOMIC INEQUALITY IN DEVELOPING COUNTRIES

Lars Rudebeck, Olle Törnquist and Virgilio Rojas *(editors)*
DEMOCRATIZATION IN THE THIRD WORLD
Concrete Cases in Comparative and Theoretical Perspective

Benu Schneider *(editor)*
THE ROAD TO INTERNATIONAL FINANCIAL STABILITY
Are Key Financial Standards the Answer?

Howard Stein *(editor)*
ASIAN INDUSTRIALIZATION AND AFRICA
Studies in Policy Alternatives to Structural Adjustment

William Vlcek
OFFSHORE FINANCE AND SMALL STATES
Sovereignty, Size and Money

International Political Economy Series
Series Standing Order ISBN 978–0–333–71708–0 hardcover
Series Standing Order ISBN 978–0–333–71110–1 paperback
(outside North America only)

You can receive future titles in this series as they are published by placing a standing order. Please contact your bookseller or, in case of difficulty, write to us at the address below with your name and address, the title of the series and one of the ISBNs quoted above.

Customer Services Department, Macmillan Distribution Ltd, Houndmills, Basingstoke, Hampshire RG21 6XS, England

---

Offshore Finance and Small States

Sovereignty, Size and Money

William Vlcek
Lecturer in International Politics
Institute of Commonwealth Studies
University of London

palgrave
macmillan

First published 2008 by
PALGRAVE MACMILLAN
Houndmills, Basingstoke, Hampshire RG21 6XS and
175 Fifth Avenue, New York, N.Y. 10010
Companies and representatives throughout the world

PALGRAVE MACMILLAN is the global academic imprint of the Palgrave Macmillan division of St. Martin's Press, LLC and of Palgrave Macmillan Ltd. Macmillan® is a registered trademark in the United States, United Kingdom and other countries. Palgrave is a registered trademark in the European Union and other countries.

ISBN 13: 978–0–230–52220–6 hardback
ISBN 10: 0–230–52220–3 hardback

This book is printed on paper suitable for recycling and made from fully managed and sustained forest sources. Logging, pulping and manufacturing processes are expected to conform to the environmental regulations of the country of origin.

A catalogue record for this book is available from the British Library.

A catalogue record for this book is available from the Library of Congress.

10 9 8 7 6 5 4 3 2 1
17 16 15 14 13 12 11 10 09 08

Printed and bound in Great Britain by
CPI Antony Rowe, Chippenham and Eastbourne

Contents

Acronyms

AOSIS	Alliance of Small Island States
BIS	Bank for International Settlements
CAP	Common Agricultural Policy
CARICOM	Caribbean Community
CHOGM	Commonwealth Heads of Government Meeting
CIMA	Cayman Islands Monetary Authority
CMGSS	Commonwealth Ministerial Group on Small States
CVI	Commonwealth Vulnerability Index
ECCB	Eastern Caribbean Central Bank
ECCU	Eastern Caribbean Currency Union
EU	European Union
FATF	Financial Action Task Force
FDI	Foreign Direct Investment
FTAA	Free Trade Agreement of the Americas
GATS	General Agreement on Trade in Services
GATT	General Agreement on Tariffs and Trade
GDP	Gross Domestic Product
GNI	Gross National Income
HTCI	Harmful Tax Competition Initiative
IBC	International Business Company
IFC	International Financial Center
IFSA	International Financial Services Authority
IGO	International Governmental Organization
IMF	International Monetary Fund
IRS	Internal Revenue Service
ISO	International Organization for Standardization
ITIO	International Trade and Investment Organization
LDC	Less Developed Country
LLDC	Lesser Less Developed Country
MNC	Multinational Corporation
NCCT	Non-Cooperative Countries and Territories
NGO	Non-Governmental Organization

OECD	Organization for Economic Co-operation and Development
OED	Oxford English Dictionary
OFC	Offshore Financial Center
RNM	Regional Negotiating Machinery
SAR	Special Administrative Region
SDEs	Small and Developing Economies
SIDSnet	Small Island Developing States Network
SIE	Small Island Economy
UN	United Nations
USA PATRIOT Act	Uniting and Strengthening America by Providing Appropriate Tools Required to Intercept and Obstruct Terrorism (USA PATRIOT) Act
VAT	Value Added Tax
WTO	World Trade Organization

List of Tables and Figures

Tables

Figures

Preface and Acknowledgments

While there are a number of journalistic accounts about offshore finance, there have been few academic book-length analyzes of the phenomenon. Similarly, there are a number of popular statements concerning the detrimental impact for development and social welfare as a result of tax competition, yet outside of the ongoing debate within the economics discipline there are few studies that consider the *politics* of tax competition. This study seeks to contribute to the wider debates involving globalization and global finance through an analysis of the understudied arena that is the international politics of offshore finance and tax competition. It is, as stated quite clearly in the title of this study, all about sovereignty, size, and money.

The introductory chapter of the book investigates the size variable and here it is about the size of the jurisdiction and not the size of the financial sector within that jurisdiction. Specifically, size is used to distinguish a specific group of jurisdictions that have come to use the offshore financial sector specifically as an economic development path. In the early days of decolonization, solutions were sought as a way to assure the economic independence of soon-to-be new states. The first new states including India, Pakistan, and Ghana all possessed populations, natural resources and manufacturing capabilities sufficiently large that they readily provided opportunities for economic development. Some later, smaller states were not so blessed and in fact, there were debates in the British government during the mid-1950s over the question of whether some of the smaller British colonies could ever become an economically self-sufficient independent jurisdiction. Some in government argued that an offshore financial center (OFC) provided a low-impact, high-gain approach to economic development in a small island jurisdiction, a viewpoint that had its supporters up until the time of the case study that sits at the center of this analysis.

Sovereignty is the critical variable in this study, for as explained in Chapter 2 it is state sovereignty that provides these small states the opportunity and means for regulatory arbitrage and the redesignation of national identity. These features are extremely useful in international finance to minimize tax and take advantage of investment opportunities designed to benefit a specific form of capital. One example of this would be 'round-tripping', in which domestic capital is transferred to a foreign – offshore – jurisdiction before returning as a 'foreign' direct investment in order to benefit from the tax reductions or holidays established to attract foreign investment capital in preference to domestic investment capital. States make the rules about business regulation, finance and accounting, yet they very often treat foreign-sourced capital and foreign-based corporations differently from domestic capital and corporations. OFCs hosting banking facilities and international business company registrars provide the means for domestic businesses to manipulate legislation in ways there were not intended by their drafting legislatures. At the same time, keep in mind that any sovereign jurisdiction is effectively 'offshore' to any other sovereign jurisdiction. Consequently, the United States is just as much an offshore jurisdiction for purposes of a European citizen as is the Cayman Islands, Dubai, Singapore and Hong Kong.

The third variable is money, though truthfully it is not a variable so much as it is a constant, a constant that serves to facilitate and motivate international commerce and the late twentieth century phenomenon known as globalization. International flows of capital in pursuit of a higher rate of return and diversification of investment vehicle have driven first the emergence and then the growth of the international banking center that operates in multiple currencies. Admittedly, this variable also takes us into the 'dark-side' of globalization, for while money may have a color (think US greenbacks) it has no loyalty or sense of morality. Money is ethically and politically neutral, a means to an end and a medium of exchange in the marketplace. Consequently, any encounter with offshore finance also brings up questions about money laundering and the various predicate crimes that bring about the need to clean money of its illegal or illicit origins. Since 2001, this dark-side of globalization has also brought about questions of terrorist financing and the pursuit of ways and means to combat terrorism via a reduction, and ultimately the elimination, of the flow of money to the terrorist. These matters will also be discussed when and where appropriate in the following analysis.

Charles Kindleberger recognized the essential hurdle confronting any solution to the problems of cross-border taxation and tax competition. 'Harmonization, whether in complete or in optimal deregulation, however the latter may be defined, means of course a loss of national sovereignty for the harmonizing countries.' (Kindleberger, 1987: p. 73) Conceding sovereignty is not something states, large or small, are readily willing to undertake. To control their tax structure (fiscal sovereignty) is to control many (if not all) aspects of their domestic economy. Issues of national culture, preferred approaches to social welfare, and income re-distribution are merely items at the top of the list impacted by tax harmonization. Because of the obvious difficulty in achieving global tax harmonization, the Organization for Economic Co-operation and Development (OECD) appears on the surface to be approaching this problem by forcing small non-member states to undergo changes that are in the best interests of OECD members with its representation as a global problem and the resolution as a global public good. The complexities of this case study are outlined in the first chapter along with a discussion of the offshore concept and its place in global finance.

The tax competition project has been constructed as global in scope and execution. To analyze it in its entirety would be a formidable task and consequently, this book is limited to a specific consideration of several Caribbean jurisdictions associated with the Commonwealth. These constraints provide for an evaluation of a number of factors that influenced the evolution of the OECD project, and the efforts of small states to resist it. As already suggested, the common legal tradition of most Commonwealth members is fundamental to the regulatory structures of offshore finance. In support of these small states the Commonwealth Secretariat provides assistance in a number of areas, including the development of model laws, guidance for economic development, and as a collective voice within international fora against the OECD position on tax competition.

The second chapter lays out the theoretical foundations for sovereignty as a state practice in international politics. It introduces to the discussion non-self-governing territories, because these *semi*-sovereign entities in some cases also use offshore finance as a method for economic development. It considers taxation in the modern state, legal differences between states over questions of tax avoidance and tax evasion, and representative viewpoints on state responsibility for providing tax-related information to another state. The chapter then considers the impact of state sovereignty on this issue of taxation and tax competition, and in particular the choice of whether or not, and how much, to tax its residents and citizens. In the argument made by the OECD, globalization has reduced the ability of the state to collect the tax it is owed. State borders are no longer the barrier to the movement of capital they once were, yet they remain a barrier to the transfer of taxpayer information.

The discussion turns to global financial governance and tax competition in Chapter 3. The OFC has been implicated across four significant threads in the discourse of global financial governance: money laundering, tax evasion, capital flight and terrorist financing. In large measure these threads are conflated in public debate and upon occasion the distinctions between them have been intentionally blurred by policy promoters. These issues must be kept separate, however, because there are clear legal and social implications emerging from each problem. The prior presence of a global anti-money laundering initiative has led to its use as a 'smoke screen' for the OECD's campaign against tax competition. Chapter 3 opens with a discussion of the global anti-money laundering regime, while the specific economic and legal consequences for the Caribbean jurisdictions from this regime are addressed in Chapter 6. The third chapter then explains the OECD's argument for the existence of harmful tax competition, analyzes its argument that the problem is global in nature and therefore requires a global response. After introducing the OECD's Harmful Tax Competition Initiative (HTCI) as its proposed method to counter these 'harmful' tax regimes, the chapter presents a critique of the project that emerged from inside the organization itself, from those member states with significant financial services business sectors.

The response of the small states to the OECD project is presented in Chapter 4. These small states made three significant arguments against the OECD project: firstly, that it was a violation of the internationally accepted principle of state sovereignty; second, that the OECD was not the correct international forum to produce a global solution because, as a club of thirty developed states, it does not possess appropriate global representation; and third, there was the appearance of differential treatment between the OECD members and the non-OECD states identified by the project. Then the chapter provides the OECD rebuttal to these criticisms, and closes with a review of the role and influence of the United States in this case study, where it first supported the OECD project in 1998 and then withdrew that support in 2001.

From this specific review of the OECD tax competition project, the book turns to the larger context in which these events occurred. In Chapter 5 the Commonwealth is introduced as a site of collective action for the many small states that were formerly part of the British Empire. The Commonwealth Secretariat facilitated discussions and engagement with the OECD on behalf of its members and these activities are recounted with an analysis of their effectiveness for the goals desired by small Caribbean states. There are a number of non-self-governing jurisdictions which host an OFC yet are not independent members of either the Commonwealth or many other international organizations. One solution for this situation was the creation of an international organization representing the interests of all OFCs.

The focus in Chapter 6 is placed on the specific circumstances of offshore finance in four representative Caribbean OFCs. It opens with a survey of the many challenges confronting a small island economy; particularly those affecting development and those that arise from the geographic particularities of an island. Then the chapter analyzes the contribution made by the OFC to the economies of three Caribbean states, the Bahamas, Dominica, and St. Vincent and the Grenadines, and the non-self-governing territory (and exemplar of the OFC) the Cayman Islands. The chapter closes with a consideration of the wider implications of offshore finance as part of global capital flows through the Caribbean.

The concluding chapter summarizes the argument and draws out several very specific observations about small states and sovereignty within the global political economy. The resistance of small states toward the OECD and its project demonstrates the continuing importance placed on sovereignty by post-colonial states. Moreover, it reminds us that small states can exercise influence within international politics when able to achieve some form of collective or coordinated position. Naturally, there is an acknowledgment that the actions and decisions of the United States, as a major (if not the most significant) participant in the OECD and the world economy more generally, was an important influence upon the progress of the HTCI. This review leaves us to consider the implications to be drawn from this specific case study for the position of small states in the global political economy of the twenty-first century.

This book emerges from a PhD dissertation (thesis in the lexicon of the British university system) completed at the London School of Economics and Political Science in 2005. I have endeavored to make it more readable than is common to a dissertation, as well as incorporated new material and data from the past couple of years. The reader should understand, however, that the case study at the center of this analysis remains an unresolved matter in international finance and consequently this analysis addresses only a snapshot of the events and institutions involved. At the same time, it is my hope that after reading this text many will gain an improved understanding of the present state of affairs regarding offshore finance, tax competition between states and the complexities of global financial governance, whenever that present point in time may be.

In addition to the acknowledgments contained in the dissertation addressed to all and sundry family, friends and colleagues I have accumulated further debts along the path to the production of this book. I must also thank my colleagues at the Institute of Commonwealth Studies in the University of London, where I spent the year in which I revised this manuscript as Lecturer in International Politics and Convener of the MSc in Globalization and Development program. The convivial and supportive atmosphere provided by the academic, administrative and library staff was beneficial to making the task more pleasant than I could have expected. Further thanks are due to Professor Christopher Hill, my supervisor for his continued support, Professor James Mayall and Dr. Paul Sutton, my examiners for their encouragement to publish this manuscript, and Professor Timothy Shaw for accepting it for his International Political Economy Series (and also for the subtle reminders anytime I ran into him at conferences, seminars and on the streets of London to keep working on it). Finally there is a very good friend, Linda Dilley, who tackled the full manuscript with little prior knowledge of the discipline and provided numerous probing questions and aesthetic feedback intended to help me produce a readable text. Notwithstanding all the help and support from these many people I remain solely responsible for all statements, opinions and critiques contained in this text.

Acknowledgments

Chapter 6 includes revised material previously published as 'Why Worry? The Impact of the OECD Harmful Tax Competition Initiative for Caribbean Offshore Financial Centres', *The Round Table: The Commonwealth Journal of International Affairs*, vol. 96, no. 390 (June 2007), pp. 331–346.

My thanks to Columbia University Press for permission to reproduce the quotation that serves as the epigram for Chapter 3 from Robert Andrews, Mary Biggs and Michael Seidel, et al., eds, *The Columbia World of Quotations* (New York: Columbia University Press, 1996).

The population data in Tables 1.1–1.5 is reprinted with kind permission of the United Nations Population Division.

The Cayman Islands Government Economics and Statistics Office has permitted the inclusion of excerpted data from the *Cayman Islands Annual Economic Reports* in Chapter 6 when accompanied by the following disclaimer:

> "The Economics & Statistics Office (ESO) takes care to ensure that the information supplied in our publications and website is correct. However, no warranty, expressed or implied, is given as to its accuracy and the ESO and Government of the Cayman Islands do not accept any liability for error or omission. ESO and the Government of the Cayman Islands are not responsible for how the information is used, how it is interpreted or what reliance is placed on it."

The epigram for Chapter 6, from Shridath Ramphal, 'Small is Beautiful But Vulnerable', *The Round Table: The Commonwealth Journal of International Affairs*, no. 292 (1984), p. 369, published by Taylor & Francis Ltd, http://www.informaworld.com, and reprinted by permission of the publisher.

The Eastern Caribbean Central Bank has granted permission for the inclusion of statistical data in Chapter 6, subject to the disclaimer and copyright notice found on its web site, http://www.eccb-centralbank.org/disclaimer.asp.

1
International Norms and the Practice of Sovereignty

> One lesson seems clear: that the difficulty of damming money flows in separate countries will require cooperation, achieved with intermittent gains and setbacks, in surveillance of money and capital markets when disturbed, and ultimately in the coordination of monetary and fiscal policies.
>
> – Charles Kindleberger[1]

In the closing decade of the twentieth century, the end of the Cold War brought with it a flowering of multilateralism that seemed to flourish in a zeitgeist of globalization (Rosenberg, 2005). State interactions were no longer framed in terms of an East-West conflict and consequently it seemed as if this change opened up a freedom of action on the part of all states and not simply those with significant military or economic power. Freed from the confines of this ideological conflict, the impression developed that every voice would be heard and every issue discussed, with equal treatment for all in a renewed drive towards the collective benefit of humanity.

As the global community adjusted to the absence of Cold War rivalry, it became increasingly apparent that while it was a new day the same old song continued to play. Only now, it was more often economic power that dominated inter-state relations, rather than military power. The problem remained that small states generally lack economic power as much as they lack military power. Within this global situation resides the question considered here – how have small states been able to maintain a sense of sovereign independence when confronted by pressures to change that originate from their larger peers? Of particular interest is the variety of ways in which the influences of large states operate behind the guise of multilateral initiatives. These global governance initiatives are often represented to the public under a rubric claiming that, if they succeed, they will create a harmonious environment for the betterment of humanity through multilateral cooperation and by providing global public goods.

Against a backdrop painted with images depicting globalization debates, a retreating state, and humanitarian interventions, this book argues a case for the continued relevance of state sovereignty in an international society of states. Indeed, not only does sovereignty remain relevant, but it may also be that its most jealous guardians are the smallest of states. Whatever the argument made about the decline and evisceration of state sovereignty, the fact remains that the world is composed of states which constrain and construct the lives of those existing within their borders, both actual (natural) persons and corporate (legal) persons. The essential concern behind the case study analyzed below was recognized by Charles Kindleberger twenty years ago – regulatory arbitrage permitted by state sovereignty permits opportunities for some that may be detrimental to the welfare of others.

> [T]here should be some harmonization of various national laws, making differences in legal approaches unimportant as incentives for movement of capital. Such harmonization is difficult to achieve in a world of sovereign states. It involves ganging up on the Luxembourgs, Liechtensteins, Bahamas and the like to undermine their advantage as tax havens emanating from the sovereign right to set levels of taxation and to protect business dealing within the jurisdiction with laws ensuring secrecy. (Kindleberger, 1987: p. 73)

As will be seen, this problem maps on to both the North-South axis of disagreement and a trans-Atlantic axis of disagreement, due in part to differing perceptions of sovereignty, and in particular taxation as an element of *fiscal* sovereignty.

The argument presented here involves small states and their participation in international society at the beginning of the twenty-first century. The elements of this account of small state sovereignty are the Organization for Economic Co-operation and Development (OECD), tax collection, and offshore financial centers (OFCs). In using the OECD initiative to eliminate harmful tax competition as a case study, the focus is not on tax competition or the political economy of taxation. Naturally, these matters must be discussed in order to understand some of the background and premises behind the disagreement between the OECD and a number of small states. Nevertheless, the main point of interest and focus here rests on an effort guided by the OECD to overturn the domestic decisions made by sovereign states for their economic development. The changes demanded by the OECD affect the domestic politics of taxation and financial (banking) legislation. These events are framed as a case of intervention by the OECD (and its member states) in the sovereign independent status of those states hosting an OFC. Individually and collectively, a number of small states with an OFC responded to this intervention, as they strove to maintain their sense of sovereign independence while pursuing economic development for the general welfare of their residents.

The justification for this act of international intervention emerges from a domestic problem experienced particularly by OECD states, that is the collection of income taxes from their own recalcitrant residents. Fiscal sovereignty, as one facet of state sovereignty, anticipates that not only is a society free to choose its preferences about taxation (whether to impose a tax, what to tax, and how much tax to apply), but that it possesses the capability to collect these taxes from the members of that society. Increasing economic links between different tax jurisdictions exacerbate a problem that tax administrations have struggled with since their earliest days – the avoidance and evasion of paying taxes.

This Harmful Tax Competition Initiative (HTCI) of the OECD has been used by several authors to analyze norms in international relations. Michael Webb, for example, framed the entire conflict between the small states and the OECD as one in which norms represented the pivotal feature.

> The havens tried to persuade the OECD to abandon its campaign against HTC by framing the campaign as inconsistent with norms promoted by OECD countries. ... The HTC initiative was depicted as inconsistent with multilateralism, which the havens (like small countries everywhere) argued was a long-standing norm of international diplomacy. (Webb, 2004: p. 807)

A problem with Webb's approach is the fact that it ignores the innate 'actorness' of the small states as sovereign entities. It is not simply the fact that the small states seek to operate within the prevalent norms of international society when arguing that the actions of the OECD (or individual members) are 'inconsistent with multilateralism'. But it is also the fact that they were operating as sovereign actors when first they decided to establish an OFC and then later when forced to defend their decision and to question the relative value of cooperation with the OECD versus their own economic development. In effect, the small states have challenged the other sovereign states that belong to the OECD not only to 'talk the talk' of inclusive multilateral decision-making processes, but also now to 'walk the walk'. Jason Sharman argues that the continued resistance of the Pacific island OFCs 'can be explained by the suspicion that the new standards simply cannot be met by individual countries, and even pooling resources at the regional level may not be sufficient.' Consequently, because they lacked the capacity and means required to cooperate these small states had nothing to lose through continued recalcitrance. (Sharman, 2005: p. 317) Sharman indicated that a frank offer to cooperate with the Financial Action Task Force's (FATF) anti-money laundering initiatives for US$10 million was made by Nauru. He suggested that side-payments for cooperation from the Pacific jurisdictions would be low cost relative to the reputed lost tax revenues attributed to these 'tax havens'. However, he reported that 'no such deal looks likely in the near future.' (Sharman, 2005: pp. 319–321) On the other hand, William Wechsler depicted this response as not 'constructive', ignoring completely in this request for compensation the fundamental contribution to economic development made by Nauru's financial center (Wechsler, 2001: p. 54). In addition to these normative arguments about the interchange between the OECD and the small jurisdictions with OFCs, a *legal* argument that 'offshore structures and policies are inherently legitimate' was also developed (Antoine, 2001).

The arguments made by these authors concerning the importance of norms within the engagement (negotiations) between the OECD and the small states are interesting and relevant in, and of, themselves. However, they explain what (norms as a measure of legitimacy) or how (norms as a 'weapon of the weak' in the discourse) without explaining the *why*. The conclusion from the analysis presented here is that sovereignty (as a concept) is the answer to the *why* question. The desire to retain freedom of choice and action as a practice of the sovereign state explains why small states first, chose to pursue an economic strategy involving offshore finance, and second, why some have resisted the efforts of the OECD that they concede their sovereignty by cooperating fully and completely with the desires of developed states' own economic strategies. The point is not whether it is norms or interests that are used by small states to resist the efforts of the OECD. It is the fact that they persisted in resisting, in asserting their sovereign independence and insisting upon their freedom to choose and act in a fashion that serves to advance their domestic economic development. In this view, small states are the same as large states – for it is their sovereign independence and freedom to act in support of their domestic economies that drove the OECD member states to establish the tax competition initiative in the first place.

From this brief outline of the situation, this chapter now turns to explain the relevance of size as a factor in relations between states. This explanation is followed by a short discussion on several fundamental issues involving taxation. The third section of the chapter presents the emergence of OFCs as a component of the global financial system in the second half of the twentieth century. In presenting the story of the evolution of the offshore it also discusses the role of the legal tradition found in many of the OFCs and the use of an OFC for economic development.

What does size have to do with it?

Small states exist on the margins of international relations research in a fashion reflecting the very nature and structure of international society itself. This may be because they are not as 'sexy' as powerful states and imperial powers as a research topic. On the other hand, it may result from the fact that they lack an indigenous research establishment large enough to aggressively promote a research agenda focused on the interests and issues of the small state. Very often small states are viewed as existing on the periphery of the major powers – either as the victims of political action, or as suppliers and consumers of the goods and services produced by major states. This is certainly the situation within much of the research that includes the small states of the Caribbean.

World events in the closing decade of the twentieth century opened different opportunities for the economic potential of the small state to be realized. Whether we identify present circumstances as interdependence (1970s terminology) or globalization (1990s terminology) the redistribution of production that is facilitated by technology (telecommunications), transportation (containerization) and labor cost differentials (that may now be extensively utilized because of the first two factors) provides a space in the global economy in which a small state with limited capabilities/capacities may still prosper. The significant point to emphasize is that it is *global*, that opportunity exists beyond the nearest neighbors of the small state to encompass any potential customer and supplier. And global capital flows are the lubricant to this engine of commerce.

Success, however, involves competition, and competition has losers, as well as winners. Moreover, the redistribution of production applies to illegal and illicit goods and services just as much as it does to the legal/licit economy.[2] If a small state, or the ruling coterie of a small state, is so inclined there are also avenues of profit available from the illegal as well as from legitimate economic endeavors.[3] The economic subsector considered in this book permits the opportunity to benefit from illegal conduct, and in several instances this opportunity has been taken, much to the reputational detriment of the financial industry as a whole in these small economies. Throughout, the case remains that these jurisdictions insist upon an acknowledgment of their *sovereign* status as a participant in the society of states. Even when and where the constraints of a given situation limit the opportunities for independent action, the small state *expects* equal treatment and recognition for their sovereign independence, irrespective of their size, when it impacts/involves their population and economic well-being.

A number of these small jurisdictions exercise some influence within the realm of international finance. They operate as nodal points in the web of banks and financial institutions that interlace the world via electronic connections. A reference to any one of these jurisdictions is likely to sprinkle the conversations of financial analysts and government regulators, and the specific jurisdiction identified will only differ as a result of one's location or range of interests – the Bahamas, Luxembourg, Vanuatu. Along with these sovereign states are a number of non-self-governing territories that also participate in the offshore financial industry, most prominently the British Overseas Territory of the Cayman Islands. In the discussion that follows 'jurisdiction' is the inclusive word that will be used when referring to these non-self-governing territories in addition to the independent sovereign states.

In any discussion of offshore finance, the most frequently mentioned feature is taxation, or rather the general absence of income taxes imposed by these jurisdictions. This feature is widely believed to be the only purpose, function and rationale for the existence of financial institutions in these locations, particularly when combined with banking confidentiality. However, as will be seen, the circumstances behind the emergence and expansion of offshore finance extend beyond mere taxation, and many of these jurisdictions support other offshore services. Nonetheless, it is this particular concern over taxation that led the OECD to conduct a campaign against those jurisdictions it believed were engaging in 'harmful' tax competition. The organization (and some of its members) was concerned about losing *potential* tax revenue because mobile capital had been transferred through institutions located offshore.

To counter this practice, the G7 member states of the OECD encouraged the organization to undertake a campaign to change the situation and restore their ability to identify all tax owed to them. By preparing a case that portrays the existence of foreign accounts as the point of origin for 'harmful tax competition', they expected to force mobile capital to return to its source. Without the opportunity for tax arbitrage, capital has no reason to travel.[4] Therefore, it is necessary to look at the OECD's use of the phrase, harmful tax competition, and the intent behind its use. How can competition be considered harmful, particularly since competition, as a principle, is fundamental to the theory and operation of a capitalist economy? The question is meaningful only if we agree that some harm results from tax competition. The term itself suggests the occurrence of some 'damage, hurt, or injury' to a 'person, party or institution'. In this case, *how* is the harm inflicted, and upon *whom (or what)* is the harm inflicted by tax competition? Is there an alternative approach negating the harm if it is not possible to change the practice that is perceived as harmful?

At issue is the fact that at the same time that the OECD strives to intervene and change the tax policies of non-member states, they have been unable to resolve this issue internally amongst themselves. The apparent hypocrisy in this circumstance is among the first issues raised by any critique of the merits of the project.

> Issues arise not only about the consultation and the determination process, but also about the fact that the international regime being developed is driven and controlled by a group of countries, which are themselves major perpetrators of the 'offending' actions. (Persaud, 2001: p. 204)

Moreover, there are differing conclusions about the impact of tax competition on an economy, which further stokes the debate. One reason is that the economic research on tax competition arrives at different conclusions depending on the starting assumptions as well as the economic model employed by the researcher.

A common and simple example of tax competition has been its use to attract business, especially manufacturing facilities. The use of favorable tax policies (tax holidays, preferential rates, special exemptions or deductions) by a community to attract new enterprises is widely acknowledged, and in many cases encouraged. The specific use of the term 'community' is necessary here because the competition for a prospective facility may be between two (or more) towns, provinces, regions, or states. Consequently, any distress over the impact of the favorable tax regime for other jurisdictions may be domestic (national) as often as it is international. The competition for a new Intel chip fabrication plant to be located outside of the United States in the mid-1990s for example included communities in thirteen different states: Argentina, Brazil, Costa Rica, Chile, China, India, Indonesia, Korea, Mexico, Puerto Rico, Singapore, Taiwan, and Thailand. Narrowed to four states (Brazil, Costa Rica, Chile and Mexico) Intel ultimately selected Costa Rica in 1996. Some of the reasons identified were 'political and social stability; high quality of life; rule of law and low levels of corruption; relatively high levels of economic freedom, particularly with regards to international trade and capital flows; [and] relatively high levels of education.' (Rodríguez-Clare, 2001: p. 316) Similar items were noted for a new Intel manufacturing plant to be located within the United States. In that instance, Charles Pawlak (vice president of Intel International and corporate manager of real estate and site selection) stated that 'Our preference would be to get *no* special concessions; we just want a place that meets our needs. Incentives are only important if there's a deficiency.' In this second example, the competition for the new facility was between 10 communities located in Arizona, California, and Oregon (Lyne and Venable, 1994: p. 1009).

A study published in 2000 by the Foreign Investment Advisory Service (FIAS, a joint service of the International Finance Corporation and the World Bank) investigated the use of tax incentives to attract foreign direct investment. In doing so, the authors found,

> Tax incentives neither make up for serious deficiencies in a country's investment environment nor generate the desired externalities. But when other factors – such as infrastructure, transport costs, and political and economic stability – are more or less equal, the taxes in one location *may* have a significant effect on investors' choices. This effect varies, however, depending on the tax instrument used, the characteristics of the multinational company, and the relationship between the tax systems of the home and recipient countries. (Morisset and Pirnia, 2000: p. i, emphasis mine)

This conclusion echoes the above quotation from the Intel executive. Consequently, a reader of the FIAS report may conclude there are too many variables affecting the analysis behind the site selection process for one to conclude authoritatively that tax incentives have an influence (or not) on investment decisions. In the case study explored here, the OECD has explicitly excluded foreign direct investment (FDI) from their investigation of harmful tax competition. The authors of the OECD report acknowledged 'that the distinction between regimes directed at financial and other services on the one hand and at manufacturing and similar activities on the other hand is not always easy to apply.' (Organization for Economic Co-operation and Development, 1998: p. 8) Nonetheless, the variety of conclusions reached about the harm or benefit arising from tax competition in this instance is present also in research on finance capital taxation.

In a frequently cited International Monetary Fund (IMF) report, some 69 jurisdictions were identified as providing the home for an OFC (Errico and Musalem, 1999: p. 11). The intersection of this list with membership in the Commonwealth produced a subset of small sovereign states with an offshore business sector. My choice of the

Commonwealth Caribbean jurisdictions is in part one of size and the presence of a number of OFCs and in part recognition for the participation of the Commonwealth Secretariat in multilateral discussions over the harmful tax competition initiative. This limitation reflects the legal norms dimension of the 'offshore' and related perceptions of taxation (tax competition) and it takes account of the fact that a number of Caribbean states have actively resisted the OECD's project.

Variety in definition – What is 'small'?

It is important to understand what is meant by a *small* state in this book, because 'small' is very much in the eyes of the beholder. A variety of approaches has been used to define a small state and this question challenges any attempt to conduct a comparative study of small states. Taking a qualitative approach, the contributors to *Small States in World Politics: Explaining Foreign Policy Behavior* started from a concept of the small state based on perceptions, 'if a state's people and institutions generally perceive themselves to be small, or if other state's peoples and institutions perceive that state as small, it shall be so considered.' (Hey, 2003b: p. 3)

On the other hand, the Commonwealth has built a body of literature based on empirical measurements in an effort to quantify the effect of size on development. The Commonwealth has provided a forum and a voice for the small state since the early 1980s. A wider awareness of the issues that concerned small states was first accomplished by the Commonwealth Secretariat with the publication of *Vulnerability: Small States in the Global Society* in 1985. This analysis of small states was revisited in 1997, with a study that broadened the scope to include the environment and the evolving nature of the global economy after the Cold War. In *A Future for Small States*, the authors defined a small state as one possessing a population of 1.5 million or below (Commonwealth Advisory Group, 1997: p. 9). This updated the earlier definition from one million and reflected the global population increases between 1983 and 1995. In 1997, this cut-off point identified 49 states with a population of 1.5 million or less. Of these states, 28 were members of the Commonwealth, and 42 were considered part of the developing world (Commonwealth Secretariat, 1985: p. 9).[5]

The varying approaches taken to define a small state result in the use of different adjectives to qualify the state. Where some authors used the word 'small', others used 'mini' or 'micro'. Several tables categorizing small states and jurisdictions by population are provided below. These tables break down the roster of states by population size, the first lists those states with less than 5 million people, the second less than 1.5 million, and the third less than 500,000. The fourth table lists all remaining states with populations less than 100,000 as of the 2007 UN Population Report. The final table identifies the non-self-governing territories with population data reported by the United Nations.

Fundamentals of taxation (and tax competition)

The attitudes of individuals and societies about taxes, collecting taxes and paying taxes, have become the moral justification (and in some sense elitist self-righteousness) for the action of states and international organizations as played out in this story of 'peaceful' international intervention. In addition, the different conclusions variously reached by economists, politicians, and analysts emanate from their individual initial position on the question of state taxation. These attitudes are fuel for the debate between the OECD and small states over the OECD's accusation that offshore finance promotes *harmful* tax competition.

There are two fundamental reasons to collect taxes – to provide benefits to citizens, and to redistribute wealth amongst them. Taxes collected to provide benefits are essentially user fees. They are contributions made by citizens to finance the goods and services received from the government. Taxes collected for the express purpose of redistributing wealth (transfer payments in the form of poor relief, food subsidies and unemployment benefits) transform the state into some sort of Robin Hood, taking from the rich and giving to the poor (Cappelen, 2001: p. 97).

> The distinction between redistributive and benefit taxes may not be as clear. One could also argue that at least some redistributive taxes could be understood as benefit taxes in the sense that wealthy individuals pay them for the benefits (e.g., lower crime rates, a better educated workforce) that more egalitarian societies provide (Cappelen, 2001: footnote 2, p. 97).

Table 1.1 Small States by Population, 1.5 to 5 million

Country or area*	Total population in thousands, 2007
Turkmenistan	4965
Eritrea	4851
Norway	4698
Croatia	4555
Costa Rica	4468
Singapore	4436
United Arab Emirates	4380
Central African Republic	4343
Ireland	4301
New Zealand	4179
Lebanon	4099
Occupied Palestinian Territory	4017
Bosnia and Herzegovina	3935
Moldova	3794
Congo	3768
Liberia	3750
Lithuania	3390
Panama	3343
Uruguay	3340
Albania	3190
Mauritania	3124
Armenia	3002
Kuwait	2851
Jamaica	2714
Mongolia	2629
Oman	2595
Latvia	2277
Namibia	2074
TFYR Macedonia[a]	2038
Lesotho	2008
Slovenia	2002
Botswana	1882
Gambia	1709
Guinea-Bissau	1695

Source: United Nations Population Division, 2007.
Note: Commonwealth member states are italicized.
[a] The former Yugoslav Republic of Macedonia.
*This was the United Nations' terminology; they qualify this phrase in the report with the statement – 'The designations employed and the material in this publication do not imply the expression of any opinion whatsoever on the part of the Secretariat of the United Nations concerning the legal status of any country, territory or area or its authorities, or concerning the delimitation of its frontiers or boundaries.' (p. iv)

Table 1.2 Small States by Population, 500,000 to 1.5 million

Country or area*	Total population in thousands, 2007
Estonia	1335
Trinidad and Tobago	1333
Gabon	1331
Mauritius[a]	1262
Timor-Leste	1155
Swaziland	1141
Fiji[b]	889
Cyprus	855
Qatar	841
Comoros	839
Djibouti	833
Bahrain	753
Guyana	738
Bhutan	658
Cape Verde	530
Equatorial Guinea	507

Source: United Nations Population Division, 2007.
Note: Commonwealth member states are italicized.
[a]Including Agalega, Rodrigues and St. Brandon.
[b]Commonwealth membership suspended in December 2006 following a military coup.
*See the note with Table 1.1 – Small States by Population, 1.5 to 5 million

Thus, redistribution in a limited sense finances a more egalitarian society. Yet it might be equally true that an expanding economy that provides increased employment would lead to lower crime rates (crime is no longer necessary to pay for the necessities of life) and a better educated workforce (paid by employers seeking to further expand their successful business). It is on this basis that an argument can be made that excessively taxing the rich is self-defeating for the community at large. Notwithstanding this counter argument, the OECD project is an effort to assure that taxes may continue to be collected from the wealthy residents who have shifted their assets offshore.

The specific challenge to sovereignty explored here occupies a space within the wider debate about globalization as a modern/late-twentieth century phenomenon. One frequently identified aspect of globalization has been the *velocity* of capital mobility, facilitated both by telecommunications technology advancements and by the

Table 1.3 Small States by Population, 100,000 to 500,000

Country or area*	Total population in thousands, 2007
Solomon Islands	496
Luxembourg	467
Suriname	458
Malta	407
Brunei Darussalam	390
The Bahamas	331
Maldives	306
Iceland	301
Barbados	294
Belize	288
Vanuatu	226
Samoa	187
Saint Lucia	165
Sao Tomé and Principe	158
Saint Vincent and Grenadines	120
Micronesia (Fed. States of)	111
Grenada	106

Source: United Nations Population Division, 2007.
Note: Commonwealth member states are italicized.
*See the note with Table 1.1 – Small States by Population, 1.5 to 5 million

elimination of capital controls. Consequently, one school of thought finds in this set of circumstances a threat to the welfare state, from a perceived 'race to the bottom' in corporate tax rates, and taxation more generally, that will eventually lead to reduced state revenues (Tanzi, 1995). A reduction in tax receipts would lead to a reduction in welfare provision that will undermine the foundations of the welfare state, particularly as established in continental Europe. These views on capital mobility and tax competition are embedded in the initiative of the OECD to force compliance with a program to eliminate tax competition between states.

A basic argument of the tax competition (and public choice) literature was published by Charles Tiebout in 1956 under the title 'A Pure Theory of Local Expenditures'. This article engaged with an earlier work by Paul Samuelson concerning individual preferences for public goods (Tiebout, 1956; Samuelson, 1954). The hypothesis of Tiebout's article posits that, *contra* Samuelson, individuals are

Table 1.4 Small States by Population, less than 100,000

Country or area*	Total population in thousands, 2007
Tonga	100
Kiribati	95
Seychelles	87
Antigua and Barbuda	85
Andorra	75
Dominica	67
Marshall Islands	59
Saint Kitts and Nevis	50
Liechtenstein	35
Monaco	33
San Marino	31
Palau	20
Tuvalu	11
Nauru	10
Holy See (Vatican City State)	1

Source: United Nations Population Division, 2007.
Note: Commonwealth member states are italicized.
*See the note with Table 1.1 – Small States by Population, 1.5 to 5 million

able to express a preference for public goods. This expression is performed through the act of choosing their place of residence, given that this choice was predicated upon the local availability of public goods. Preference for any specific public good would involve the support of public expenditures to provide it, and therefore a corresponding consent to pay the taxes that provide the public good. This argument was applied to the case of local government taxes and expenditures, in the United States, and relied upon labor force mobility. The fact that labor is somewhat immobile, along with the problem of free riding in connection with access to public goods, are two of the criticisms raised with this particular argument.

The impediment to a cross-border application of Tiebout's theorem is that labor is fairly immobile given the widespread existence of immigration controls and the general desire of citizens to live in a familiar culture. This situation remains the case even within the European Union for EU citizens.[6] Nonetheless, in presenting an idealized situation of consumer choice about local taxation, the Tiebout theory has become a basic part of public choice economics, with respect

Table 1.5 Non-Self-Governing Territories by Population

Country or area*	Total population in thousands, 2007
Reunion	807
Guadeloupe	445
Martinique	399
French Polynesia	263
New Caledonia	242
French Guiana	202
Netherlands Antilles	192
Guam	173
Channel Islands	149
United States Virgin Islands	111
Aruba	104
Nothern Mariana Islands	84
Isle of Man	79
American Samoa	67
Bermuda	65
Greenland	58
Faeroe Islands	49
Cayman Islands	49
Gibraltar	29
Turks and Caicos Islands	26
British Virgin Islands	23
Wallis and Futuna Islands	15
Cook Islands	13
Anguilla	13
Saint Helena[a]	7
Saint Pierre and Miqueleon	6
Montserrat	6
Falkland Islands (Malvinas)	3
Niue	2
Tokelau	1
Pitcairn[b]	0

Source: United Nations Population Division, 2007 and CIA Factbook, 2008.
Note: British dependent territories are italicized. The Christmas Islands, Cocos (Keeling) Islands and Norfolk Island were included in the population figures for Australia by the United Nations.
[a]Including Ascension and Tristan da Cunha.
[b]The population of Pitcairn was estimated at 48 in July 2007.
*See the note with Table 1.1 – Small States by Population, 1.5 to 5 million

to tax competition and public expenditures. And in this fashion, it serves as a corollary to Charles Kindleberger's characterization of capital flight: 'A narrow economic reading might regard the action as a speculative position based on the prospect of currency devaluation. A broader socio-political view would call it a middle-class strike.' (Kindleberger, 1987: p. 58) Just as capital flight may be viewed as a form of middle-class protest against the state and its management of a national economy, the same may be said of tax avoidance on the part of individual citizens. Suffering not from a tyranny of the majority, but rather from the tyranny of a tax-imposing minority in control of the government, these dissenters duck and dodge away from the *impôt*, whether on ethical/moral grounds or simply to resist the confiscation of their wealth by the state (Vlcek, 2004). Therefore, even though citizens are disinclined to move, which would clearly establish their preferences for existing or proposed public goods (and thus the level of tax that they felt to be acceptable), they are inclined to move their capital in an effort to reduce their tax contributions. Thus, tax avoidance indirectly indicates citizen preferences about their tax contributions to the state. In sum, the difficulty with this theory at the end of the twentieth century is the fact that while residents may express their preference for public goods in their choice of residence, they may now more easily avoid contributing to these public goods. By demonstrating their desire to retain their wealth by choosing to locate their financial assets 'offshore', these residents reproduced the 'free rider' problem described by the OECD as justification for the harmful tax competition project (Organization for Economic Co-operation and Development, 1998: p. 14).

The structure of offshore finance exists within the nature of international politics, and the traditions of state sovereignty. These traditions include both independence of action over domestic activities, and a proscription against intervening into the domestic activities of *another* sovereign state. It is within these traditions that states are free to design governing structures for banking, finance and taxation which are independent, and therefore potentially different, from those of other sovereign states. Yet, the proscription against intervention has developed exceptions in the past several decades. Stephen Krasner argues that the non-intervention principle of state sovereignty has been substantially porous from the very beginning (Krasner, 1999). The argument here is that the citizens of a sovereign state are taught to believe otherwise and consequently they strongly resist the interference of others into the domestic affairs of their country. This viewpoint was a central argument made by Hochstetler, Clark, and Friedman concerning state sovereignty.

> Outside of the realm of military power, sovereignty emerges as less central to states' material interests and more central to their asserted social identities than standard arguments over sovereignty suggest. (Hochstetler *et al.*, 2000: p. 592)

Moreover, having established the widespread understanding that all sovereign states are entitled to equal treatment (as reflected for example in the United Nations' Charter and the UN system of international organizations) for some states to act otherwise is a problem.

Thus, if there are processes, procedures or activities that would directly impact the lives and welfare of the citizens of a sovereign state, then that state should be involved and its representatives should be participants in those activities. In the case of large developed states, it generally has not been a problem as they are frequently the initiators and hosts of the relevant multilateral meetings. The participation of small states on the other hand is hampered by the limited resources (both personnel and finance) available to them in order to participate in the full range of international fora. This resource limitation should not be used, however, to justify their exclusion from those gatherings likely to develop proposals intended to direct a change to their domestic legal or social structures. This exclusion was one problem with the OECD's project – the small states with OFCs were not included in the process that created the harmful tax competition project that now demanded their cooperation and compliance.

Offshore – small state development within the terrain of global finance

In order to limit the extent of discourse surrounding the OFC, one must appreciate the use, and potential misuse, of the term *offshore* within the context of global finance. Clearly, in the nautical sense the word offshore is meant to describe an entity (ship, rock, or island) located at some distance from the coast of a larger island or mainland (continental) territory. Ronen Palan suggested that for the purposes of politics and domestic regulation, the use of the term might be derived from the pirate radio stations of the 1960s. Radio Caroline, off the coast of the United Kingdom for instance, sought to emulate Radio Luxembourg while at the same time avoiding the national regulation on broadcasting in the UK. This regulatory avoidance was achieved by floating at sea just beyond the territorial limit (3 miles at this point in time) of domestic UK regulations (Palan, 2003: pp. 21–23). This point of view suggests to a present day reader a sense of the permeability of boundaries (territorial borders) and an emergent sense of the globalization of information (in this instance, rock music and advertising) in a time before we had imagined such developments. Most literature covering offshore finance associates the usage of the term offshore with the emergence of the Eurodollar markets during the economic recovery following World War II. The etymology of offshore provided by the Oxford English Dictionary refers to an article from the 8 May 1948 issue of *The Economist* – 'The 16 nations will be provided with "off-shore" dollars for buying from Germany.' (OED, 2002)

The logical (and natural) counterpoint to offshore is *onshore*. However, if the text does not involve offshore in any circumstance, then the use of the term onshore (to describe for example, the nature of banking regulation in Germany) is completely absent. Consequently, onshore does not appear to exist in the absence of the offshore. Within the constraints of financial markets, this term is used to refer to those institutions and agencies that exist within the regulated domains of sovereign states. Specifically, it is often used to designate the institutions and agencies regulated by the large, developed sovereign states, and represents a counterpoint to the situation believed to exist in an OFC. At the same time, however, these OFCs also exist within regulated sovereign states, simply ones that chose a path of minimum regulation on those aspects that encourage and support their (offshore) business environment. In the main, they strive to meet the capital adequacy ratios mandated by the Basel Concordat and other international supervisory requirements. Consequently, in this conception the use of onshore in opposition to offshore creates the image of an irregular landscape of financial institutions and regulation, containing offshore entities located at sea and surrounding the several landmasses of onshore regulation (United States, Europe/EU, Japan, India, and Australia/New Zealand).

Placing offshore and onshore onto a virtual map depicting such a landscape produces most of the visualization behind the use of these terms. Yet it leaves to be described a number of jurisdictions that include small territories of the United Kingdom – the non-self-governing territories. These territories exist in a semi-independent, semi-autonomous condition that is not full sovereign statehood. The nature of their constitutional relationship with the United Kingdom nevertheless permits them the space in which to create domestic legislation on taxation and financial regulation independent from British regulation. Thus the Channel Islands, Gibraltar, the Isle of Man, the Cayman Islands, and other Overseas Territories possess a strong geographical/political/legal connection to the onshore state, yet at the same time have a space in which to reproduce characteristics of an offshore state, given that these territories host 'offshore' financial centers.

Thus, nautical terms of physical geography have been captured for use in political geography and political economy. And perhaps in the minds of some, when visualizing this regulatory landscape of onshore and offshore finance, they have introduced, or painted in, the presence of liquidity pipelines. These pipelines serve to convey the flows of global capital from one domain to the other, but they are not metered and do not contribute (via *appropriate* taxes) towards the maintenance of the state institutions that provide a peaceful global environment and its infrastructure. It was from the existence of unmetered (untaxed) financial flows, which generated the accusations that the OFCs are free riders on global public goods.

Since 1960, improvements and new technologies in the area of telecommunications (satellites, a global infrastructure of high-speed, large bandwidth fiber optic cabling, miniaturization of electronics, and finally, the Internet) have dramatically changed the operation of financial services. Dedicated and secure telecommunication networks have been created, which now allow immense quantities of near-instantaneous commercial/financial transactions to occur globally, 24/7. This technology has facilitated an immense growth in the financial services industry globally (for the Eurodollar market alone, with a size of $11 billion in 1964, it grew to $1 trillion in 1984 and stood at $3 trillion in the early 1990s).[7] This growth included the sizeable expansion of the offshore sector.

A common legal tradition

In addition to the points noted above, another reason to focus on Commonwealth small states with regard to issues of offshore finance is their common legal system. The existence and operation of the offshore realm has a strong association with the British legal tradition. Most jurisdictions outside of Europe with some history as a financial haven possess a legal system based on British (English) common law. This includes most Caribbean and Pacific OFCs, in addition to the unique relationships maintained by the Channel Islands and the Isle of Man with the United Kingdom.

In a broad sense, the legal space in which the offshore business sector has been built exists within a fundamental difference between the English and Continental legal systems. The difference lies within the foundations of each legal system – for the continental legal tradition *explicitly* identifies what is permitted, whereas the English legal tradition *explicitly* identifies what is *not* permitted. Thus, an action is banned in the continental tradition, unless the law has expressly permitted it. Conversely, any action not specifically identified as an illegal action is permissible in the English tradition, until such a time as it has been defined as illegal by legislation (Palan, 2003: p. 29; Antoine, 1999: pp. 29, 31). This underlying legal tradition appears to be embedded within cultural perceptions of the law, and expectations as to what is considered either legitimate or illegitimate. The legal structures of society shape the conduct of citizens in a variety of ways, both large and small and particularly with entrepreneurial business developments.

As a consequence of European colonialism, European legal traditions were promulgated around the globe. The English common law foundation for Caribbean legal systems was described by Rose-Marie Antoine in her textbook *Commonwealth Caribbean Law and Legal Systems*. 'The term common law tradition, although originating in England and founded on English law, speaks to all the English-speaking countries and the geographical area known as the Commonwealth.' (Antoine, 1999: p. 29) The subsequent development of the practice of offshore finance may be understood then as an absence of any *explicit* prohibition of these financial practices. It was with the development of the Eurodollar market that 'offshore' transactions first appeared in the City of London, the product of a discrete and explicit separation of resident and non-resident deposits of foreign currencies. The British financial system was 'effectively compartmentalized' between domestic deposits in pounds sterling subject to domestic regulations, and foreign deposits in all other currencies (though primarily US dollars) which were unregulated (Burn, 1999: p. 226). This position on banking regulation intersected with earlier British case law concerning corporate taxation. As noted by Sol Picciotto, court cases, which bounded the definition of corporate residence, led to an 'anomaly that a company incorporated in the UK would not be liable to UK taxes if controlled from abroad.' (Picciotto, 1999: p. 49) This judgment led to an additional opportunity where firms could incorporate a subsidiary in the UK, which they then 'controlled' from abroad and through which they routed business activity. This technique for structuring the multinational corporation would result in avoiding British taxes on business transactions, along with any tax that would have been imposed by the parent corporation's state of residence. Taken together, these two features of the law facilitate lawful tax minimization by corporations through offshore subsidiaries and operating through a form of regulatory arbitrage.[8]

An appreciation of the history and development of this legal tradition within the Commonwealth provides an understanding of the nature and origins of offshore finance. These differences have been recognized for some time and were highlighted within internal British government documents concerning the establishment of the New Hebrides (Vanuatu) financial center. In a letter from the Treasury to the Inland Revenue in August 1974, the author noted the fact that 'legal provisions for controlling New Hebrides financial operators and for guaranteeing their secrecy derive exclusively from English law...'[9] This distinction influences the perception of various actors concerning the legitimacy of offshore finance. These perceptions of legitimacy are further aggravated for some participants 'because in some countries, to seek to frustrate the intention of the law is already a breach of an express legal principle.' (Waincymer, 1997: p. 251) One conclusion from this line of thought is that some commentators do not recognize the actions of the OECD as an explicit attack upon state sovereignty because they view the practice of offshore finance (and those using these services) as inherently illegal. An example of this was seen when the rapporteur for a European conference concerning corruption described such a viewpoint when presenting

'The nexus between corruption and offshore financial centers: an introduction'.

> If it is not correct to state that offshore financial centres exist because of a corrupted environment ..., it should be assumed that there is an indirect link between grand corruption and offshore. (Savona, 1999: p. 14)

Therefore, from this legal-cultural perspective, one could argue that the state itself has engaged in illegitimate conduct by legislating and promoting offshore finance and is therefore a 'financial pirate'. Some of the proponents of 'international standards' argue that this unacceptable conduct should be 'shunned' by law-abiding states (Kondo, 2002). This viewpoint fosters a tension between the involved jurisdictions (and their representatives) that emerged from their personal experience of differing legal traditions.

A central premise of this book is the conception that the 'offshore world' is an integral aspect of the states system. There is, however, the fact that 'offshore' jurisdictions manipulate the institutional structure of sovereignty and reproduce, as Palan argues, sovereignty as a marketable commodity for governments. Through the juridical implementation of sovereignty, the right and ability to create laws defining the structure of finance and regulation inside the state container, small states have used their sovereignty as a commodity in pursuit of economic development. This commodity (in the form of their tax administration) produces the contested ground upon which this book examines the nature of sovereignty as enacted by its smallest practitioners. This viewpoint is contested by those who argue from the standpoint that a global public good supersedes the sovereignty (and sovereign choices) of any individual state (Albin, 2003).[10] Such an argument supports the OECD position by presenting transparency and information exchange between and amongst participants in the international financial system as welfare enhancing. Consequently, transparency and information exchange represent elements of a larger structure supporting international financial stability, a goal that is regarded as a global public good. By identifying its project as one that supports global welfare, the OECD is emphasizing that it has the best interests of all states in mind, and not simply the interests of its members.

The examination of this question of small states defending their sovereign independence intersects with other debates within the discipline of international relations. First, this demonstration of the continued sovereign capability of the small members of the international society reinforces the argument that, notwithstanding the views of some proponents of globalization, states continue to matter. Contrasting this aspect of sovereign statehood as independence of action is the growth of global financial governance through the promulgation of international standards and best practices created by select multilateral groups and yet intended for worldwide implementation. This aspect extends beyond the OECD to include the FATF on money laundering and terrorist financing, and a variety of cross-national professional organizations for the insurance industry, stock exchanges and other sectors of the financial services industry.

Offshore financial centers as development

In conjunction with the development of the Eurodollar market the OFC came to be seen as one approach to economic development, and thus economic security, for small states. Small jurisdictions have considered financial services as an economic development strategy since the 1960s.[11] This strategy for economic development began in the Caribbean with the Cayman Islands in 1967, while at the same time they chose to remain a British colony (United Kingdom. Public Record Office, 1973; Roberts, 1995: p. 240). In the Pacific, the first OFC was established on Norfolk Island in 1966 (van Fossen, 2002). When the finance center in Port Vila, New Hebrides was established, among the reasons offered were that it did not occupy a lot of land, did not pollute, and did not compete with local businesses. At the time, officials from the British Residency sought advice on the regulated development of a 'tax haven' from the already existing British tax havens in Bermuda, the Bahamas and the Cayman Islands (United Kingdom. Public Record Office, 1970).

Bishnodoat Persaud reiterated the attractive environmental and economic features of an OFC in 2001:

> Offshore financial services have become a significant part of the economy of many small states. These activities generate a substantial amount of license fees which belie the notion of a no tax

> situation. They also generate employment involving secretarial, administrative, accounting, information technology and professional skills. (Persaud, 2001: p. 209)

These features, in conjunction with the revenue from licensing fees, help to explain the efforts taken by small states to defend and maintain the *status quo*.

The development and success of OFCs in small states depended upon the nature of the international economic structure established after World War Two by the Bretton Woods Agreement. This structure permitted variations between states in banking regulation, capital controls, interest rate ceilings and the effective rate of taxation (Goodman and Pauly, 1993: pp. 52–60). The circumstances of post-war recovery and the burgeoning Cold War conflict fostered the development of the Eurodollar market, and subsequently a growing recognition of the arbitrage possibilities in international finance. Business opportunities developed for financial institutions outside of the major, regulated financial markets, leading to the creation of OFCs of varying quality (in terms of local regulation, control and oversight) (Francis, 1985; Hampton, 1996).

At the same time that the number and size of the OFCs grew there have been periodic warnings for the difficulties that faced them. An evaluation of offshore banking in 1979 suggested that 'it seems possible, indeed probable, that there is little unsatisfied demand for new offshore centers' (McCarthy, 1979: p. 48). A few years later the author of a study on offshore banking in the Bahamas observed that 'recent international developments ... appear to threaten the future survival of offshore banking centres.' (Francis, 1985: p. 91) While global financial markets liberalized throughout the 1980s, the offshore financial sector continued to grow. In his analysis of the OFC as an economic development strategy in 1994, Mark Hampton concluded that while a state might be successful in establishing a new OFC, that success was dependent upon satisfying a niche in the marketplace. He cautioned that 'hosting an OFC is clearly not a panacea for SIE [small island economy] development.' (Hampton, 1994: p. 248)

2
Sovereignty and Taxation

> Martin Wight points out that 'it would be impossible to have a society of sovereign states unless each state, while claiming sovereignty for itself, recognized that every other state had the right to claim and enjoy its own sovereignty as well.'
>
> – John Gerard Ruggie[1]

Sovereignty, as a feature of a state amongst the community of states, has come to be used as a development tool by small states. One analysis of this strategy suggests that the fundamental factor is the ability to establish municipal law within a defined and bounded territory.

> First, there is a shared perception that a sovereign right to write the law – whether at the municipal, state, or national level – combined with a competitive system can be used as a competitive asset. In other words, a link between a competitive system of jurisdictions and the potential for the commercialized use of the right to write the law is well recognized (Palan, 2002: p. 159).

For Ronen Palan, the small state 'sold' its sovereignty when choosing to establish an offshore financial center (OFC). In effect, the small state used its sovereign status to pursue a comparative economic advantage to offset the other limited capabilities that accompany its small size. The use of this strategy may be an approach to counter the loss or decline of a comparative advantage for some other commodity. The benefits from hosting an OFC include increased employment in the service sector, which can increase the education and training prospects for citizens, and revenue from associated fees and taxes. Thus, state sovereignty has been used to provide the means to increase and enhance the domestic economy of the small state.

However one may view this use of state sovereignty, it is necessary first to understand what is meant by the concept and several viewpoints are presented in the next section of this chapter. After looking at the more general concepts of sovereignty, the discussion focuses on what the concept means for these small states. From here the discussion turns to concepts of taxation, and finally to the combination of these two sets of concepts, in the form of fiscal sovereignty.

Concepts of sovereignty

There exists an extensive literature on the topic of 'sovereignty' within international relations, international law, and political science. The concept, definition, and even the word itself have been challenged since at least the sixteenth century.[2] The debate on the nature and validity of the concept has been re-invigorated since the end of the Cold War with the evolving development and use of humanitarian intervention. The condition of sovereignty has also been questioned in light of globalization, with some authors suggesting not only that the sovereign state may be in decline, but also that the very concept of sovereignty has become redundant. Before addressing concerns for the continued relevance of state sovereignty, the traditional understanding of the concept should first be considered.

Defining the sovereign state

The Montevideo Convention on Rights and Duties of States (1933) defined the state in its first article as a 'person' in international law possessing four qualifications. These qualifications are: a defined territory, a permanent population, a government, and the capacity to conduct relations with other states. For international law scholars however, the Montevideo Convention is an inter-American convention and it only applies to its limited number of signatories (Crawford, 1989: p. 280). This convention for international law established the bounds for a political community, which is to be identified as a state. This political community is sovereign with respect to the territories it occupies. As F. H. Hinsley stated when laying the foundation for his study of sovereignty

> ... the idea of sovereignty was the idea that there is a final and absolute political authority in the political community; and everything that needs to be added to complete the definition is added if this statement is continued in the following words: '*and no final and absolute authority exists elsewhere*.' (Hinsley, 1986: p. 26, emphasis in the original)

Therefore, the sovereign state is a political community exercising control over a piece of territory. Further, this condition must be recognized and acknowledged by similar political communities. With peer recognition comes the acknowledgment that the territory is a juridical equal able to enter into agreements with other states and to participate in a variety of suitable international organizations. This approach to establishing and maintaining that status of the 'sovereign state' accords power to the existing members of the international community of states, and serves as a control mechanism to limit the participation of aspiring members to the community. Clear examples of the use of this power include the denial of recognition to the Soviet government in Russia following the October Revolution until 1934 by the United States; and the continued recognition of the government in Taiwan as the sovereign representative for China, instead of the Mainland government, until the 1970s by a number of Western states, including most prominently the United States (Krasner, 1999: pp. 14–20).[3]

There is also a strong aspect to sovereignty that is necessarily *socially constructed*. The construction of sovereignty is tied to the perception (self-recognition) of a group of people as a nation. And, as a nation, they have identified some bounded territory in which they wish to exercise self-determination. For well-established states, this construction is reinforced by a history (or perhaps a mythology) as a nation-state, which then provides a rationalization and justification to the claims for existence as a political society. Similarly, for groups possessing a history as a nation, yet lacking status as a state and desiring self-determination, it fuels the desire for independence from the existing political entity of which the territory claimed presently is a part, in order to form a new political entity (or to join with an another, already existent political entity established by members of the same group). However, the focus of the group (nation) is on the territory from which the sovereign state emerges. Gaining recognition for them hinges on the possession of territory, and to a (sometimes variable) extent, exercising control over this territory.

Acquisition of sovereignty at this point provides the social recognition of the state – and the rights and responsibilities attendant to this recognition – by the international community. The state is sufficiently autonomous to seek a position amongst other states, while able to conduct internal affairs as desired without external interference. This ideal, or imagined, perspective of sovereignty may not function within the international system in precisely this fashion, as discussed by Stephen Krasner in *Sovereignty: Organized Hypocrisy*. It is however, the image or perception resident in the minds of the leadership within the state that counts, and this image influences the actions they take both in relation to other states, and internally with the populace. For as noted by Krasner, 'Rulers, not states...make choices about policies, rules, and institutions.' (Krasner, 1999: p. 7) This choice includes both the recognition of other political entities as sovereign states and acting to maintain its rights and status as a sovereign state.

Accompanying the status of recognition as a sovereign state is the perception of the rights associated with that status. A list of such rights would include:

- control of the passage of people, goods, and services through territorial borders
- monopoly of the means of violence
- authority to enter into agreements with other states

In constructing a definition of sovereignty, we need to ask whether these rights are divisible, i.e. – can a state give up the right (say) to control the passage of individuals across its border with a neighboring state, and remain sovereign? The experience of the European states that have signed the Schengen Agreement suggests the answer is yes. They have conceded this control mechanism to the outer borders of the group of member states, accepting that individuals go through passport control upon first entry to the Schengen group of states. Once admitted, individuals have free right of passage, without further passport and immigration control amongst the member states. Nonetheless, the member states feel/perceive that they remain sovereign. This view of sovereign rights was described by Michael Fowler and Julie Bunck as the Basket Approach to sovereignty, '...a basket of attributes and corresponding rights and duties. While every state has a basket, the contents are by no means the same.' (Fowler and Bunck, 1995: p. 70ff) Sovereignty is thus relative, and elements of these rights are freely ceded in the process of negotiation. States are therefore willing to relinquish some aspect of their freedom to choose a course of action in exchange for some benefit. The key aspect of this perspective of sovereignty is that it is a product of willing cooperation and negotiation, and that should circumstances change the right in question could be reclaimed (at least theoretically). In presenting this approach to sovereignty, Fowler and Bunck quoted Hans Blix comparing sovereignty to property rights,

> As ownership is described as a bundle of rights, sovereignty may perhaps be described as a bundle of competences. There is no inherent reason against the voluntary acceptance of limitations upon the freedom of action in one field or in several fields, upon one or more of the competences in the bundle. Of course, such limitations do reduce the freedom of action of the state and thereby nibble at the sovereignty – as the concept is defined here. Most of that freedom will remain, however.[4]

This conception of sovereignty, particularly with reference to competences, is a foundation for the operation of the European Union.

The alternate approach is to treat sovereignty as a unitary value, 'a monolith, like a chunk of stone'. (Fowler and Bunck, 1995: 64) In this Chunk Approach to sovereignty, a state either is, or is not, sovereign; just as a woman cannot be half pregnant, a state cannot be 75 per cent sovereign. In this tradition, all sovereign states are equal, in what Krasner and others identify as international legal sovereignty. Therefore, sovereignty is based upon reciprocity amongst states, with similar rights and duties. A state is also party to a collection of treaties and conventions, which further refine the conduct of a state relative to its rights and duties, and which may lead to a relative imbalance amongst states' rights (Fowler and Bunck, 1995: p. 64ff).

Sovereignty for small states

Many small states, and most especially those considered here, are relatively new and consequently concerned about perceptions of sovereignty. Thus for a new state, the construction of a social identity as a 'state' (no less than as a 'nation') is also relatively new. As already mentioned and widely noted in the literature on post-colonial states, self-determination, and nationalism, many new states are not homogenous territories, in part because of *uti possidetis* (Ratner, 1996). These former colonies came to sovereign status with pre-existing internal problems of nationalism and self-determination (along with secessionist and recidivist demands). The partition of the Subcontinent into India and Pakistan for example, did not resolve such problems there, as East Pakistan became Bangladesh in 1971, and the Kashmir province remains a flashpoint between India and Pakistan. Another residual effect of decolonization has been the condition known as the failed state or quasi-state. For Robert Jackson, 'Sovereign states are legally but not necessarily physically insular and today most of them are economically dependent or interdependent.' (Jackson, 1990: p. 33) He takes the chunk approach to viewing sovereignty, which is challenged by the situation present in a large number of states. Jackson described the consequences of this situation as a proliferation of quasi-states. Quasi-states are political entities possessing international recognition as a state (possessing territory and conducting relations with other states) but without effective control of the internal affairs of their territory. 'Their governments are often deficient in the political will, institutional authority, and organized power to protect human rights or provide socio-economic welfare.' (Jackson, 1990: p. 21)

This viewpoint may be further advanced by the suggestion that the continued existence of quasi-states is at the same time a social construct of the international system. Their status as *sovereign states* has been constructed by the rest of the international community, which insists on dealing with a unitary actor. This unitary actor is the territory and population previously defined as a state, even if the situation is contested domestically. It is not so much a matter of *degrees* of statehood, as simply one of continuing to treat the territory *as a state*. Various external organizations (including IGOs and NGOs) maintain their expectations for modes of governance and organizational structure, and continue to act as if they exist to represent this notional state. Consequently, these territories continue to perform as states internationally even when they are unable to function as a state domestically (Sørensen, 1999: pp. 397–399). Somalia serves as the most profound example of this difficulty for the international system.

The concept of sovereignty is integral to political organization, and thus to the perceptions of the society which forms that political organization. The essence then of sovereignty may be characterized as the collective concept resident in the collective social/communal mind.[5] These shared public perceptions, as reflected in the images displayed by the media, academic writing, and the public comment of political leaders, all serve to refine and reproduce the concept of sovereignty, thereby influencing the actions of the state, through the conduct of its government. This condition is recognized by small states, which may be particularly sensitive to the actions that reinforce their self-perception of sovereign independence. At the same time, these societies are sensitive to the external forces that undermine their self-perception.

An example of the latter situation may be found in the negotiations for 'shiprider' agreements between the United States and a number of Caribbean states in the 1990s. As described by Holger Henke, the difficulty in concluding these negotiations arose from differing perceptions about state sovereignty. The shiprider agreements would permit search and seizure actions by US Coast Guard vessels inside the territorial limits of Caribbean states as part of the war on drugs. Without these agreements, potential law enforcement actions would be a violation of territorial sovereignty. For Henke this controversy demonstrated that the United States lacked an 'understanding and appreciation of the value and significance which ex-colonial societies, like the Caribbean countries, assign to their independence and right of self-determination.' (Henke, 1998: p. 42) This conclusion was echoed by other authors concerning US-Caribbean state relations over the 'war on drugs'. Moreover, some of the 'negotiation' tactics used by the United States to reach a resolution on the shiprider agreements demonstrated this disregard for Caribbean perceptions of sovereignty. When Jamaica, for example, expressed its reluctance to signing the initial agreement proposed by the US, subsequent discussions included the threat that Jamaica could be 'decertified' as a result of the lack of cooperation in the war on drugs (Munroe, 2000: p. 196).[6]

The sensitivity of small states, particularly the ex-colonial societies discussed by Henke, to sovereign independence while ultimately acquiescing to the demands of larger states (as was the case with the shiprider agreements) raises a point about concepts of liberty connected to this discussion of small state sovereignty. Quentin Skinner has suggested that in addition to positive and negative liberty, as explicated by Isaiah Berlin, there is a third concept of liberty. Essentially, this concept suggests that when the individual is subject to the capricious rule of a sovereign they will constrain their actions. This response is not because of any actual interference or threat of interference in their lives, but because they recognize that they are dependent upon the goodwill of the sovereign. Thus, it is 'by the mere knowledge that we are living in dependence on the goodwill of others' that our liberty to act as we would desire is thereby constrained (Skinner, 2002: p. 247). This third concept of liberty aptly describes the position of small states in international society, since their decisions and actions reside within such a space, one that is created by the continual awareness that they are dependent upon the goodwill of larger states. And none more so than the Caribbean small states that live in the shadow of the United States.

Remnants of empire

A question initially raised after World War Two concerning the transition of colonies to sovereign states was one of capacity and viability. As the pace and pressure of decolonization increased, these concerns became less critical to the process. The question was no longer 'can this territory survive as an independent state', but rather 'why is this territory not yet independent'? The pressure came in particular from the United Nations' General Assembly Fourth Committee (Special Political and Decolonization), as well as from the citizens/residents of the territories involved. This assertion is not to suggest however that the urge for an independent sovereign status was universal amongst the residents of these territories. Nor does it mean that there are no colonies left in the international system of states. While the descriptive name applied to them may have changed over time, to British Overseas Territory or the French Département d'Outremer for example, these jurisdictions have remained 'non-self-governing territories' in the language of the General Assembly (Anonymous, 8 Nov 2000).

Reviewing the list of territories, the reader will recognize the presence of many as locations for OFCs. This fact introduces an additional dynamic to the debate on harmful tax competition, as the *administering state* becomes a participant in efforts to constrain OFCs. Furthermore, the administering state may have competing and conflicting interests within the debate on taxation, as in the case of the United Kingdom which is a member of the European Union, a member of the Commonwealth, and the administering state for a number of jurisdictions (Clegg, 2006). Even though the emphasis here is on those jurisdictions possessing sovereign status, and treated as sovereign states within the international system, nonetheless the non-self-governing jurisdictions must be discussed with the context of offshore finance and the Organization for Economic Co-operation and Development (OECD) project against tax competition because they include prominent participants. As already mentioned, a number of these Overseas Territories host an OFC, including the frequently mentioned Cayman Islands. Before looking at those aspects, the next section introduces some of the basic concepts involved in taxation.

Taxation in the modern state

The economic literature covering taxation, tax policy coordination and tax rate harmonization frequently utilizes mathematical or game theoretic models. Generally absent, however, is the application of these models to 'real world' circumstances or testing against empirical data (Andreoni *et al.*, 1998: pp. 850–852). In some cases, the representative two-state model is modified, from presenting two symmetrical states to presenting two differently sized states, or introducing a third, non-participating state (a.k.a. a tax haven) to the model (Huizinga and Nielsen, 2002b; Wilson, 1991). Nevertheless, use of empirical data to demonstrate these models within the messy domain of inter-state politics is limited. Research by a number of authors, including Eggert, Fuest and Huber, Perroni and Scharf, and Huizinga and Nielsen, contain equations that suggest the potential results deriving from tax coordination amongst states (the EU Savings Tax Directive as one example), but it offers no suggestion over the taxpayer action likely to result from such coordination efforts (Eggert, 2001; Fuest and Huber, 2001; Perroni and Scharf, 2001; Huizinga and Nielsen, 2002a).[7]

Fortunately, the essence of 'real world' taxpayer conduct has been captured elsewhere and in particular by the literature on tax avoidance/tax compliance.[8] Broadly speaking, there is 'tax avoidance' and 'tax evasion' – the first term describes those transactions which are within the letter of the law, even to the point of using unintended legislative loopholes. The second term, tax evasion, is of greater concern as it involves transactions that are intended to escape legal tax obligations via fraudulent means (Gordon, 1981: pp. 60–61). Furthermore, the treatment of tax evasion, and thus its criminalization, varies from country to country. Notably, in Switzerland tax avoidance/evasion has not been a crime, whereas in other jurisdictions it is, to a greater or lesser extent.

This basic determination of two aspects (avoidance and evasion) was further refined by Ramon Jeffery, who concluded that the problem for tax compliance actually possessed three aspects – evasion, avoidance, and mitigation.

> Tax evasion is the intention to evade an existing tax liability, which often involves an element of criminality or fraud, such as the failure to disclose income. The *unacceptable* reduction of one's tax liability by ordering one's affairs in a particular way constitutes *tax avoidance*, while the *acceptable* reduction of such liability constitutes *tax mitigation*. In both the domestic and international contexts, the seemingly intractable difficulty is that of distinguishing between acceptable and unacceptable transactions where there are beneficial tax consequences for a taxpayer; that is, in differentiating between tax mitigation and tax avoidance. (Jeffery, 1999: p. 98, emphasis in original)

These definitions represent a case of semantic hair-splitting, as attempting to determine (much less agree on) the difference between acceptable and unacceptable would be as effective as attempting to determine the state of mind of the taxpayer when they made a particular decision which had tax consequences in order to determine that it was *illegal* tax avoidance. The approach followed here is in keeping, however, with the increasing enactment by states of *anti*-avoidance laws in their on-going efforts to collect and keep tax revenue. Moreover, the attempt by the judiciary (or prosecutors to convince the judiciary) of the validity of such anti-avoidance legislation appears to be an effort to actively interpret not only the legislation, but also the legislators' intent (state of mind) to increase revenue collection and reduce *abusive* tax avoidance activity.

In the legal literature, frequent reference is made to precedent-establishing court cases. Statements made by judges concerning the conduct and action of taxpayers have particular cogency. For the United States, Vanistendael cited Judge Learned Hand (*Gregory versus Helvering*, 1934) – 'Any one may so arrange his affairs that his taxes shall be as low as possible; he is not bound to choose that pattern which will best pay the Treasury; there is not even a patriotic duty to increase one's taxes.' From the British judicial record comes *Commissioners of Inland Revenue versus Duke of Westminster* (1936), in which the judges wrote – 'Such behaviour is perfectly legal, because most countries recognise the right of the taxpayer to arrange his affairs in such a way as to pay less tax.' (Vanistendael, 1997: p. 132). A broad assessment of the situation found that taxpayers simply

> ... behave in such an idiosyncratic manner in tax matters. As Wheatcroft puts it, 'when dealing with other areas of law citizens tend to stick to well-trodden paths; with tax law, they seek new ones.' (Cooper, 1997: p. 17)

The legal approval of tax minimization would certainly stimulate government (legislative) action to find any means and measures necessary to enhance revenue collection.

Consequently, the trend in the past several decades has been in the other direction, with states enacting anti-avoidance laws. These laws are particularly difficult to enforce, however, as they attempt to assess the 'state of mind' of the taxpayer at the time the suspect activity occurred. This action is necessary in order to determine if the *intent* was to *avoid* paying tax.

> This view of tax avoidance seeks to define it by reference to a state of mind although the state of mind might be presumed from identifiable external criteria such as the form in which the taxpayer organised the transaction. (Cooper, 1997: p. 28)

In other words, even though no concrete and indisputable evidence of tax evasion exists, the tax administration continues to believe that the intention of the transaction was to avoid paying tax. Therefore, it must demonstrate that the evidence available is sufficient to imply that the underlying intention in the mind of the taxpayer was tax avoidance.

There is also a common perception expressed in the literature that 'Given that tax evasion is so widespread, it is unlikely that information will be provided directly by taxpayers and full information thus requires the participation of foreign authorities.' (Bacchetta and Espinosa, 1995: p. 104) Because of the very nature of tax avoidance and tax evasion, an accurate assessment of the extent and prevalence of these activities continues to be difficult. This situation has not prevented attempts to gauge the size of the tax evasion problem. In *Justifying Taxes*, Agustín Menéndez used estimates of the size of the 'shadow' (or underground) economy to extrapolate the extent of tax evasion in Europe. Nonetheless, 'the increase of the shadow economy has not reduced the money collected through taxes, but it has led to the placement of a heavier tax burden on the official economy.' (Menéndez, 2001: p. 107)[9] Yet, following this logic, if the growth of the shadow economy has not reduced the amount of revenue collected by the state, then its existence has not placed a heavier tax burden on the open (official) economy. Should the shadow economy disappear overnight, it would not decrease the tax revenue collected, and the government would continue to operate as before. What this statement suggests, however, is that the shadow economy has reduced *growth* in the tax revenue collected by the state. In response to the level of taxation, the population has restricted the size of government and public goods, not through tax competition, but by displacing economic activity to the untaxed realm.

Among the factors influencing taxpayer conduct is the role of the state and its use of the tax revenue collected. Consequently, the views held by citizens concerning the value and benefit from the use of their tax contribution would influence their support for, and acquiescence in, taxation. This development is reflected by the OECD in statements such as 'harmful tax competition diminishes global welfare and undermines taxpayer confidence in the integrity of tax systems.' (Organization for Economic Co-operation and Development, 1998: p. 8) The growth of the shadow economy as presented in Menéndez between 1960 and 1994 is very suggestive of the argument that taxpayer confidence in their tax system has declined. In his data the citizens of these OECD countries have essentially 'voted with their feet' by taking measures to avoid paying taxes. As Menéndez described the situation, 'Firstly the lack of satisfaction with tax systems has tended to be expressed through the private act of evading taxes and less so through a public criticism of the tax model.' (Menéndez, 2001: p. 108) The purpose behind a discussion of tax compliance and the underground economy at this point is to emphasize the domestic basis of taxation. The problem presented by OFCs to other states in the global economy is that they represent an opportunity for citizens to relocate savings and investment beyond the territorial boundaries of their home state. It is this problem that leads the OECD to frame the OFC and tax competition as detrimental to global well-being.[10] Nonetheless, there is research suggesting that tax compliance is not a rational choice, given the level of deterrent measures implemented within OECD states to force compliance. The analysis of Lars Feld and Bruno Frey attribute the level of tax compliance to 'tax morale', which is the willingness of taxpayers to pay their taxes, rather than suggesting that compliance is simply a response to the threat of prosecution (Feld and Frey, 2002b). For their research work, tax morale is a product of the relationship between the taxpayer and the tax administration within a state's legal and constitutional structure. Thus, when it is widely recognized by taxpayers as a good relationship (they are treated respectfully) tax compliance is higher. When the situation is one of low tax morale and the relationship between taxpayer and tax administration is adversarial, tax evasion is more prevalent (Feld and Frey, 2002a).

Leviathan state or benevolent state?

Economists typically depict the state as one of two ideal types. The approach fits very well with the frequent use of game theory to model the decision-making process. The first view of the state positions it as a Leviathan, an 'intrinsically untrustworthy revenue-maximizer'. Accompanying this view is the perception that tax competition serves as a constraint 'on the intrinsic pressures towards excessively high tax rates implied by policy-makers' pursuit of their own interests.' (Edwards and Keen, 1996: p. 115) The opposite view, without the simple Hobbesian label, presents the state as a benevolent maximizer of citizens' welfare. For a benevolent maximizer state, tax competition produces inefficient outcomes, which detract from its ability to provide public goods. In other words, competition prevents the state from increasing taxes in order to fund additional public goods.[11] The tension inherent between these ideal types is implicit in questions focusing on government policy-making, government efficiency, and the extent and depth of government presence in society (Edwards and Keen, 1996: pp. 114–115). In reaching their conclusions Jeremy Edwards and Michael Keen found circumstances where the government was at neither extreme (neither revenue-maximizer nor benevolent-maximizer), yet tax coordination between states could still result in benefits for the representative citizen. The results reached would depend on two factors, income effect and relative price, and they could just as easily cause a welfare loss for the representative citizen instead of producing a benefit (Edwards and Keen, 1996: pp. 130–131). Nonetheless, these extreme depictions of state government are often used by authors to frame their work on taxation and tax competition.

The relative social demand for public goods (and thus tax revenue) has also been framed in terms of fairness and redistribution. Perceptions of fairness, and of the need for both benefit taxation and redistributive taxation, shape public attitudes about tax competition and influence policy-makers. As summarized by Alberto Alesina and George-Marios Angeletos, individuals possess some innate desire for what they consider a 'fair' outcome (Alesina and Angeletos, 2003).[12] Yet, the perception of 'widespread tax evasion' seems at odds with this assertion.

Do individual desires to minimize tax payment (as reflected by efforts for tax avoidance) overcome this desire for fairness? Writing about *The Shadowy World of Tax Evasion, Capital Flight and Fraud*, Ingo Walter suggested that it does.

> And the growing complexity of tax codes and their use for a broad range of political purposes other than raising revenue has added further to the impression of unfairness, gradually undermining tax morality and stimulating the search for escape even among otherwise law-abiding people. (Walter, 1989: p. 79)

For Walter this taxpayer perception of unfairness may be directed at the imposition of taxes, or it may be focused on how the tax revenue is used. Nonetheless, given a perception that the state was not achieving a fair outcome, citizens were opting out. In order to counteract this tendency the opportunities to opt out on paying taxes must be reduced, which leads to the objective of the OECD tax competition project. The assumption here is that by reducing tax competition the project would in turn reduce tax avoidance and restore the 'lost' tax revenue.

The argument that tax competition reduces public welfare is not conclusively established. The authors of a survey of economic and public finance literature reviewed studies supporting both sides of the topic, and analyzed their arguments. Günther Schulze and Heinrich Ursprung found that '[i]t appears that the final judgement on the welfare effects of increased tax competition depends critically on how one views government behaviour.' (Schulze and Ursprung, 1999: p. 311) While concluding that empirical evidence 'does not appear to have given rise to any significant retrenchment of the welfare state, it cannot be rejected out of hand that the tax *structure* may have been influenced by the globalisation process...' as the decline and convergence of corporate tax rates between states appear to suggest (Schulze and Ursprung, 1999: p. 346, emphasis in the original). But they also point out that the corporate income tax base, and the revenue collected from it, is small when compared with those of the income and value added taxes of developed states. Therefore, Schulze and Ursprung have also concluded that the ability of states to maintain existing welfare programs will only be seriously affected should 'the income and value added tax bases become significantly more mobile in the future course of global market integration.' (Schulze and Ursprung, 1999: p. 346) Moreover, one might add, it is this concern that is behind EU efforts for tax harmonization in Europe – cross-border shopping (taking advantage of lower VAT) and the existence of capital collecting interest in foreign bank accounts, untaxed – could seriously erode the national and collective tax bases (Vlcek, 2004).

Taken together, the arguments of Menéndez, Feld and Frey, and Alesina and Angeletos support the contention of the OECD that taxpayer confidence has been undermined. But it is not tax competition itself which undermines the confidence (and thus the tax morale) of the representative taxpayer. Instead, it is the response of the state to the presence of competition. While there has been an increase in the size of the underground economy (as shown by Menéndez), taxpayers desire or seek a fair outcome. Consequently, if they trust the tax administration they pay taxes. The study of Feld and Frey concludes that participation in the democratic process fosters support for the tax administration. 'In such systems of direct democracy, taxpayers know that the public services they consume are worth the taxes they pay. Taxpayers therefore feel obliged to pay their taxes honestly.' (Feld and Frey, 2002a: p. 6) It is not the existence of yet another way to avoid taxes (such as an OFC) that undermines tax morale. It is the relationship between taxpayers and the tax administration that affects taxpayer confidence. As Feld and Frey wrote, 'trust breeds trust'.

A sovereign right to tax?

When reading the debates over international tax harmonization, one often encounters the statement that states have a sovereign right both to tax, and to determine the amount of tax. The point frequently emphasized by opponents of tax harmonization is that of the sovereign independence of the state on matters of taxation, that is, their fiscal sovereignty.

> A country's right to levy taxes is a fundamental aspect of its sovereignty. Without the power to tax, a government would be unable to redistribute resources among its citizens and provide public goods. The question of how tax rights should be distributed is

> therefore one of the oldest and most important problems of tax theory (Cappelen, 2001: p. 97).

This perspective takes us a step beyond the discussion of state sovereignty already presented. Moreover, it addresses the question of how the state is to achieve self-sufficiency. A similar perspective is present in the tax harmonization debate within the European Union.

> Another holistic approach, much favoured in the European discussion as well as by economists focusing on world-wide allocative efficiency as the most relevant international tax policy objective, is some form of imposed harmonization or uniformity. At one level, this implies international tax police again, or cession of national sovereignty. (Bird and Wilkie, 2000: pp. 100–101)

The redistributive aspect of tax revenue, between wealthy and poor, is an element of the debates domestically as well as internationally. These debates engage with the question over the preferences held in a given society for public goods and the allocation of state revenue.

A contrasting perspective from small developing states also concerns the question of fiscal sovereignty. To answer the question – who has the right to tax? – Rosemarie Antoine approaches it as a matter of jurisdiction, in the legal sense of the word. Can a state claim the right to tax entities (or individuals) located outside their territorial boundaries? The answer involves the difference between the 'origination' approach and the 'residence' approach used to establish a tax liability. With the origination approach, income is taxed in the territory in which it originates (also known as the territorial approach or principle of territoriality). Under the residence approach, the income is taxed by that jurisdiction wherein the citizen (or firm) resides (also known as the domicile approach). Developed states frequently take the residence approach for corporate income tax, with the consequence that tax collection has in effect become an extra-territorial application of domestic law. Antoine states that this method is contested by developing states, asserting that 'they, and not the country of original residence, have the right to tax.' (Antoine, 2001: p. 11).

Accompanying the distinction between origination and residence in taxing income is the state's approach for determining the extent of income subject to taxation. For the individual, there are two approaches, one based upon the individual's place of residence (territorial) and the second based upon the individual's citizenship (worldwide). It is a question of jurisdiction, 'In Britain, the Inland Revenue is not very interested in the colour of your passport – its primary concerns are with residence, ordinary residence, and domicile.' (Kay and King, 1990: p. 204)[13] This approach produces a potential for complex income tax submissions, and promotes the development of an entire sub-discipline within law and finance for tax consultation in the United Kingdom. Citizens of the United States on the other hand are obligated to report their worldwide income, from all sources to include non-US employment and non-US investment and savings. This requirement holds even if they are not resident in the United States. It is because the US maintains a worldwide tax administration, based on citizenship and not residence, and laws exist to increase the difficulties experienced when renouncing citizenship for presumed reasons of tax minimization. Tax deductions and credits are available to reduce the impact of double taxation in most states' tax structure for their residents. Nevertheless, under worldwide-based tax laws *all* income is considered. To forget to declare the interest income from an account in the Cayman Islands is tax evasion, not avoidance, for a US citizen.

For the United Kingdom, with a territorial-based tax administration, it is not so clear-cut. It becomes a question of its remittance basis. In this instance, the possession of an offshore account is a form of potential tax avoidance. The citizen may not be obligated to declare the income, until it is repatriated (remitted) to the United Kingdom. If the income is utilized, e.g., consumed while on holiday abroad, it is tax avoidance, but is it tax evasion? This is open to some debate as the question of intentionality is raised.[14] However, if the same citizen walks up to the automated teller machine (ATM) around the corner from their home, and withdraws money from their offshore account, the transaction should now be accountable to the state's tax administration, to whatever extent it was earned income.

The treatment of corporations is far more complex. Firms are the predominant rationale behind double taxation treaties, firms conduct individual negotiations with local officials before making significant new investment, and firms are treated to a variety of tax credits/deductions. Moreover, firms may engage in transfer pricing, a problem that becomes increasingly problematic for tax administrators as international trade becomes more a matter of intra-firm trade. The multinational firm is able to manipulate pricing between divisions or subsidiaries located in different states, effectively transferring taxable income, and deductible business expenses, to the benefit of the firm. Tax treaties include provisions to tackle transfer pricing, but to deal with the problem effectively requires coordination between the affected states' tax administrators (Deprez, 2003; Graham, 1996). Another tactic used by multinational corporations (MNCs) has been to establish a holding company in a location offering preferential treatment for the firm's tax status. The holding company 'owns' patents or other intellectual property that it then 'licenses' to subsidiaries (likely including the original firm) located in less tax-friendly locations. This approach also effectively transfers the MNC's global income and profits to the low tax jurisdiction.[15]

Sovereignty also has been identified as hindering the achievement of an 'efficient allocation of revenue between countries inuring to the benefit of taxpayers' (Jeffery, 1999: p. 22). The author of *The Impact of State Sovereignty on Global Trade and International Taxation* contends that state sovereignty no longer serves the needs of the political community and its citizens. Instead, sovereignty is preventing the coordination activities required to eliminate international tax distortions.

> In the light of international economic integration it is no longer sufficient just to look at the equity considerations which arise between taxpayers. It is now essential also to look at the equitable relativities between nations: inter-nations equity. This requires that the worldwide tax base be fairly shared between nations. (Jeffery, 1999: p. 11)

To achieve this goal requires the cooperation of all states, which must cede their sovereign right to set, collect and distribute tax revenue to a global authority.

The essential problem, as identified by Ramon Jeffery, is 'State reluctance to enact international norms for fear of losing "sovereignty".' (Jeffery, 1999: p. 37) The solution to this problem is found in the extraterritorial enforcement of municipal (state) law. Jeffery suggested that while a state's enforcement jurisdiction may be limited by territorial boundaries, its legislative jurisdiction is not limited by those boundaries.[16] Therefore, Jeffery argued that the refusal of one state to enforce the tax laws of another state merely facilitates and promotes tax evasion. His contention was that 'world-wide economic integration' has fundamentally changed the situation for international relations and international law. Globalization therefore justifies, or at least legitimates, the extraterritorial enforcement of a state's laws.

> [I]t no longer follows that one State, by exercising its prerogative power in the territory of another, is necessarily challenging that other State's sovereignty. The reason for this is that the basis of the enforcing State's economic power is no longer circumscribed by territorial boundaries. (Jeffery, 1999: pp. 123–124)

The objective is to give up all notions of state sovereignty (at least for economic matters) in order to remove all barriers to tax collection, and further, to establish a global tax regime in order to create an equitable global society.

State sovereignty also includes the norm that no state is obligated to act as the tax collection agent for another sovereign state. Bilateral agreements are intended to overcome this difficulty, while not expecting a state to enforce the laws of another state within its sovereign jurisdiction. The inability of a state to request and collect financial data concerning any accounts held by its citizens in an offshore jurisdiction without a prior information exchange agreement obstructs the capability of the state to pursue tax evasion, much less impose tax. However, the existence of a bilateral agreement does not assure information exchange, as the agreements often require mutual recognition of possible criminal conduct by the account owner, for example the accusation of money laundering. Tax avoidance or evasion in one state may not satisfy the mutual recognition requirement, as that activity may not be similarly defined in the second state (van der Bruggen, 2001). Part of the objective of the OECD project is to resolve these difficulties.

Economic development within global finance, and the burgeoning nature of globalization, impacts the sovereignty of small states. In particular it impacts the space in which small states are allowed fiscal sovereignty. At the same time, the different approaches used for taxation discussed here require fiscal sovereignty amongst states in order to continue to function. These differences are fundamental to retaining the ability to choose, and thus to enable each state to pursue and achieve the goals and aspirations for social welfare and the distribution of public goods desired by its citizens. It appears hypocritical on the part of developed states to retain the freedom of choice concerning taxation for themselves, while insisting that other states must forego similar sovereign choices. Thus, we now turn to the efforts of the OECD to eliminate what it has determined to be 'harmful' tax competition as produced by the choices made by sovereign states.

3
Global Financial Governance and Tax Competition

> He will place a tax on the air you breathe and on the bread you eat; he will give you a legislation which is as legitimate as it is unjust and instead of reasons, he'll give you laws. These will grow in the course of time, until you no longer exist for yourselves but for others.
>
> – Franz Grillparzer, *Libussa*, Act 2 (1872)

Sovereignty, and the sovereign right to tax (or not), rest within the structure of the state. This state-centric perspective may be subject to criticism for ignoring other, non-state, influences on the lives of citizens.[1] However, the situation prevails that it is the state, with its attendant structures and institutions, which remains concerned with the well-being of its residents and citizens. Whether that concern involves a minority or a majority, nevertheless revenue is required to satisfy expectations for political goods. State revenue is generally collected via either tariffs or taxes, yet the scale and extent of this collection may be manipulated to achieve a variety of purposes beyond simply government operations. This manipulation may be intended to attract new or additional sources of revenue to the state. These efforts lead observers to characterize the result as a 'competitive' state, for the government strives to enhance the political goods available to its citizens, while competing with other states (who also seek to enhance their public's welfare).[2] Among the political goods pursued are jobs (or full employment), improved infrastructure, improved educational opportunities, and additional business opportunities ancillary to the investment attracted to the state.

One arena for competition amongst states that has emerged over the past few decades concerns the taxation of individuals and firms. The competitive nature of the rate of taxation and the items subject to tax have been stimulated by the growth and pervasiveness of modern transportation and communication. Consequently, individuals and firms are no longer constrained by the physical geography of their resident (home) state. This further stimulates the competition, to a point where it has been characterized as 'harmful' by some observers. One might argue however, that it is only the losers in this competition who complain – that it is 'unfair', that the playing field is not level, and that consequently the competitive situation causes harm. The situation is described as one where the tax policy variance amongst states has skewed investment decisions. This in turn denies some states tax revenue, as well as providing a motivation and avenue for capital flight (whether or not it is to avoid expropriation or simply to seek higher returns on investment).[3]

International cooperation is required in order to resolve this competition between states collectively. However, different domestic needs could influence the level of cooperation forthcoming from the involved states. The next section introduces the global campaign against money laundering. This initiative for global financial governance is often associated with similar efforts to control tax avoidance/evasion, such as the Organization for Economic Co-operation and Development (OECD) project. This section serves as background to a more detailed examination of the project objectives within a context of state sovereignty. The documents published by the OECD to explain and promote the Harmful Tax Competition Initiative (HTCI) are analyzed. The examination is composed of subsections describing the OECD case against tax competition. The definition developed by the OECD for 'harmful' tax competition, and the tactics the OECD proposed to counter this harmful tax competition are both outlined. The next subsection explores the phrase frequently used to identify the goal of the OECD initiative. This phrase, 'to level the playing field', served to identify both the goal and the concern with competition among states over taxation. It required the creation of a special working group to establish a common definition of the phrase. The discussion in this chapter on the harmful tax competition project concludes by briefly presenting some of the dissenting views offered by OECD member states concerning the project.

Money laundering – smoke screen for the harmful tax competition initiative

Offshore financial centers (OFCs) are frequently accused of providing the methods and means to launder money and in the minds of some authors, they explicitly encourage the activity (Kochan, 2005). In general, the objective of money laundering is simply to place money into the financial (banking) system in a way that successfully disguises its origins, whether illegal or legal. The illegal source originally targeted for money laundering investigations was the profits from drug trafficking. An example of a legal source would be to place the proceeds of a business transaction into the banking system in a way designed to avoid paying the tax due on any profits. Within Europe, the earliest money laundering initiative was a recommendation of the Council of Europe to track the introduction of illegal money entering the banking system (Council of Europe, 1980). This recommendation was not, however, directed at drug trafficking; rather its objective was to intercept the proceeds from crimes committed by the left-wing terrorist groups plaguing Europe at the time, including the Red Brigades and the Red Army Faction (Pieth, 2002: p. 365).

The move to criminalize money laundering began with the US in 1986, well after the emergence of offshore finance. To define money laundering as an independent crime for American law enforcement served to open up a second front in its war on drugs.[4] After domestic criminalization, the US government actively undertook the initiative to establish money laundering as a crime internationally, given the cross-border nature of the activity and with illegal drug trafficking identified as its primary source. The Financial Action Task Force (FATF) was created to support the anti-money laundering campaign by identifying the financial activities and techniques used to launder money. From this information, the FATF produced evaluation criteria that are now used to determine the susceptibility of any firm, agency or national financial system to money laundering activities (Financial Action Task Force, 1990). With these objectives in mind, the FATF created the Forty Recommendations as guidance for states to criminalize money laundering. It has overseen the development of 'typology' documents to describe the methods and techniques used to conceal money laundering (Financial Action Task Force, 2003b). Another product of the FATF was the Non-Cooperative Countries or Territories

(NCCT) list. From its first publication in 2000, this document served to identify jurisdictions that had not met the Forty Recommendations as the standard for anti-money laundering legislation and enforcement. As one part of a strategy towards global compliance/cooperation against money laundering, it would appear to have been successful. Most states that were listed in turn rapidly re-wrote laws or drafted new laws in order to pass muster with the FATF. The first NCCT list evaluated twenty-nine jurisdictions selected by the FATF and found fifteen of them to be non-cooperative with the anti-money laundering recommendations (Financial Action Task Force, 2000). The experience of the Caribbean jurisdictions included in this first 'blacklist' is discussed as part of the analysis of their OFCs in Chapter 6.

Some commentators argue that the information exchange regime of the harmful tax competition project will enhance the enforcement of anti-money laundering legislation and efforts to combat the financing of terrorism (Witherell, 2002; Biersteker, 2004). In a similar fashion, the OECD argues that there are 'substantial similarities between the techniques used to launder the proceeds of crime and to commit tax crime.' (Centre for Tax Policy and Administration, 2001: p. 33; Organization for Economic Co-operation and Development, 2002) The intense scrutiny placed on OFCs by a number of international organizations has mitigated their general usage for disguising the origins of criminal money. Furthermore, some of the most widely publicized cases of money laundering have not involved OFCs, but instead implicated a number of large international banks located in the major global banking centers. For example, there was the specific case of the Bank of New York and US$7 billion of Russian funds (thought to be foreign aid monies) laundered for the benefit of a small group of Russian citizens (Minority Staff of the Permanent Subcommittee on Investigations, 2001: pp. 253–254).[5] For purposes of the present discussion, it is sufficient to note that there is an international consensus on the criminality of money laundering, if not the means to eradicate it. As noted already, there is no such international consensus for tax crimes (evasion, avoidance or abusive) as they are state-specific in their identification as well as enforcement.[6]

The story of the Harmful Tax Competition Initiative

It can be suggested that the roots of the OECD project sprouted from the European Union's Tax Harmonization campaign, which itself began in the 1960s (Holzinger, 2005; Genschel and Plümper, 1997; Genschel, 2002; Sanders, 2002).[7] From this vantage point, the issue was not so much a problem of tax avoidance by corporations, as much as it was tax avoidance and tax evasion by countless anonymous individual citizens. Any figures reported for the size and magnitude of extraterritorial wealth are perforce estimates, and thus they should be considered with some skepticism. In particular we should be alert to any pre-existing assumptions embedded in the estimates, such as the desire to support a particular political agenda. Further, it is difficult to segregate the accounts of individuals from accounts possessed by corporate business entities (which could actually mask and conceal an individual). The veracity of figures presented for offshore wealth could be compared with those suggested for money laundering, 'Figures of $300 billion to $500 billion for international flows are banded [sic] around and become "facts by repetition," but there is very little evidence to justify them.' (Levi, 2002: p. 184) In June 2000 for example, Oxfam UK reported 'recent estimates' that there were between $6–7 trillion in OFCs, and that between $3–4 trillion of this sum 'consists of savings held abroad by wealthy individuals' (Oxfam, 2000: p. 7).[8] The report goes on to calculate that this results in a tax revenue loss of 'at least US$50 billion a year'. Another data point comes from testimony offered to the United States Senate, Permanent Subcommittee on Investigations, in July 2001, when the District Attorney for Manhattan declared 'Deposits of U.S. dollars in the Cayman Islands have been increasing by about $120 billion a year; according to the Federal Reserve Bank of New York, there are now more than $800 billion U.S. dollars on deposit in Grand Cayman.' (Committee on Governmental Affairs, 2001) There was nothing to suggest however in this testimony from the Manhattan District Attorney just how much of this amount he believed were deposits by US citizens or corporations, versus how much belonged to non-citizens seeking the security of deposits in a hard currency. And an article published in *The Nation* in June 2001 quoted a financial consulting firm's 'World Wealth Report' – 'According to Merrill Lynch & Gemini Consulting's "World Wealth Report," one-third of the wealth of the world's high net-worth individuals, or nearly $6 trillion, may be held offshore. Offshore havens also hold an estimated 31 percent of the profits of US multinationals.' (Komisar, 2001)

These figures locate a motivation for the OECD, whose initial document for the project was titled *Harmful Tax Competition: An Emerging Global Issue*. Immediately, starting with the very cover of the report, the OECD established this project as involving a 'global' concern, by using an image of a globe in the cover artwork. The message to be received is that 'we' (the OECD) were tackling this issue, on 'our' own initiative, for the betterment of all. In the introduction of this report, the authors stated that it

> ... is intended to develop a better understanding of how tax havens and harmful preferential tax regimes, collectively referred to as harmful tax practices, affect the location of financial and other service activities, erode the tax bases of other countries, distort trade and investment patterns and undermine the fairness, neutrality and broad social acceptance of tax systems generally. *Such harmful tax competition diminishes global welfare and undermines taxpayer confidence in the integrity of tax systems*. (Organization for Economic Co-operation and Development, 1998: p. 8, emphasis mine)

The subsequent paragraph then stated that the report covered both member and non-member states and their dependencies. It was important to be clear that not only was the problem global, but the analysis and attendant recommendations were also global in nature. However, the report refrained from addressing the issues of foreign direct investment (FDI) and consumption taxes. It focused solely on 'general income tax systems, as well as those taxes levied on certain types of income.' (Organization for Economic Co-operation and Development, 1998: p. 8)[9] The totality of the work contained in this report 'needs to be seen in the context of the OECD's role in a world where the pace of globalisation is accelerating.' (Organization for Economic Co-operation and Development, 1998: p. 8)

Establishing the case against competition

The first chapter of the report, 'Tax Competition: A Global Phenomenon', developed the argument that 'The accelerating process of globalisation of trade and investment has fundamentally changed the relationship among domestic tax systems.' (Organization for Economic Co-operation and Development, 1998: p. 13) One may read this as a 'hyperglobalist' statement – the situation was new, mobility of capital was new, and while this 'globalisation has had a positive effect on the development of tax systems [it] had the negative effects of opening up new ways by which companies and individuals can minimise and *avoid* taxes...' (Organization for Economic Co-operation and Development, 1998: p. 14, emphasis mine)[10] In keeping with criticisms made on this perspective of globalization, the argument here suggests otherwise. The ways were not new, and the means of minimizing and avoiding taxes were not necessarily new, only technologically more advanced. Looking at the history behind the development of global finance and tax havens, one finds that corporate domicile and capital flight were aspects of the financial landscape prior to this latest wave of internationalization. Switzerland has been used to protect individual wealth from confiscation in unsettled times since the seventeenth century (Faith, 1982). Corporate case law concerning taxation, and in a sense the inter-state transfer of corporate profits, in the United Kingdom dates from 1876 (Picciotto, 1999: p. 73, footnote 5). At a time when London was recognized as the world financial center and global financial hegemon, this fact suggests that corporations (both joint-stock and individuals) have found spaces in the financial regulatory landscape to avoid taxation for at least the last 130 years (and likely much longer).

Nonetheless, *Harmful Tax Competition* starts from the premise that the situation is 'new'. Individuals that utilize the services of tax havens, and the tax haven jurisdictions themselves, are characterized as 'free riders' – the individuals because they benefit from public spending but don't contribute towards those same public goods; and the tax havens (and their residents) because they benefit from the 'general public goods created by the non-haven country.' (Organization for Economic Co-operation and Development, 1998: pp. 14–15) The OECD report acknowledged the complexity of the issues involved in taxation, and the use of tax laws by many states to encourage and facilitate development and investment. The report also recognized the paucity of data available to perform 'a detailed comparative analysis of the economic and revenue effects involving low-tax jurisdictions.' Nonetheless, its authors found that 'the available data do suggest that the current use of tax havens is large, and that participation in such schemes is expanding at an exponential rate.' (Organization for Economic Co-operation and Development, 1998: p. 17) The figure provided in the report is that

> ... foreign direct investment by G7 countries in a number of jurisdictions in the Caribbean and in the South Pacific island states,

which are generally considered to be low-tax jurisdictions, increased more than five-fold over the period 1985–1994, to more than $200 billion, a rate of increase well in excess of the growth of total outbound Foreign Direct Investment (Organization for Economic Co-operation and Development, 1998: p. 17).

Let us pause for a moment and consider this example – first, as already noted, FDI itself was explicitly excluded from consideration in this report, yet it was necessary to use FDI data to support the argument, presumably due to a lack of more relevant data. The absence of detailed figures to support this statement is also interesting in that a different OECD publication provides data identifying 'direct investment abroad (outflows)' for the G7 states in 1994 as US$188 billion (out of an OECD total of US$248 billion) (Organization for Economic Co-operation and Development, 2004b: p. 32). Yet, it is quite likely that the capital flows identified in the OECD report were simply transiting the offshore centers onward as FDI in other locations.[11] The facilities offered by OFCs have been utilized extensively in this manner and certainly there are limited investment opportunities in these low-tax jurisdictions themselves.

One method for using a low tax jurisdiction with FDI involves leasing equipment. This can be a more profitable strategy than owning the same equipment at a specific location, given the proper treatment of capital depreciation rules in the home state tax regulations. The technique was to lease the equipment from an intermediate company, located in a low-tax jurisdiction, for use in a third state. The lessor collected payments in a low-tax jurisdiction, while the parent company located in the high-tax jurisdiction claimed deductions on the business expense for leasing the equipment. In addition, the intermediate firm might have been able to claim capital depreciation deductions on the equipment that it owned. If all of these firms were in the same corporate structure, all monies stayed within the family, as it were (Doggart, 2002: 10th ed., pp. 72–73). Furthermore, this strategy may serve to limit exposure to the risk of expropriation or nationalization of a firm's capital equipment. Captive insurance companies, similarly located in low-tax jurisdictions, also facilitate the management of risk. While the captive company insured the risks of the owning firm, it collected its premiums (and thus profits) in a low-tax jurisdiction. At the same time, the parent firm benefited from the deduction on insurance premiums available in some high-tax jurisdictions. Again, the monies remained within the corporate family (Doggart, 2002: pp. 87–88).[12] An underlying point to these transnational tax minimization methods is the fact that they followed the letter of the legislation of the home (OECD) state, even if for objectives not explicitly intended by the legislature.

Reports appeared in the Australian media in early 2003 (and echoed by the media in Bermuda) concerning large capital outflows passing through 'tax havens'. The reports dramatically stated that 'According to figures compiled by the federal government's financial intelligence agency, Austrac, $5.01 billion flowed out of Australia to 41 OECD-designated tax havens in the June 2002 financial year, and $3.56 billion flowed back in.' This observation was accompanied by a statement from the opposition party's (Labor) assistant treasury spokesman,

> 'This isn't just high-wealth individuals or big companies', Mr Cox said. 'Certainly hundreds of millions, probably billions of dollars in Australian tax are being lost each year.' (Mellish, 2003: p. 1)[13]

However, the reply offered by the Australian Taxation Office reflects the complexity of the issue, and again the problem with collecting and reporting relevant data.

> 'The $5 billion refers to the amount of funds identified as transferred to haven countries, it does not refer to the amount of tax avoided or evaded', Mr Fitzpatrick [First assistant commissioner] said yesterday.
>
> 'It says nothing about the profit derived from those funds, the tax payable on those profits, tax that is payable in Australia or tax that has actually been paid in Australia.
>
> 'Not all tax-haven use is offensive. For example, Bermuda provides special regimes for shipping and insurance.' (Buffini, 2003: p. 3)

As this Australian example illustrates, the authors of *Harmful Tax Competition* were justified in their concern over the lack of relevant, applicable data. The lack of data is in part a result of the complexities of the tax code. It is because of this problem that the OECD continued 'to attach importance to collecting additional data on developments in tax havens and in the use of preferential tax regimes.' (Organization for Economic Co-operation and Development, 1998: p. 17) At the same time, the report acknowledged that 'there are no particular reasons why any two countries should have the same level and structure of taxation.' Most issues of taxation are domestic and reflect social preferences for the type of tax and how it is used, however, there are increased spillover effects due to globalization. 'Countries should remain free to design their own tax systems as long as they abide by internationally accepted standards in doing so.' These efforts by the OECD are intended, in part, to provide OECD-certified acceptable international standards (Organization for Economic Co-operation and Development, 1998: p. 15). But, if taxation is a domestic concern for the sovereign state, why is there a need for *internationally* acceptable standards? If we agree that a need exists for international standards, is it then valid that they be created by a select group of states? This approach is not the technique used by the International Organization for Standardization (ISO) to provide standards in other areas of commerce and business, for example standards for automotive emission diagnostic controls (see www.iso.org). Under the structure of the ISO a group of experts (either national or international) prepares a draft standard that is then submitted for review, comment and vote (with or without comments). Each national standards agency has the document reviewed by national experts, and then it submits its *one* vote. The ISO is a universal organization rather than a club with membership restrictions like the OECD.

Creating a definition of the harmful competitor

Listed in the second chapter of the report, 'Factors to Identify Tax Havens and Harmful Preferential Tax Regimes', are the criteria used to determine and discriminate between tax haven states and non-tax haven states. Within this determination exists a further subset of states, those non-tax haven states with preferential tax regimes. There are a number of problems posed by these criteria which left them open to debate. First, the report recognized that 'a precise technical definition' of a tax haven is not available, yet insisted that 'a useful distinction' between states that raise significant tax revenues with those that don't collect tax served as a selection criteria. (Organization for Economic Co-operation and Development, 1998: p. 20) Second, the terms tax evasion and tax avoidance were conflated, while the issue of money laundering has been introduced – because if access to information for tax purposes (transparency) was constrained, 'it facilitates tax evasion and money laundering' (Organization for Economic Co-operation and Development, 1998: p. 24). Finally, there is the effort made to distinguish between a tax haven and a preferential tax regime which would exist in a non-haven state. Each of these problems will be discussed in more detail, as they were pivotal to the aims of the project, and to the criticisms made about the initiative.

First, in developing a definition of a 'tax haven' the authors of the report found that it was possible to distinguish 'three broad categories of situations' where the tax imposed in one state on a 'geographically mobile activity' would be different (lower) than that imposed by another state for the same income. The first category (situation) established the state as tax haven, a state that collected 'no or only nominal tax on that income.' The second category identified was a situation in which, while the state 'collects significant revenues from tax imposed on income at the individual or corporate level', the source of this particular income received preferential treatment such that it was 'subject to low or no taxation'. Finally, the third category noted was simply that the state 'collects significant revenues from tax imposed on income at the individual or corporate level' but the rate of tax imposed was less than that of another state (Organization for Economic Co-operation and Development, 1998: pp. 19–20). The value of the adjective 'significant' was not quantified, presumably because it was obvious, and thus recognizable in the eyes of the beholder. However, what is considered a significant level of taxation by a US citizen may be viewed as a low level of taxation by a UK citizen. Michael Keen described this particular distinction in discussing five specific differences between the US and UK tax systems in 1997 (Keen, 1997). The ambiguity that is possible here could lead to further misunderstandings and miscommunication in those cases where there is not a shared appreciation for what qualifies as a 'significant' level of taxation (Picciotto, 2007).

The text of *Harmful Tax Competition* referred back to an earlier paragraph in the text, and acknowledged that 'globalisation has had a positive effect on the development of tax systems'; therefore this third category was considered beyond the scope of the report.[14]

> It is not intended to explicitly or implicitly suggest that there is some general minimum effective rate of tax to be imposed on income below which a country would be considered to be engaging in harmful tax competition. (Organization for Economic Co-operation and Development, 1998: p. 20)

So the first category identified any no/low income tax collecting state as a tax haven, the second category identified tax-collecting states that provide preferential treatment for mobile capital, and the third category recognized the distinction between and amongst sovereign states to establish their own levels of taxation (as long as *some* amount of income tax was collected).

Consequently, states are permitted fiscal sovereignty to establish rates of tax imposed on income, so long as there is a tax imposed and there is no preferential treatment of non-residents over residents. Yet this perception contradicts the sentence, quoted above, that the report 'is not intended to' establish some minimum expected level of taxation. Globalization has introduced acceptable competition amongst those states which impose taxes, and this has 'thereby [minimized] tax induced distortions' (Organization for Economic Co-operation and Development, 1998: p. 20). Nevertheless, a perception also exists suggesting that those states imposing little or no tax have induced a 'race to the bottom'.[15] Surely, this perception anticipates the expectation for some minimum level of taxation upon individual and corporate income by every national government. And if this level has not been met, if the state was not collecting those 'significant revenues' from individual and corporate income, then it qualified as a tax haven, by the definition promoted in this report.

This brings us back to the question, what is a tax haven? Again, the report acknowledged that 'the concept of a "tax haven" does not have a precise technical meaning'. Nevertheless it continued to assert that it is possible to discriminate between states, between those that are 'tax havens' from those states that offered preferential tax regimes (Organization for Economic Co-operation and Development, 1998: p. 20). The discriminating characteristic between these two categories was between minimal taxation and the preferential treatment of a specific source of income. For the authors of this report – 'the absence of tax or a low effective tax rate on the relevant income is the starting point of any evaluation.' (Organization for Economic Co-operation and Development, 1998: p. 21)[16] After this declarative point in the report, the text proceeded to explore the factors used to determine if a state qualified as a tax haven, or possessed a preferential tax regime.

Chief among the determining factors identified to differentiate between these two categories was the level of transparency, a particularly popular term in the vocabulary of globalization and global governance. In this report the argument was that transparency is hampered by the existence of legislative, legal or administrative provisions preventing the 'effective exchange of information' (Organization for Economic Co-operation and Development, 1998: p. 24). Transparency is not simply cooperating in the exchange of information between states but, it is also the elimination of secret tax agreements and any legal barriers preventing the disclosure of beneficial ownership. The lack of transparency was identified as also preventing an exchange of information for other 'tax-related' financial matters such as money laundering. Here again, the concern is really with laws permitting banking confidentiality. It is important to note that the report at this point spoke of 'criminal tax fraud' (Organization for Economic Co-operation and Development, 1998: p. 24). This phrase has different (or non-existent) meanings within different state legal systems. Consider for example the analysis arranged by the OECD on 'Access for Tax Authorities to Information Gathered by Anti-Money Laundering Authorities'. The analysis was conducted on data provided by OECD *member* states and found that there were significant differences in the exchange of information even permitted within the individual legal systems of the survey respondents for this specific criminal activity (Organization for Economic Co-operation and Development, 2002). The results indicate that significant challenges hinder the way forward for states to achieve the level of transparency desired. To accomplish the crossflow of data that was desired between law enforcement and revenue collecting authorities would require legislative action in many states. A lack of transparency and limitations on the effective exchange of information were two of the four key factors used to identify and categorize a particular jurisdiction as a tax haven.

The other two factors used to identify a state to be categorized as a tax haven were 'no or nominal taxes' and 'no substantial activities'. As already noted, the factor concerned with the level of taxation was identified as 'a necessary condition for the identification of a tax haven.' Moreover, if the jurisdiction was 'perceived to offer itself as a place where non-residents can escape tax in their country of residence' then this may be a sufficient condition (Organization for Economic Co-operation and Development, 1998: p. 23). The desire for 'substantial' activities was deemed important because otherwise it appeared that the jurisdiction was merely 'attempting to attract investment and transactions that are purely tax driven.' Substantial activities might include for example full-time employees and offices, however, the report conceded that determining if 'an activity is substantial can be difficult.' (Organization for Economic Co-operation and Development, 1998: p. 24) In response to criticisms related to this problem, the substantial activity factor was reassessed, and it was dropped as an evaluation criterion with the 2001 Progress Report (Organization for Economic Co-operation and Development, 2001a: p. 10).

So one might conclude that a jurisdiction was a tax haven if one perceived that it offered an escape from taxation. Described this way, the tax competition proposition appeared flexible enough to be applied to any jurisdiction, small state or large state, as long as the observer was sufficiently perceptive. In 2002, the United States for example, did not tax the income activities of non-resident non-citizens (no or nominal taxes), or report the possession of such accounts to the country of residence of these individuals (lack of effective exchange of information) (Langer, 2002).[17] Therefore, at that time the United States was a tax haven – for non-resident aliens. Yet this last point, the fact that this situation applies only to non-resident aliens, is a discriminating factor between the tax haven and the preferential tax regime; the US does collect 'significant revenues' from individual and corporate income taxes. As a result, the US should have been categorized as possessing a preferential tax regime rather than as a tax haven, yet neither identification was made in the OECD reports.[18]

Similar in nature to the tax haven, the preferential tax regime is the second category where there are differences amongst states in the amount of tax imposed on mobile capital. Three of the four key factors for this category are identical with those of the tax haven category. These factors are no or low effective tax rates, lack of transparency, and the lack of effective exchange of information. The difference here was with the fourth factor, 'no substantial activities' which had been replaced with the 'ring fencing' of tax regimes (Organization for Economic Co-operation and Development, 1998: p. 27). The concept of 'ring fencing' got directly to the heart of the matter and was the factor that made the tax regime in question a preferential one. As defined in the report, ring fencing was the situation where the regime is restricted to non-residents; or those who benefited from the regime are 'explicitly or implicitly denied access to domestic markets'. Since residents were excluded from the preferential regime, it was clearly intended to attract mobile capital seeking to avoid the taxation of the country of origin. And this approach 'effectively protects the sponsoring country from the harmful effects of its own incentive regime' while it caused harm to foreign tax bases (Organization for Economic Co-operation and Development, 1998, pp. 26, 28). In addition to mobile capital, the description of a preferential tax regime could be applied to other areas of taxation excluded from this report, for instance the tax-free export-processing zone. But in the case of preferential tax regimes, the report did not limit itself to these four key factors (as it did with the definition of a tax haven).

The additional factors, which may be used to identify a preferential tax regime, occupied the remainder of the chapter in *Harmful Tax Competition*. The chapter then concluded with several questions for use in 'assessing the economic effects of a preferential tax regime in terms of its potential harmfulness.' Recall that the second category identified jurisdictions which 'collect significant revenues' from income taxes, with the exception of this preferential regime. The list of remaining factors comprised a roll-up of all remaining elements that could identify those jurisdictions where citizens from a high-tax OECD state might have an account and avoid excessive taxation on their income. These factors were: an artificial definition of the tax base, failure to adhere to international transfer pricing principles, foreign source income exempted from local income tax (the territorial taxation system used in the UK for example), negotiable tax rate or tax base (as famously used by Switzerland for Elizabeth Taylor, as one amongst a collection of celebrity personalities over the years[19]), existence of secrecy provisions, access to a wide network of tax treaties, regimes which were promoted as tax minimization vehicles, and places where the regime encouraged purely tax-driven operations or arrangements (Organization for Economic Co-operation and Development, 1998: pp. 30–34).

Taking action against the competition

Having determined that harmful tax competition exists, that it is a global problem, and having suggested how to identify the sources of this competition, it only remained for the report to propose the methods for use in 'Counteracting Harmful Tax Competition'. This is the title of Chapter 3 of *Harmful Tax Competition*, the first paragraph of which reads,

> Governments cannot stand back while their tax bases are eroded through the actions of countries which offer taxpayers ways to exploit tax havens and preferential regimes to reduce the tax that would otherwise be payable to them. (Organization for Economic Co-operation and Development, 1998: p. 37)

It is a situation wherein individual states are attempting to protect their tax base, but feel that international coordinated action is necessary, because 'the activities which are the main focus of this report are highly mobile.' (Organization for Economic Co-operation and Development, 1998: p. 38) More accurately, because the income they are seeking to impose a tax upon is highly mobile, only international cooperation can monitor or control it.

To achieve this international coordination, action is necessary from the major regional finance centers (Frankfurt, Paris, Hong Kong, Chicago), as well as the global finance centers (New York, London, Tokyo), if the project is to succeed. A leak anywhere in the global financial system, that allows an OFC under sanctions to transfer funds into the system, will negate the efforts of the OECD project. Any space in which one may place untaxed income and continue to have access to it provides a tax haven alternative for any person so inclined. Therefore, the OECD is not only relying on the participation of state governments, but also the cooperation of the major multinational financial firms with branches, subsidiaries, partners and affiliates resident in the OFCs (implicitly anticipated via state regulation and enforcement). To achieve this level of participation, it appears the OECD is also implicitly going to depend upon a specific and widely recognized feature of the successful financial center, the value of its reputation and the consequential fragility of a reputation. We need only consider the circumstances surrounding one historical case to demonstrate this feature for an OFC. On the Isle of Man, a 'lax regulating regime enabled a series of business failures to [occur] in the early 1980s in particular, [sic] the devastating crash of the Savings and Investment Bank Limited (SIB) in 1982' (Cobb, 1998: p. 16). This bank failure affected the reputation of the financial center, and resulted in a loss of confidence in the remaining financial institutions on the island. There was also the cost of dealing with various legal actions and of compensating depositors in the failed institution (Solly, 1994: p. 90). The implementation of new legislation increased regulatory oversight and supervision. However, it has taken years for the Manx financial services industry to recover from the effects of this one failed bank.

The OECD report divided its Recommendations for countering harmful competition into three categories. These categories collected together recommendations concerning domestic legislation, tax treaties, and the 'intensification of international co-operation' (Organization for Economic Co-operation and Development, 1998: p. 39). The Recommendations of specific interest here were all under this latter category of international cooperation, viz.: the establishment of 'a Forum to implement the Guidelines and other Recommendations of this Report' (#15); the production of a list of tax havens (#16); and a recommendation that states with particular links to tax haven jurisdictions ensure these links do not promote harmful tax competition (#17). Thus the intention was to create the mechanism through which to force the uncooperative jurisdictions, which would be 'named and shamed' on the official OECD list of tax havens, to become cooperative. Finally, those states possessing colonial vestiges (overseas territories) were expected to use their 'particular links' to eliminate harmful tax competition from these non-self-governing jurisdictions.

In pursuit of the 'level playing field'

In conjunction with describing tax competition as a source of global harm, the supporters of the harmful tax competition project identified as their goal the creation of a 'level playing field.' This sports analogy is consistent with a view of an international system composed of competing states. Such a conception also reinforces a belief in a limited tax base from which to draw state revenue. Therefore, it is a zero-sum game where one state's loss is another state's gain. In order to maintain their existing tax base, high tax states are pursuing a campaign to 'level the playing field' upon which high tax states competed against the low or no tax states. And because its usage is so prevalent in the documents analyzed here it is necessary to consider the application of the term to global finance. A usage suggested by small states was that all states 'must be subject to the same rules for any given activity' (Stikeman Elliott, 2002: p. xi). This viewpoint was contradicted by the solution reached in February 2003 for *European Union* tax harmonization, which did not advance the project for a *global* level playing field in taxation. It is a contention that results from the differential treatment accorded three EU member states on the matter of information exchange as a negotiated compromise to reach agreement.

As with the OECD's stated objective for the tax competition project as a whole, this definition does not involve a level playing field for competition in tax rates. Rather, it addresses the means by which the OECD would overcome the obstacles of fiscal sovereignty and banking confidentiality for collecting tax on residents' foreign accounts. As a matter of fairness amongst states the level playing field involves tax regime transparency and the exchange of tax-related financial information. In this fashion, the existence of a difference in tax rates becomes immaterial as a factor in international finance. With the establishment of the information exchange regime, states would have the information required to collect taxes from their residents at domestic rates, no matter where the income was earned. In effect, this solution will supersede all existing territorial tax administrations by assessing all tax obligations against globally earned income, as opposed to income earned within the jurisdiction of the taxpayer's state of residence. The objective accomplished by the global implementation of this definition would be to overcome the barrier created by principles of state sovereignty.

One could argue that efforts to create a level playing field are not intended to redress an imbalance, but instead are intended to establish common rules of play. If all participants are following the same global rules for 'acceptable' conduct, than competition (where it exists) will be 'fair'. To use a sports analogy is to allude to a sports event, whether football, rugby, baseball, or cricket. Yet even in sports competitions, the fact that the playing field is level, does not guarantee that the competition is equitable or 'fair'. Consider the status for example of Manchester United and the New York Yankees as representative professional sports franchises. Both are well-funded organizations able to use their economic position to maintain their dominance by acquiring the best available players. They are analogous to the large developed states, competing against less well-endowed smaller organizations. Consequently, they possess an economic advantage that has translated into a competitive advantage that overwhelms the level circumstances of their playing field. Extending this analogy to the OECD states suggests that forcing a global level playing field, in whatever market sector, provides large developed states with a competitive advantage to maintain their market position and to continue to dominate the economic efforts of smaller states. As discussed in the next section, these circumstances worry the smaller members of the OECD just as much as they worry non-member small states.

An immanent critique from OECD abstentions

Support for this project was not unanimous among the member states of the OECD. Annex II of *Harmful Tax Competition* contains the statements made by OECD members Luxembourg and Switzerland outlining their concerns with the document (Organization for Economic Co-operation and Development, 1998: pp. 73–78). In its statement, Luxembourg acknowledged its participation in both the OECD and EU activities on taxation. However it argued that this report presented 'a partial and imbalanced approach' that did not satisfy the group's mandate. Luxembourg was particularly concerned with 'the Report's implicit belief that bank secrecy is necessarily a source of harmful tax competition.' Consequently, 'Luxembourg shall not be bound by the Report nor by the Recommendations to counteract harmful tax competition.' (Organization for Economic Co-operation and Development, 1998: pp. 74–75)

In reaching a similar conclusion regarding the report, Switzerland also raised its concern that the report did not take into account the non-tax factors involved in economic competitiveness. Similarly, Switzerland noted the point made earlier, that the OECD Report acknowledges that states possess fiscal sovereignty, while at the same time it uses lower tax levels as a criterion for identifying harmful regimes. On this point, the conclusion reached by Swiss officials was that 'this results in unacceptable protection of countries with high levels of taxation, which is, moreover, contrary to the economic philosophy of the OECD.' (Organization for Economic Co-operation and Development, 1998: p. 77)

The progress report in 2000, *Towards Global Tax Co-operation*, mentioned in its footnotes that the 1998 report was approved with abstentions from Luxembourg and Switzerland. Belgium and Portugal would join them in abstaining from the 2001 progress report.[20] This later report contained a footnote in which Luxembourg and Switzerland 'recalled' their earlier abstention to the 1998 report. Luxembourg regretted 'that the 2001 progress report is further away from the goal of combating harmful tax competition with respect to the location of economic activities.' In addition, Switzerland noted that its earlier abstention applied to any subsequent work (Organization for Economic Co-operation and Development, 2001a: p. 4, footnote 1). As states possessing a substantial financial services industry, Luxembourg, Switzerland and Belgium would experience an economic impact similar to the small, non-OECD member states hosting OFCs. However, as members of the OECD, they are inside the club and may participate in the discussions on harmful tax competition. The small states on the outside find their participation is limited to the 'Global Forum' where they can neither schedule meetings nor strongly influence the agenda.

Conclusions

Hopefully it has become clear from this analysis of the OECD reports on harmful tax competition that the OECD approached this issue with a limited conception of fiscal sovereignty. That is, a conception that demands a significant level of state revenue will originate from taxes and one that anticipates the existence of internationally accepted standards for designing the necessary tax administration. At the same time, there are significant differences among OECD member states in the construction of their tax systems, specifically in the allocation of tax rates to individual income, corporate income, capital income, consumption, and sin (i.e. – tobacco, alcohol and fossil fuels). Within these tax administrations are various measures intended to encourage certain businesses while discouraging other activities (e.g. – measures promoting family-owned farms and taxes to discourage smoking). A state's tax code reflects the social preferences of its society for the construction and distribution of public goods, or at least the legislature's interpretation of those preferences.

The argument developed by the OECD that competition is harmful was clearly built upon the idea that the state is a benevolent maximizer of public welfare. As such, economic analysis starting from this premise supports the initiative, while analysis premised on the viewpoint that the state is a *Leviathan* contests the purpose behind the OECD project. At the same time, the question of taxation and the provision of public goods has become abstracted from the free market ideology promoted by a number of OECD states in other venues, such as the trade in goods and services. In general then, one's opinion of the project against harmful tax competition reflects the basic understanding they hold of the role of the state in society, and the extent of taxation required to satisfy that role. In this fashion, the argument that globalization has changed the nature of global economic exchange is really an argument that the capability of the state has been diminished. That argument contends that globalization has reduced the ability of the state to manage its national economy including specifically the control of capital and the extraction of taxes.

The specific criticisms made against the OECD's HTCI, largely by smaller states, are not framed against the perceived loss of state control over the domestic economy. Rather they are concerned with matters of state sovereignty (independence and non-intervention), equitable treatment (for members and non-members alike), and the origination of the project within a club organization limited to already developed states. These criticisms, followed by various statements made by OECD representatives to rebut them, are presented in the next chapter.

4
Resistance and Withdrawal

> For the citizen of many smaller, poorer, weaker states, however, the international secretariats look more like enemies, instruments of a new kind of collective colonialism devoted to the preservation of the capitalist system and the hierarchies of power represented in it, even at considerable cost to their material welfare, the dignity and sometimes even the survival of individual men, women and children in a neocolonial society.
>
> – Susan Strange[1]

In February 2003, an article in the *Nassau Guardian* identified the European Union's latest efforts towards tax harmonization as contrary to the Organization for Economic Co-operation and Development (OECD) goal of a global 'level playing field' for taxation. The reporter identified three jurisdictions (Panama, Antigua and the Cayman Islands) that had immediately registered their criticism of the EU Directive on the Taxation of Savings with either the EU or the OECD. Their protests concerned the apparent preferential treatment accorded some EU member states concerning information exchange as part of the negotiated resolution that finally put in place the Savings Tax Directive (Delaney, 2003). The OECD also expressed a concern at the potential impact the directive could have on its Harmful Tax Competition Initiative (HTCI).

> Donald Johnston, OECD Secretary General, wrote privately to the heads of EU Governments in January [2003] saying Europe had

> endangered a global drive to crack down on criminal tax cheats, by excusing three member states from exchange of information. (Ausenda, 2003b)

These events highlight the status of the OECD project in early 2003, four years after the publication of the initial report. In particular it demonstrates a heightened awareness on the part of residents in the targeted small states for the potential impact of these external events on their lives. In the previous chapter, the main elements of the OECD project on harmful tax competition were outlined. This chapter discusses the reaction of small states to the coercive and disciplinary nature of this project. In the first section is a discussion of their main points of criticism – that it challenges state sovereignty, that the OECD is not appropriate as a site for global governance, and that the treatment of non-cooperative jurisdictions must be equitable. This is followed in the second section with elements of the OECD rebuttal to these criticisms. The third section is focused on the role and influence of US support for and subsequent disengagement from the OECD project. The final section provides a summary of the debate between the opponents and proponents of tax competition present in the OECD's harmful tax competition project.

A critique from the islands

The critique of the OECD's project emerged from a variety of locations, and offered several points of contestation. Perspectives were provided in the financial press, and by the media in general from among the affected jurisdictions. Suggestions were offered concerning the legal ramifications of the sanctions proposed in the OECD report. A potential conflict between these sanctions and World Trade Organization (WTO) obligations was identified. Moreover, accusations framing the HTCI as an attack on state sovereignty were made by various commentators. The major points of criticism of the OECD project explored here are: that it was an attack on the sovereignty of the identified states (and particularly small states); that the OECD was not the appropriate forum for the question of tax competition amongst sovereign states; and that the OECD had not fostered or promoted actions consistent with its intended goal of a 'level playing field'.

A subversion of sovereignty

The first and most basic criticism made about the OECD project was that it subverts the sovereignty of states. Externally-driven attempts to force a change in the domestic decisions made about taxation is contrary to the principle of non-intervention in the domestic affairs of a sovereign state. By initially presenting the issue as one of lost tax revenue, many observers concluded the OECD was motivated solely by this problem and nothing else. 'But such motivation implies interference in the sovereign right of nations to determine their own tax regimes.' (Persaud, 2001: p. 205) Bishnodat Persaud highlighted the further point that the objectives of the harmful tax competition project exceeded any previous attempts at tax cooperation that OECD member states had accomplished successfully among themselves. The particular problems encountered by the European Union in its drive towards tax harmonization were mentioned, including the continuing intransigence of Austria and Luxembourg. Within the EU, they exercised their sovereign independence whenever necessary on matters of financial legislation and regulation (Persaud, 2001: p. 206).

The OECD project's insistence on transparency, discussed in the last chapter, conflicts with historical traditions of banking confidentiality and privacy. The most frequent argument made against banking confidentiality was that it served only to protect the 'guilty'. Nevertheless, even the fact that one is innocent (and therefore has nothing to hide from the government) does not mean that they are willing to have their financial data become a matter of *public* knowledge. It is a simple desire to keep financial information private, away from the perusal of neighbors, co-workers, and litigating lawyers. Fundamentally, this is about a society's option to choose not only the structure of taxation, but also the level of confidentiality regarding information and the privacy of the individual.

From a legal perspective, Rosemarie Antoine has suggested that legal questions about banking confidentiality involve state sovereignty, especially within the context of offshore financial centers, because it involved more than one state's municipal law.

> Questioning offshore confidentiality laws is more than a mere legalistic inquiry. To some extent it is also questioning the right of sovereign governments to create laws in harmony with their

> own nationalist and developmental perspectives. As such, the protection of confidentiality should be seen as a duty in the public interest, even by the courts (Antoine, 2001: p. 12).[2]

As with matters of taxation and public goods, confidentiality and data privacy are also a matter of social preferences. Nonetheless, banking secrecy laws are not impervious to all outside inquiries. On this aspect of confidentiality laws, Antoine discussed the appropriate procedures and legal measures available to override the legislation. Such measures are often a part of a mutual legal assistance treaty (MLAT) between two states and are specifically intended for use when investigating *criminal* activity. (Antoine, 2002)

The option, or opportunity, for mutual legal assistance has been ignored upon occasion, particularly in cases that involved a large state seeking information from a small jurisdiction. The United States in particular has failed to use its existing MLATs to wage its 'war on drugs' (and associated money laundering activity) and the simple civil cases that are part of its pursuit of tax evasion. The result is the extraterritorial enforcement of the US legal system throughout the Caribbean. In one case (United States v. Field) the Canadian manager of the Cayman Islands branch of the Bank of Nova Scotia was subpoenaed for an Internal Revenue Service (IRS) investigation of the bank's activities while he was in transit through the Miami airport (Antoine, 2001: p. 18; Hudson, 1998: pp. 546–549). As Alan Hudson described the dilemma for the bank manager and the bank, it was the fact that they 'operated across state boundaries and found themselves caught between two sets of laws.' (Hudson, 1998: p. 547) The US Court of Appeals recognized it was an extraterritorial application of US law, but nonetheless found that

> conflicts are inevitable. ... This court simply cannot acquiesce in the proposition that US criminal investigations must be thwarted whenever there is conflict with the interest of other states. (Hudson, 1998: p. 548)[3]

Essentially, US courts supported the country's hegemonic position in the Caribbean by exhibiting this attitude that US law superseded the law of other states. As Antoine commented, 'The Supreme Court argued [against seeking international assistance] on the somewhat flimsy basis that such judicial assistance was costly and time consuming.' (Antoine, 2002: pp. 287–288) In sum, the US is likely to use its existing treaty structure only when convenient for its purposes. For the broader question of the OECD project and state sovereignty, the answer is similar. The members of the OECD will use the threat of sanctions to force small states to comply with an information exchange regime and, in essence, intervene in the domestic law-making processes of these small jurisdictions.

The right place?

The next most common criticism after the issue of the subversion of state sovereignty is the contention that the OECD is not the appropriate forum for this project.

> It should be recalled that the OECD is a multinational grouping of 30 countries. It is not an international organization and it has no legal authority to speak for the world or to establish rules, norms or standards for any state except its own members. Nonetheless, it is now dictating terms on what, in short, could be described as cross-border tax matters (Sanders, 2002: pp. 339–340).[4]

If one accepted the argument that a global problem involving tax competition existed, then another international organization, it was argued, should be the location for any discussions on the problem. Persaud suggested either the WTO or the International Monetary Fund (IMF), as 'more representative and relevant international organizations.' (Persaud, 2001: p. 204) However, he noted that just as with the OECD some of the states identified as tax havens were not members of either of those two organizations. Consequently, he suggested it was an opportunity for a multilateral organization such as the Commonwealth (where many of the affected states are already members) to coordinate a global discussion on taxation.[5]

One element of the argument that the OECD was not the correct forum involved the question of participation in the decision-making process. The OECD has acknowledged that if harmful tax competition is framed as a global problem, 'it is critical that as many countries as possible are involved in the dialogue.' (Organization for Economic Co-operation and Development, 1998: p. 10) In pursuit of this goal, the OECD Committee on Fiscal Affairs 'used its extensive outreach programme to engage in a dialogue with non-member countries.' (Organization for Economic Co-operation and Development, 1998: p. 10)[6] It is unfortunate that of those states identified as having attended one of the three regional seminars held preceding the publication of the first report, only Jamaica is a member of the set of small states considered here. In addition, none of these meetings included the participation from any jurisdiction identified in 2000 as an 'uncooperative tax haven'. (Organization for Economic Co-operation and Development, 2000: p. 17)[7] Viewed from this perspective, the suggestion that the Commonwealth could facilitate a broadening of participation in the discussion over harmful tax competition is understandable. At the same time, the absence of small states in the outreach program may also help explain the involvement of the Commonwealth in subsequent discussions.

Accompanying the suggestion that the WTO would be a more appropriate venue for discussing the issue of tax competition, were suggestions that any sanctions directed by the OECD could be challenged under the provisions of the dispute settlement mechanism of the WTO. 'The targeted jurisdictions, acting together, could yet request the establishment of a tribunal to test the legality of any sanctions imposed by OECD countries against targeted jurisdictions in the context of the HTCI [Harmful Tax Competition Initiative].' (Sanders, 2002: pp. 340–341) The former legal counsel (until December 2000) in the OECD also suggested this tactic. Mark Warner highlighted the discriminatory nature of some of the proposed measures, which could be in violation of the prohibitions against trade discrimination that are part of the General Agreement on Tariffs and Trade (GATT) and General Agreement on Trade in Services (GATS). These sanctions would be particularly problematic if they were applied only against harmful tax regimes and not against states with preferential tax regimes (Scott, 24 April 2001).

Common rules for a common problem?

As mentioned, the sanctions proposed against the tax havens (non-OECD members) were not equivalent to those proposed for use against the preferential tax regimes (OECD members or their non-self-governing jurisdictions). As a tactic to resolve this differential treatment, several of the jurisdictions identified as tax havens submitted *conditional* commitments to support the OECD project. These commitments were conditional on the position that *all* states (whether or not a member of the OECD) must accede to identical conditions for transparency and effective exchange of information.[8] This tactic attempts to place normative pressure concerning tax competition back upon the OECD. However, in the 'commonly asked questions' Annex to a conference paper presented by Jeffrey Owens (Head of the Centre for Tax Policy and Administration at the OECD), the response to question eighteen indicates that he did not view this as a constraint upon the OECD's freedom of action. 'The OECD would not accept a commitment to progress by any one country that is conditioned on the actions of all other countries.' (Owens, 2002: p. 7)[9] Nevertheless, the reply provided to Aruba's commitment letter, from the Secretary General of the OECD, stated:

> I can confirm that it is the OECD Members' understanding that your commitment is made on the basis that:
>
> - The principles that are applied to Aruba will also be applied to the assessment of regimes in OECD Member states; and... (Johnston, 2001)

Given that the Secretary General of the OECD speaks for the organization and on behalf of its members, this reply was in sharp contrast to the statement made by the head of its Centre for Tax Policy and Administration. It is also important to note that any sanctions would be applied individually by states, and not by the OECD, *per se*.[10]

Ronald Sanders remained cautious concerning the engagement of the OECD towards the non-member states in 2002. He noted that, logically, a level playing field for all should lead to the application of sanctions against OECD member states.

> A level playing field also means that countries such as the USA and the UK may also have to change existing regimes in financial services that compete with many of the targeted jurisdictions. (Sanders, 2002: p. 344)

The EU Savings Tax Directive has already been identified as demonstrating the unequal treatment afforded to some states, and justified

Sanders' cautious viewpoint. This method of pursuing 'fair' treatment has been attempted in a variety of economic sectors (e.g. the importation of bananas to the EU) other than financial services as explored here. It was described by Armstrong and Read as 'the increasing dominance of multilateralism over bilateralism' in international trade and typified by the operation of the WTO. The level playing field, as an approach to trade, is compelled by an increase in 'more rigorous international trade rules'. (Armstrong and Read, 2002b: p. 40) With the increased use of a multilateral approach, the individual trade preferences contained in many bilateral trade agreements with developing states are deemed illegal. This approach is to the detriment of the small developing economy where it occupies a niche in the marketplace that, combined with a trade preference, affords it a comparative advantage. The relevant example here is the cultivation of bananas in the Windward Islands. Leveling the agricultural playing field (at least in the developing world) has removed the comparative advantage previously created by a trade preference, and leaves European consumers to purchase what is now the cheaper product, bananas grown on the larger plantations of Central American states (Royle, 2001: 141–142; Griffin, 2000: pp. 118–119; Lewis, 2000).

In a similar fashion, the campaign to level the financial services playing field (under the guise of eliminating tax avoidance/evasion opportunities with increased transparency and the establishment of an information exchange regime) is anticipated to reduce the size of the financial services sector in the economies of these small jurisdictions. The market niche they serve is not likely to disappear, however. It will just relocate to a more amenable jurisdiction, as already demonstrated with regards to the EU Savings Tax Directive (Bilefsky, 2006). Quite probably, this shift will benefit any jurisdiction able to withstand the pressures of the OECD project, for instance those states with preferential tax regimes. This probability further justifies the case made for equivalent treatment between harmful tax regimes and preferential tax regimes. Otherwise, it appears that the whole effort to eliminate harmful tax competition is in actuality intended to displace funds from their offshore locations back to financial centers in OECD states. The nature and consequences of this aspect of the OECD project for the Caribbean is discussed in Chapter 6.

The OECD rebuttal

State sovereignty is not under attack

In a variety of ways and in a number of forums, the OECD attempted to refute these criticisms and to keep the discussion limited to its definition of harmful tax competition and the dangers confronting global society from tax competition. The Head of Fiscal Affairs at the OECD characterized the above issues as 'misunderstandings', and responded to them in an article posted to the OECD website (Owens, 2001).[11] The first misunderstanding identified was that the 'OECD is threatening the fiscal sovereignty of Small States.' The first point made in response to the accusation was to acknowledge that this claim was a recurring theme about the harmful tax competition project. Jeffrey Owens offered three reasons to demonstrate that it was a misunderstanding. First, the OECD has no power to tell a government what it should do, it is simply a multinational organization encouraging economic cooperation. Second, the OECD believes global cooperation will result in '*more* and not less fiscal sovereignty', though it is obviously an untested proposition. Finally, just as 'tax policy must remain the sovereign right of national governments', these governments also have a sovereign 'right to take action to protect [their] revenue base.' (Owens, 2001: emphasis in the original) From these remarks, one would expect that the OECD should be encouraging global cooperation because it will enhance fiscal sovereignty, yet leaving it to each individual state to take whatever action it finds appropriate – domestically.

It is also agreed that the OECD does not posses the power to *tell* a state what action it should undertake. As mentioned in Chapter 3, the organization could not even achieve unanimous support amongst its members for the project report in 1998. However, just as the OECD's 'extensive outreach programme' may induce the involvement of non-member states in its discussions on harmful tax competition, so may it *persuade* member and non-member states alike to take some punitive action as part of the project. In this instance, the OECD possesses a power of *moral suasion*. Non-cooperation by a jurisdiction, for example, on the issues of financial transparency and the exchange of financial information could be treated in a fashion similar to non-cooperation with the global anti-money laundering program. If this approach were taken by OECD members, the targeted jurisdiction could find itself in a position similar to the Philippines in early 2003. Having failed to pass anti-money laundering legislation acceptable to the Financial Action Task Force (FATF) that organization threatened to have the state's financial institutions blacklisted. In tandem with this perception of the status of financial institutions and legislation in the Philippines, the Asian Development Bank announced it would withhold a needed loan package until the acceptable legislation had been passed. These two multilateral organizations are similar to the OECD in that while they putatively have little power to tell a state what to do, the threat of sanctions worked (even though it did so in the face of nationalist criticism from a number of Philippine Senators) (Lucas, 2003; Martin, 2003).

Among the issues raised by the Philippine Senators with respect to the changes directed by the FATF were a concern for a reduction in financial privacy (the relaxation of banking secrecy laws), and the sanctioning of bank account investigations in the absence of a court order. There were also accusations that the US was interfering in the domestic political process of the Philippines, because it emerged that the US government had provided funding to a lobby group in the Philippines (ABS-CBN News, 2003; Cadacio, 2003; Casayuran, 2003). The mere threat of sanctions appears to have had an immediate impact on the Filipino economy. Potential sanctions were 'cited by officials and foreign exchange traders as one of the reasons for the peso's recent weakness. The currency plunged to a two-year low of 54.58 to the US dollar on Monday. It closed Tuesday [4 March 2003] at 54.50.' (ABS-CBN News, 2003) In addition to this immediate impact on the economy, blacklisting Filipino financial institutions held the potential for a much greater long-term impact to the economy. The increased surveillance of all cross-border financial transactions that would accompany any sanctions was predicted to slow their processing and consequently all capital transfers. Sanctions would impact currency transfers originating from Filipinos living abroad. These remittances were reported to amount to US$7 billion in 2002, and are a valued source of foreign currency and revenue for the Philippines' economy (ABS-CBN News, 2003). Compare this amount to the US$1.2 billion in official development aid received in 2002 (Central Intelligence Agency, 2004).

The potential effect on the economy from FATF-directed sanctions was emphasized with a reminder of the potential for capital flight.

Senator Edguardo J. Angura recalled the experience of 1999, when anti-money laundering legislation was first discussed in the Philippines. At that time, a relaxation of banking secrecy laws was suggested as well. He believed that simply entertaining suggestions to change the financial privacy regime reduced investments. 'Inward remittances dwindled and our local banks suffered. Local deposits were siphoned abroad or transferred to foreign banks or to domestic banks with overseas branches.' He linked this capital flight with the depreciation in the exchange rate of the Filipino Peso that occurred in the same time period (Angara, 2003). As would be expected from a former colony, the debate among the politicians included statements declaring that the Philippines' sovereignty would be 'undermined by the government's apparent subservience to the demands of FATF.' The former Senate Majority Leader Francisco S. Tatad declared 'that Filipinos must learn to fully stand up and to behave like an independent country.' (Casayuran, 2003)

In the end, a compromise was reached between the FATF and the Philippines. The FATF believed that 'the new legislation addresses the main legal deficiencies in the Philippine anti-money laundering regime previously identified by the FATF.' (Financial Action Task Force, 2003a) At the same time, the interest of the Philippines in maintaining the existing checks and balances between state authority and financial privacy was upheld. Philippines' Senate President Franklin Drilon announced following a meeting with the FATF regarding the legislative changes, '[FATF] officials agreed that the Philippine requirement for a court order to probe a bank account was in accordance with international standards and could remain.' (ABS-CBN News, 2003) The passage of new legislation only removed the immediate threat of sanctions. The Philippines remained on the FATF's list of non-cooperative countries and territories (NCCTs) until 11 February 2005, and will continue to be monitored by the FATF to ensure 'adequate implementation' of the new anti-money laundering legislation (Financial Action Task Force, 2005: p. 8).

The experience of the Philippines with the FATF serves as a cautionary example for the jurisdictions under threat of sanction by the OECD from the harmful tax competition project. This example highlights the influence exercised in financial markets by the threat of blacklisting independent of concerns about the reputation of a financial center. At the same time, this impact is exactly what those promoting the use of a campaign to name and shame desire (Wechsler, 2001: p. 49). The connection frequently made between the project against harmful tax practices and the campaign to prevent money laundering suggests that failing to cooperate with the former project will be treated as a failure to cooperate with the latter project.

The OECD is the correct forum

Concerning the second criticism (or misunderstanding) asserting that the 'OECD is the wrong Forum,' Owens did not directly reply to this accusation. At the same time, he also did not provide a clear statement explaining why the OECD was in fact the correct forum. He did assert however, that while the OECD is an organization of only thirty countries, it 'does have a global reach. We cover small and large countries and rich and poor countries.' (Owens, 2001) For the most part one can agree with this statement. However, the membership of the OECD does not include a developing country, less developed country (LDC) or lesser less developed country (LLDC). The claim for participation by a poor country could be accepted as a valid one, but only if most of the members of the United Nations were first eliminated from consideration in the pool of potential OECD members. In looking at the league tables for states' Gross National Income (GNI) per capita, one finds the membership of the OECD exists solely within the top 95 (of 208 jurisdictions). Moreover, if Turkey were not a member of the club, this would leave the remaining members within the top 80 (World Bank, 2003). The claim that the OECD has 'poor country' membership is therefore a bit specious. One should also note that the membership of the OECD reflects the industrialized states of North Asia, Europe and North America, along with Australia and New Zealand from the Southern Hemisphere. Representation for Africa, South America, and the vast populations of China and the Indian Subcontinent is conspicuous by its absence.[12]

A former Special Advisor to the US Secretary of the Treasury wrote that the involvement of the OECD served a different purpose. The fact that the organization had a limited membership was precisely the reason to give it the responsibility 'for investigating tax evasion and establishing a consensus...on how to tackle harmful tax practices.' (Wechsler, 2001: p. 51) Acting in the belief that urgent action was required, it was necessary to use an organization with limited membership. Otherwise, 'if the debate were brought to the UN General Assembly, for example, nations with underregulated financial regimes would easily outvote those with a commitment to strong international standards.' (Wechsler, 2001: p. 49)

The next argument made in favor of the OECD being the correct organization for this issue was the fact that 'we have recently created a Global Forum on Taxation in which all participating countries will have the same status.' Owens' statement continued by encouraging the establishment of further partnerships with other regional or global organizations. The OECD, however, remains identified as the focal point for all discussions of taxation, either by creating a forum serving their purpose, or accepting the cooperation and acquiesce of other multilateral organizations within the OECD domain. None of the preceding responses from Owens directly addressed the contention made that the OECD was not the appropriate forum in which to consider global tax competition. Nor does the creation of a 'Global Forum' necessarily mean that the group will hold meetings or possess representative participation. This point was emphasized by a conclusion raised by the participants at the October 2003 meeting of the Global Forum on Taxation, 'that ways should be explored to involve significant financial centres that are not currently participating in the Global Forum process.' (OECD Global Forum on Taxation, 2003a)

All states are treated equally

While Owens' document did not contain the phrase 'level playing field', it did address the issue indirectly by discussing the criticism/misunderstanding that 'there are two standards – one for the OECD member countries and another for other jurisdictions.' The response to this criticism was that 'our work makes no distinction' between member and non-member states, only 'between those countries that wish to be part of the international community (cooperative jurisdictions) and those countries that do not (uncooperative jurisdictions).' (Owens, 2001) While Owens may feel that the work of the committee made no distinctions, a review of the documents finds that only OECD member countries were identified as possessing preferential tax regimes, whereas the list of uncooperative jurisdictions presented in the *Towards Global Tax Co-operation* contained only non-member states. The 'Tax Haven Update' on the OECD website is no different in that it only contains non-member jurisdictions (OECD, 2003).

Again, the OECD established the project and its initial agenda without prior consultation with the target jurisdictions. Small states were not involved, and according to Weschsler, the absence of 'under-regulated financial regimes' was intentional. Since the publication of the first report in 1998, representatives of the OECD have had to counter this accusation of differential treatment towards non-member states. As long as the organization continues to control the agenda of this Global Forum, the perception of unequal treatment will continue to exist.

US domestic politics and harmful tax competition

The prevalence of offshore financial centers in the Caribbean is itself in part a consequence of the US presence and economic influence in the region. Several authors identified the emergence of the Caribbean OFCs as partly in response to US financial regulation and capital controls, particularly Regulation Q (Strange, 1998: p. 30; Hampton, 1996: pp. 56–59; Johns, 1983: pp. 10–15). As already suggested, a major difficulty facing the OECD project rests not with uncooperative non-member states, but with its own members. In particular this difficulty has been with its largest member. As one American opponent to the OECD project has commented, having a tax cartel without the US 'would be like trying to set up a hardware store cartel without Home Depot or a software cartel without Microsoft.' (Mitchell, 2001b: p. 2) (Obviously, the OECD would resist any characterization of their project as being an effort to create a tax cartel.) At issue is the simple fact that at that time the US did not collect tax on non-resident non-citizens' accounts, nor did it report the existence of those accounts the account holders' home state. Consequently, the US should have been identified as the largest offshore tax haven in the world. At the end of 2002, total foreign-owned assets in the United States exceeded US$8.5 trillion, up from US$6 trillion in 1998. This figure includes over US$5.4 trillion (up from US$3.6 trillion in 1998) in direct investment composed of US Treasury securities, US currency, and liabilities reported by banking and nonbanking concerns (Nguyen, 2003). One argument made against the introduction of any information exchange was that it would lead to massive capital flight, seriously impacting the US financial system (Langer, 2002; Mitchell, 2001b).

The change of American Administration in 2001 led to a change in the official US position concerning the HTCI. Certainly, the case can be made that the Republican majority in Congress would have legislatively blocked US cooperation on the OECD project, whatever the inclinations of the White House. However, convincing officials in the Executive that US cooperation would be against the national interest is far easier than convincing sufficient members of Congress to block US cooperation.

On 26 June 2000, the US Treasury 'welcomed' the publication of the OECD progress report, *Towards Global Tax Co-operation*. The Secretary of the Treasury in the Clinton Administration, Lawrence H. Summers, was quoted in a press release.

> The identification of tax havens and potentially harmful tax regimes is a crucial step in preventing distortions that could undermine the benefits of enhanced capital mobility in today's global economy. (Summers, 2000a)

As an economist, this is a topic that Summers would understandably find very familiar. His statement followed a press release from a week earlier in support of the OECD announcement that six jurisdictions had agreed to cooperate with the harmful tax competition project. Summers justified his support for the OECD project in his comments to a tax administrators conference in July 2000. 'In today's global environment, a country cannot develop its tax policy or administer its tax laws without giving consideration to the actions of other jurisdictions.' (Summers, 2000b)

The incoming Bush Administration in 2001 was ambivalent about the HTCI. Initially, the Bush Treasury Department followed the policy of the Clinton Treasury Department, 'On February 17th, following a meeting of G7 Finance Ministers in Palermo, I [US Secretary of the Treasury Paul O'Neill] indicated that certain aspects of the OECD project were under review by the Administration.' (O'Neill, 2001b) Uncertainty about the US position in early April 2001 intersected with the Commonwealth Secretary General's strong criticism of the OECD project. One London newspaper reported an unnamed OECD official as saying, 'This is making recalcitrant countries even more recalcitrant.

If the US were to abandon its support it would be a major blow.' (Cornwell, 2001: p. 17) Nevertheless, support for the project by the United States was once again 'reaffirmed' by the Secretary at yet another G7 meeting in April 2001, 'However, [O'Neill] declined to comment on the contentiousness of offshore financial centres.' (Carroll, 2001: p. 1)

Subsequent perceptions of the emergence of a Bush Administration position on the project suggested that effective lobbying had moved critical members of the Administration out of the neutral space and on to the side of critics of the project. The Center for Freedom and Prosperity is usually identified as the focal point for the lobbying effort, but various business interests and members of Congress joined it. Lobbying activities by this organization attempted to widen the dialogue in the public sphere via editorials and articles, in addition to efforts at persuading government officials of the dangers with cooperation. At the same time, one writer observed that 'pressure is also coming from Democrats, particularly the Afro-American caucus within the US Congress, which are allying itself [sic] with Caribbean Islands against the OECD initiative.' (Carroll, 2001) The momentum of the entire OECD project would fade quickly, following a statement in May 2001 by the US Secretary of the Treasury concerning the OECD's 'working group that targets "harmful tax practices".'

> I am troubled by the underlying premise that low tax rates are somehow suspect and by the notion that any country, or group of countries, should interfere in any other country's decision about how to structure its own tax system. I also am concerned about the potentially unfair treatment of some non-OECD countries. (O'Neill, 2001a)[13]

Secretary O'Neill would make a very similar declaration before the US Senate, after which reports in the media suggested 'The threat of sanctions for small island states accused of supporting tax evasion is receding.' (BBC News, 2001) O'Neill's statement supported the case for fiscal sovereignty, without addressing the OECD's desire for information exchange.

This situation points out the role of lobbies and lobbyists in democratic politics (and particularly in US politics). As already mentioned, the one organization frequently identified by American supporters of the HTCI was the Center for Freedom and Prosperity. It was interconnected, however, with the Cato Institute (a libertarian think tank promoting limited government and free markets) through its board of directors, while another prominent opponent of the tax competition project was affiliated with the Heritage Foundation (a conservative think tank promoting free enterprise and limited government). All three of these organizations took a position against the OECD on harmful tax competition. This action fits with the policy view they present on the wider issue of taxation more generally in the United States.

Consequently, the concerns held by small states with respect to the issue of tax competition and pressure from the OECD were framed in the context of US domestic politics by think tanks and lobbyists with an agenda promoting limited government and a free market agenda. In this way, the small states benefited from what may be characterized as the 'knock-on' effect of the American domestic agenda. The issue was presented to the American government and electorate (via op-ed pieces and letters to the editor of major newspapers) as one of *American* fiscal sovereignty, with the potential to lose a significant amount of foreign investment in the American economy. Indeed, one Caribbean-based commentator urged that the Bahamas should lobby in the US against the OECD project as one of a number of policy recommendations (Morris, 2001: p. 1298). Notwithstanding the factors or motivators behind the US policy shift on harmful tax competition between the Clinton and Bush Administrations, the fact remains that a shift occurred. Because of the change, the progress of the OECD project slowed, and some small states, taking advantage of the US move, continued to resist.

Reflections upon the debate

The confrontation between the OECD and various OFCs has all the appearance of an effort to intervene into the domestic affairs of a select number of states. At the same time, the efforts by the OECD to seek consensus and the inclusion of all potentially affected jurisdictions as participants prior to the publication of *Harmful Tax Competition* appear weak. Jeffrey Owens conceded this point, but emphasized the fact that subsequent meetings sought wider participation. Furthermore, the OECD was making efforts 'to improve the process of consultation by having extensive bi-lateral and multi-lateral dialogues.' (Owens, 2001) Nonetheless, for the OECD to reply to their critics that the HTCI was not an attack on sovereignty requires a selective and limited interpretation of state sovereignty. Requests for change or cooperation backed up with the threat of sanctions constitute an intervention into the domestic affairs of a sovereign state, as reflected in the opinion of some members of the Philippine Senate. Collectively agreeing to a need for change and the extent of change required would be a less threatening approach. This approach would entail a strategy predicated upon the recognition that it was a 'one for all, and all for one' agreement. Cooperation derives from a common agreement to the presence of a problem, and of an agreed solution to the problem. The OECD collective action strategy taken against the non-cooperative jurisdictions conveyed the appearance of neo-colonialism, as suggested in the title of Sanders' article, 'The Fight Against Fiscal Colonialism'.

Since the publication of *Harmful Tax Competition* in 1998, the topic has been raised at many international forums involving the targeted jurisdictions. The global conference held in London on the Development Agenda for Small States in February 2000 contained an on-going dialogue amongst several participants. For example, the Assistant Secretary-General of the Caribbean Community (CARICOM) raised the point that it appeared developing states were always the ones to make the adjustments necessary to accommodate change in the international trade regime.

> In the OECD's project on harmful tax competition, countries with low levels of taxation were being asked to raise taxes to the level prevailing in developed countries. In the case of trade related taxes, which were higher in developing countries, the emphasis was on lowering them to levels prevailing in developed countries. (Peretz *et al.*, 2001: pp. 561–562)

There is a need to recognize the small state's limited capability or capacity to deal with the impact of adverse events upon their small economy – of their *vulnerability* to the impact of exogenous events, whether the event is a hurricane or a mandate from the FATF. In the language of the military strategist, the small state had no 'space' in which to employ a 'defense-in-depth' economic strategy – something which is inherent to the nature of a larger economy, like those possessed by OECD member states. The size and capacity of the larger economy permitted or created opportunities for jobs to shift to new market sectors.

This recognition helps explain the criticisms made by the affected jurisdictions about the OECD harmful tax competition project. The small states expect to be treated as sovereign equals, irrespective of their paucity of military and economic power. Such is the normative expectation accompanying recognition by their peers as sovereign states. Therefore they question the right of an organization composed of developed states to determine issues affecting non-members, with an expectation that the non-member states will comply, or face the consequences. The situation is especially galling, given the very limited participation initially afforded developing states in the decision-making process.

The question then involves sovereign choice, that of the individual in a democratic society, and of the state as a member of a society of states. Any international organization, as a subset of the wider society of states, is engaged in a process of decision-making, shaping the sovereign choices that mediate the interaction and cooperation of its members. The member states participate in this process, and nominally have the option to withdraw from the organization if they feel it no longer represents the interests of their citizens. However, at issue here is an instance of an international organization pursuing a course of action that it feels is in the best interests of most of its member states, but which only represents a particular subset of interests in the international community. Moreover, it seeks to impose that judgment upon the activities of non-member states. To frame the harmful tax competition project as one of global concern requiring a global response does not justify the patently *undemocratic* imposition of limitations upon states that that did not participate in their creation. If globalization is the source of this problem with tax competition, then the response should be one that the global community has agreed to implement.

This chapter has analyzed some of the replies made to the criticisms posed by small states. Subsequent actions by the OECD indicate that an effort has been made to address the issues raised, but it nonetheless sought to maintain the schedule for cooperation, or sanction, originally established. This pace was slowed by several other factors in 2001, including the efforts undertaken by a number of small states to work together and present a united front against the OECD. They have worked at the regional level (in the Caribbean this has been under the auspices of CARICOM), while a number of small states have sought to involve those OECD member states that also belong to the Commonwealth. The collaborative activities of these small states, in the Commonwealth and beyond, are addressed in the next chapter.

5
Working Together – Small States in the Commonwealth and Elsewhere

In response to the question as to why the Commonwealth, and in particular its Secretariat, has been especially involved in the issues confronting small states, there is no more apt an explanation than that offered by Peter Lyon in *The Round Table*. For many years the editor of this *Commonwealth Journal of International Affairs*, he was a cogent observer of the Commonwealth.[1]

> There is no intrinsic reason why the Commonwealth should be more concerned and more practical about the problems of small states than, say, the United Nations or the European Community. But in fact, over the last decade or so, it has been. The Commonwealth has proved to be more user-friendly for its small Anglophone members than have other roughly comparable bodies. The Commonwealth is likely to remain concerned about small states, given that about half of its current members may be so defined. (Lyon, 1996: p. 403)

Similarly, Paul Sutton described the provision of technical assistance to small states as an area in which the Commonwealth possessed 'a comparative advantage'. (Sutton, 2001: p. 88) This chapter does not seek to improve upon these explanations, rather it provides some evidence for their accuracy with respect to the particular case of offshore finance in small Caribbean states. The Commonwealth Secretariat has been involved in a variety of ways, which include sponsoring research to be discussed at meetings of Commonwealth law or finance ministers, providing the 'good offices' of the Commonwealth to facilitate further negotiations between the Organization for Economic Co-operation and Development (OECD) and offshore financial centers (OFCs), and developing model legislation for tailoring and implementation by member states.

The claim that small states benefit from Commonwealth membership (and international organizations more generally) is not universally held. The editors of one text on international political economy are among those that have suggested otherwise.

> At the time of writing this book, a prevalent view among academics and policy-makers was that small states cannot survive alone in a globalized world economy and need to join forces, preferably in regional organizations. The rationale for such organizations, however, was not entirely clear. (Palan *et al.*, 1999: p. ix)

The initial (and obvious) response to this statement is to emphasize the increased influence (voice) that might accrue from participating in a larger collective entity. Certainly there is evidence to support this assessment from the experience of the smaller members of the European Union (EU) (Thorhallsson, 2000; Arter, 2000; Hey, 2003a). The belief behind these recommendations was that membership in regional and international organizations allowed small states to 'punch above their weight' (the analogy frequently used in EU policy analysis).[2] Speaking from a security perspective of military power and strategy an alternate analogy would frame the international organization as a 'force multiplier' for the small state in an anarchic international system. The effect is that the viewpoint or opinion of a small state is magnified in impact when it becomes promoted as the viewpoint of the larger organization. By focusing upon multilateral organizations, specifically *regional* multilateral organizations, the value from participation becomes clearer. A regional organization offers more than just a means to increase the influence of any particular small state, it is also a way for neighboring states to pool resources. For small states, with their limited financial and personnel resources, this function is a great benefit. Instead of 'punching above one's weight', the regional organization provides an avenue for the small state to 'get more bang for their buck'. In this fashion, the various multilateral initiatives in the Caribbean provide a means for promoting a Caribbean vision when engaging with larger entities. An example of this is the presence of the Caribbean Regional Negotiating Machinery (RNM) in Free Trade Area of the Americas (FTAA) negotiations and in negotiations with the World Trade Organization (WTO) (Lewis, 2005).

This chapter explores the question of the effectiveness of an international organization in promoting and serving the needs and aspirations of a small state, within the context of a very specific issue. The first part of the chapter details the contributions of the Commonwealth in support of small states and specifically involving the issue of harmful tax competition. The second section of the chapter presents an analysis of an international organization formed especially to promote the interests of small jurisdictions with OFCs. The chapter's conclusions address the effectiveness of this process for collective action.

Small states within the Commonwealth

As already noted, the Commonwealth is involved in a number of activities intended to support its smaller members. The Commonwealth Ministerial Group on Small States (CMGSS) was created in 1993 to provide strategic direction for the Commonwealth activities assisting small states. A forum composed of senior officials, the Commonwealth Consultative Group on Small States, was established to provide recommendations that would be used to prioritize Commonwealth Secretariat assistance to small states. Other activities include the Joint Office for Commonwealth Permanent Missions to the UN (Joint Office) in New York City (sponsored by the Commonwealth, it has provided space at the UN for the representatives of nine Commonwealth small states) and recent joint economic studies conducted by the Commonwealth Secretariat/World Bank Joint Task Force on Small States (Commonwealth Advisory Group, 1997: p. 147; Peretz *et al.*, 2001). To assist small states with WTO trade issues, the Commonwealth Secretariat maintains a trade facility in Geneva. This facility supports small states with WTO notifications and negotiations and advises on their use of the WTO Dispute Settlement Mechanism (Small States Task Force, 2002: p. 18).

In 2003, the Commonwealth Secretariat maintained an Internet web site dedicated to the small state with its own independent Internet address (www.commonwealthsmallstates.org/), which is now part of the main Secretariat website at <www.thecommonwealth.org/small-states>. These web pages were part of the on-going effort of the Secretariat to increase international awareness for small states, and in particular to highlight the various forms of assistance that the Commonwealth Secretariat provides to its small member states. As a means of promoting these accomplishments, information available on the web site covered a range of relevant topics, including trade, economics, environment, politics, security, social aspects, and vulnerability. The text on the opening Web page today lays out the rationale beyond the close involvement of the Commonwealth Secretariat with all matters of interest to a small state.

> The Secretariat attaches high priority to supporting their integration in the global economy, building their resilience and competitiveness, and helping them take advantage of the opportunities and meet the challenges arising from globalisation.[3]

The concern with the impact of globalization on small states goes beyond just OFCs and tax competition. The Commonwealth prepared guidance for small states covering a variety of international financial issues, including money laundering, electronic commerce and international capital flows (Commonwealth Secretariat, 2006; Commonwealth Secretariat, 2000a; Commonwealth Secretariat, 2001a; Report of a Commonwealth Working Group, 1997).

The Commonwealth Secretariat also assists small states in their interactions with the WTO. As a large, complex international organization grounded in an extensive range of procedures and directives, the WTO can drain the personnel resources of the small state actively striving to participate in WTO activities. To offset this problem the Commonwealth Secretariat sponsored research, organized education and training sessions on WTO rules and related international standards, and provided technical assistance to the member states. It has published newsletters in order to disseminate information and guidance on trade matters to all its small state members (Commonwealth Secretariat, 2003b: pp. 8–9). The potential importance of this assistance for the case of OFCs is that the WTO may offer an avenue for formal protests against the imposition of any economic sanctions that may result from the OECD project.

Several other Commonwealth Secretariat activities intersect with those supporting the small state OFCs targeted by the Harmful Tax Competition project. Already in process when the *Harmful Tax Competition* report was published in 1998 were measures to address concerns with financial governance in small states. Representatives from finance ministries, law enforcement and judiciaries of Commonwealth member states have participated in a number of Secretariat-sponsored working groups. Products from these activities included 'A Model for Best Practice' to counter money laundering and 'A Commonwealth Code of Good Practice' to be used by government officials promoting private capital flows (Commonwealth Secretariat, 2000a; Report of a Commonwealth Working Group, 1997). An extensive research program on the particular vulnerability of small states led to the development of a small state vulnerability index (discussed in the next chapter).

A number of Commonwealth publications provided a favorable view concerning the use of OFCs as an economic development method prior to the 1998 OECD report. In 1997, the report *Money Laundering: Key Issues and Possible Action* contained a chapter on the topic of 'International Financial Centres'. This chapter began with an observation about the use of international finance for economic development – 'Many developing countries are looking to the development of a significant financial sector as a key to economic development.' (Commonwealth Secretariat, 1997: p. 31) Another Commonwealth report on *Promoting Private Capital Flows* included sections describing the experience of fourteen Commonwealth members with private capital flows. These discussions included the experiences of the offshore finance sectors in Mauritius and Vanuatu. In the case of Mauritius, the historical experience was one of transition from a single agricultural produce (sugar) economy to a more diversified economy.

> The country has now a strong export manufacturing sector, predominately based on textiles and clothing, and a flourishing tourism sector. The financial services sector is fast becoming an important pillar of the economy. (Report of a Commonwealth Working Group, 1997: p. 63)

Highlights of the industry and tax environment of Vanuatu preceded a discussion outlining how it had facilitated initiatives to attract foreign direct investment (FDI) to this small Pacific island.[4] The situation in Vanuatu was described as 'an example of the effects of the increased mobility of firms, people and investment capital' and therefore a symbol for the *benefits* possible from economic globalization (Report of a Commonwealth Working Group, 1997: p. 78). The strategies recommended by *Combating Money Laundering* for OFCs encouraged the development of a well-regulated and effectively supervised financial sector (Commonwealth Secretariat, 2000a: pp. 24–31).

In general, the activities of the Commonwealth Secretariat follow the guidelines determined by its member states. This guidance is developed and promulgated via the periodic meetings of the Commonwealth Heads of Government (these meetings are generally identified by the acronym, CHOGM). The report from the 1999 meeting (held in Durban, South Africa) included a brief mention of the OECD's Harmful Tax Competition Initiative (HTCI). The next meeting in 2002 reflected the increased awareness and heightened concern with the OECD project and its potential impact on small member states. The report of the 5th meeting of the Ministerial Group on Small States in 2002 (held in conjunction with the CHOGM in Coolum, Australia) recommended to the Heads of Government that the Secretariat should undertake the following action:

> *Promoting dialogue on the OECD Harmful Tax Practices Initiative.* The Secretariat should continue work under its mandate to promote dialogue between the Organisation for Economic Co-operation and Development (OECD) and non-OECD jurisdictions in this area, taking into account the OECD's attempt to respond to earlier concerns. The Secretariat should support the affected jurisdictions to mobilise assistance to meet international standards, strengthen and deepen their financial sectors and diversify their economies. The need to distinguish clearly between money laundering and tax competition was highlighted. (Commonwealth Ministerial Group on Small States, 2002)

This declaration reflected the efforts of the Secretariat in the year prior to the 2002 CHOGM. The OECD project was among the topics discussed at a meeting of Commonwealth Finance Ministers in September 2000. Several months earlier the OECD had published their progress report for 2000, *Towards Global Tax Co-operation*. The report identified 35 jurisdictions that had met its technical criteria determining that they were 'tax havens' (Organization for Economic Co-operation and Development, 2000: p. 17).[5] Prior to the publication of this report, the OECD announced that they already had advance commitments from six jurisdictions to cooperate with the OECD project, though these jurisdictions would remain unnamed in the report itself.[6] Those jurisdictions that were listed as tax havens in the report were permitted twelve months in which to decide if they would commit to cooperate with the OECD, otherwise they would be placed on a 'black list' identifying the uncooperative tax havens that was to be published in July 2001.

The communiqué from the Commonwealth finance ministers meeting conveyed their concern that this planned publication date for the list of 'uncooperative tax havens' served as an 'impediment to constructive dialogue.' At the same time these finance ministers 'strongly reaffirmed the right of sovereign nations to determine their own tax policies.' The communiqué went on to reiterate the argument that tax competition 'could in fact be helpful, and not harmful, because it can further spur governments to create fiscal environments conducive to generating growth and employment.' (Commonwealth Secretariat, 2000c) This language echoes the policy and academic discourse that supports the economic benefits that a state may derive from tax competition (Wilson, 1999). With respect to the OECD and the HTCI, the Commonwealth Finance Ministers requested that the Secretariat facilitate multilateral dialogue 'in appropriate ways.' (Commonwealth Secretariat, 2000c) The background paper prepared by the Commonwealth Secretariat for this agenda item included a point frequently overlooked in the production of international standards. 'It is important in any global dialogue that large countries understand that a solution reached must be capable of being administered in countries with severely limited human resource bases.' (Commonwealth Secretariat, 2000b: p. 9)

The requested process for multilateral dialogue was initiated by the Commonwealth Secretariat with a high-level consultation meeting in January 2001 amongst the affected small states and the OECD. A press release from 23 November 2000 announcing this meeting stated that the Secretariat was using 'its good offices to facilitate these consultations' and continued with a quote from the Commonwealth Secretary-General.

> Many Commonwealth small states which have in good faith set up offshore financial centres have found themselves on the sharp end of OECD criticism. Fortunately, four of our members are also members of the OECD, which enables dialogue. (Commonwealth News and Information Service, 2000)

Throughout this series of meetings the press releases (some of them jointly issued by the Commonwealth Secretariat and the OECD) related the confidence with which the parties entered into negotiations with no hint of the chasm that existed between the viewpoints held by the participants. The initial meeting was framed as 'high-level consultations', while the statement released immediately prior to this meeting in Barbados noted that it would 'provide the first real opportunity for multilateral dialogue between the OECD and other jurisdictions on "harmful tax competition".' (Commonwealth Secretariat, 2001b)

The multilateral nature of the meeting included not only the participation of representatives from over forty interested jurisdictions, but also a number of interested international institutions, including the IMF, World Bank, Caribbean Development Bank, Inter-American Development Bank, the Centre for Inter-American Tax Administrators, Caribbean Community (CARICOM) and the Pacific Islands Forum. The meeting itself was described as 'a frank, open and ultimately fruitful exchange of views' about the OECD project (Commonwealth Secretariat, 2001c). As a result of this meeting, a Joint Commonwealth-OECD Working Group was formed. The working group comprised tax and finance officials representing thirteen jurisdictions, including from the Commonwealth Antigua and Barbuda, Australia, Barbados, the British Virgin Islands, the Cook Islands, Malaysia, Malta, Vanuatu and the United Kingdom.[7] The other participants represented the OECD member states France, Ireland, Japan, and the Netherlands. The direction given to the Joint Working Group consisted of two wide-ranging tasks.

1. To take the broad principles of transparency, non-discrimination and effective exchange of information and to find a mutually

acceptable political process by which these principles could be turned into commitments. If successful, this process would replace the OECD's process in the context of its Memorandum of Understanding;

2. To examine how the recently created Global Forum on taxation can evolve into a truly inclusive forum which would promote global co-operation on tax matters. It will also identify further relevant tax issues for consideration by such a forum. (Commonwealth Secretariat, 2001g)

The momentum of this process of dialogue would be maintained over the next few months with two further meetings.

The first meeting of the Joint Working Group was held in London three weeks later. Here the group explored the 'participants' understanding of the scope of [their] remit' and proposals for accomplishing the two tasks quoted above. While identifying areas of agreement, the meeting 'ended with an acknowledgment that further work' was necessary (Commonwealth Secretariat, 2001d).[8] The second meeting was held several weeks later, at the beginning of March in Paris. The short press release following this meeting contained a somewhat cryptic quotation from the co-chairs of the Working Group (Owen Arthur, Prime Minister of Barbados and Tony Hinton, Australian Ambassador to the OECD).

> We are pleased by the improved understanding and progress achieved. A number of new proposals were put on the table by both parties, which we have agreed to examine further over the coming days. (Commonwealth Secretariat, 2001e)

The suggestion for the cryptic nature of this statement originates from a reading of Ronald Sanders' presentation of the activities of the working group. To begin with, he suggested that the objective behind the working group was both to avoid confrontation, and to resolve the fiscal concerns of the OECD members 'in a mutually satisfactory manner.' (Sanders, 2002: p. 337) By his account the 'targeted jurisdictions' submitted a three point proposal at the March 2001 meeting of the Joint Working Group. As Sanders described the meeting, the OECD representatives 'expressed "discomfort" with some of the details' and offered to respond with a revision more agreeable

Table 5.1 Commonwealth Members

Antigua and Barbuda	*Jamaica*	Sierra Leone
Australia	Kenya	Singapore
Bahamas	*Kiribati*	*Solomon Islands*
Bangladesh	*Lesotho*	South Africa
Barbados	Malawi	Sri Lanka
Belize	Malaysia	*St. Kitts and Nevis*
Botswana	*Maldives*	*St. Lucia*
Brunei Darussalam	*Malta*	*St. Vincent and the Grenadines*
Cameroon	*Mauritius*	*Swaziland*
Canada	Mozambique	*Tonga*
Cyprus	*Namibia*	*Trinidad and Tobago*
Dominica	*Nauru*	*Tuvalu*
**Fiji Islands*	New Zealand	Uganda
Gambia	Nigeria	United Kingdom
Ghana	Pakistan	United Republic of Tanzania
Grenada	*Papua New Guinea*	*Vanuatu*
Guyana	*Samoa*	Zambia
India	*Seychelles*	

Source: *The Commonwealth – Members*, 2007, Web page, Commonwealth Secretariat, Available: http://www.thecommonwealth.org/Internal/142227/members/ [accessed 6 March 2007]

Note: The small states, as identified by the Commonwealth Secretariat, are italicized. Zimbabwe was a member until it withdrew from the Commonwealth, effective 7 December 2003.

*The Fiji Islands was suspended from the Commonwealth in December 2006 following a military coup.

to their perspective. At the same time, a set of questions were submitted to the OECD in order 'to ascertain from the OECD whether or not its own member states would be bound by the same rules' as those directed at the non-member jurisdictions. Sanders described how when the answers were received from the OECD in July 2001 the situation did not seem to have been clarified. Instead, the reply made to these questions 'clouded the issues even more and gave rise to deeper suspicion about the motives behind the OECD's "harmful tax competition" scheme.' (Sanders, 2002: pp. 337–338)

Communication between the Commonwealth Secretariat and the OECD Secretariat was particularly tense at the time of the second Joint Working Group meeting. Reacting to a document that was purported to be meeting minutes from a January 2001 OECD Fiscal

Affairs Committee meeting, the Commonwealth Secretary-General issued a stern rebuke to the OECD in a press release. 'If this is a true and accurate record, I [Commonwealth Secretary-General Don McKinnon] am extremely disappointed.' He emphasized that the non-OECD participants to these meetings were acting 'in good faith with the OECD' and they recognized the importance of dialogue on the harmful tax competition project because of the important economic benefits they gained from their financial services sectors. Moreover, the members of the Commonwealth were 'all committed to adhering to the highest standards of fiscal probity.' McKinnon declared that the document portrayed the desire of the OECD committee not only to be 'the world's financial policeman' but also the 'prosecutor, judge, jury and jailor.' (Commonwealth Secretariat, 2001f)

The Commonwealth press release garnered a rapid reply from the OECD Secretary-General. His response declared that the document was false, and that the Commonwealth Secretary-General's statement, without first verifying the accuracy of the document, was unhelpful to the on-going discussions. This intervention by the Commonwealth Secretary-General was characterized as 'most inappropriate'. (Bingham and Andrews, 2001; Cornwell, 2001; Anonymous, 2001b; Anonymous, 2001a) The tension represented by this public display 'between two normally sedate international bureaucracies reflects deep divisions between first and third worlds'. (Cornwell, 2001) It was all the more striking given the otherwise confidential nature ascribed to the contents of these meetings. Even though the closing press release from the Commonwealth (quoted above) referred to the 'improved understanding and progress achieved' and the new proposals under consideration by both parties, this particular 'Joint Working Group' never met again. (Commonwealth Secretariat, 2001e)

The fact that the OECD did not continue participating in this particular forum would be remarked upon at a later Commonwealth-sponsored workshop. This later meeting was organized specifically for those jurisdictions 'engaged in the provision of international financial services'. The consensus opinion of the participants concerning OECD inactivity after the second meeting was to describe it as a consequence of the fact 'that OECD personnel had no real authority to speak for any one, let alone all, the OECD member states.' The concluding comments made about the effectiveness and purpose ascribed to the Joint Working Group were blunt.

> The working group owed its brief existence to asymmetrical expectations harboured by the small offshore finance centre (OFC) jurisdictions on the one hand and OECD representatives on the other. The list of specific questions agreed upon by the small states within the working group context elicited no relevant responses from the OECD. The exercise merely served to reinforce the feeling among small states that they were being discriminated against. (Commonwealth Secretariat, 2003a: p. 3)

The sentiments expressed by this quotation reflect the practicalities of the OECD as an international organization. While the Secretariat acts on *behalf* of its member states, public statements do not necessarily reflect the policy positions of any individual member, nor can it impose any policy upon an unwilling member. Consider on this latter point the abstention from the tax competition reports of four OECD states by the time the 2001 progress report was published. As Luxembourg stated when recalling their abstention to the original report, *Harmful Tax Competition*, in 2001, not only did that abstention still apply, but '[Luxembourg] regrets that the 2001 progress report is further away from the goal of combating harmful tax competition with respect to the location of economic activities.' (Organization for Economic Co-operation and Development, 2001a: p. 4)

As an international organization, this observation is just as true for the Commonwealth. The Commonwealth Secretariat does not speak on behalf of any individual member state, nor does it have a capability to enforce any policy position on its members. The Commonwealth essentially operates as a forum in which to develop a collective (consensus) opinion or a recommended course of action that member states are encouraged to pursue.[9] So while the statement from the Secretary-General concerning the fact that the intersection of the Commonwealth and the OECD (four members in common) 'enables dialogue' is true, the same circumstance carries with it the opportunity for conflict. The question emerging out of this situation is towards which set of competing goals and objectives on tax competition (OECD or Commonwealth small states) do these common members adhere? The UK is further conflicted beyond the

OECD project when it comes to tax competition issues because its EU membership involves additional obligations concerning the EU Savings Tax Directive. In this context, the foreign policy dictum that 'where you stand, depends upon where you sit' involves more than simply the ministry one represents in the meeting, it also involves the particulars of the forum or meeting in which one is participating – the OECD, the EU, the Commonwealth, or even domestic governmental meetings that involve tax revenues or the British Overseas Territories. A similar situation confronts New Zealand because of their relationship to the Pacific island jurisdictions of the Cook Islands, Nauru, and Niue. 'A senior New Zealand official said this week [3 March 2001] that the OECD's naming and shaming approach was not always helpful in the Pacific and that the Government preferred to help island Administrations.' (Bingham and Andrews, 2001)

The concluding observations quoted above from the workshop on the international financial sector represent one perspective on the situation for the joint working group between the Commonwealth and the OECD. Alternatively, the case simply may be that the objectives to be accomplished by the 'Joint Working Group' were consolidated into those of the Global Forum on Taxation. Recall that the second task presented to the Joint Working Group was 'To examine how the recently created Global Forum on taxation can evolve into a truly inclusive forum which would promote global co-operation on tax matters.' (Commonwealth Secretariat, 2001g) Given the limited resources available to the small state participants in particular, to consolidate the negotiation efforts of the Commonwealth-OECD working group into the 'global' working group would be a more efficient use of these limited resources. These limited resources would be further consolidated with assistance from the Commonwealth Secretariat to form the International Tax and Investment Organization (ITIO), which is discussed in the next section (Sharman, 2006: p. 59).

Perceptions about the OECD vary most clearly among observers and commentators when the organization moves beyond what are generally held to be its areas of expertise. As a collector of economic data concerning its members and a promulgator of 'Model' treaties and legislation, the OECD has been exemplary. The harmful tax competition project, however, was an attempt to impose a regulatory regime upon jurisdictions that are not part of its membership and as such it went beyond the organization's remit (Woodward,

2004: pp. 115–116). The difficulty experienced in this attempt by the OECD to 'go global' underscores an argument made by Jason Sharman concerning the use of 'weapons of the weak' by small states. He found that the small states engaged in tactics similar to those of NGOs in their relations with other international organizations.

> More specifically, through normative appeals, argument and rhetoric based on the principles of the 'level playing field' and inclusive, consensual standard setting, small states have often undermined the legitimacy of core state proposals (Sharman, 2003: p. 2).

More explicitly, in this specific case it was a matter of international politics and negotiations among sovereign entities. These negotiations reproduce the sovereign status of the participants as independent territorial jurisdictions that represent a distinct population with its unique interests, desires and historical experience. As an international organization, the OECD does not represent a specific constituency and instead proclaimed that it was acting on behalf of all citizens in tackling the issue of harmful tax competition as a threat to global welfare (Organization for Economic Co-operation and Development, 1998: p. 8). At the same time, the OECD report emphasized the point that it was not an attempt by the OECD to impose some optimal rate of tax upon individual domestic constituencies. 'Countries should remain free to design their own tax systems as long as they abide by internationally accepted standards in doing so.' (Organization for Economic Co-operation and Development, 1998: p. 15) Faced then with the assertions of sovereign independence that accompany the statement that the small states were absent from the discussions that produced the initial report, the OECD found itself in a position where it had to follow through and act upon its claims for multilateral participation and inclusiveness (Sharman, 2006: Chapter 5).

Statements from the Commonwealth Secretariat reinforced the individual critiques from various Caribbean states, and added a gloss of collective voice to the public debate. The OECD attempted to use its imposing size and presence (as a reflection of its membership) to convince the small jurisdictions that cooperation was required. The threat implicit in the creation of a 'blacklist' of non-cooperative jurisdictions demonstrates the hazards of the situation for small states. In the absence of cooperation, the implication is that sanctions would be recommended and, as suggested by the experience of the Philippines, these sanctions have the potential to cripple a small economy (though it depends quite naturally upon the extent of participation by the world financial community to enforce the sanctions). The progress of the OECD project from early 2001 up to 2004 was less than initially desired by the OECD Secretariat. Target dates slipped and further meetings arranged that implied progress, while delaying the achievement of the ultimate objective – the elimination of tax competition.[10]

At the conclusion of the Joint Working Group meeting in March 2001 the targeted jurisdictions were facing a July 2001 deadline to publicly commit to cooperate with the tax competition project. This deadline was later postponed to 28 February 2002, after which any 'uncommitted' jurisdictions would be formally identified by the OECD on a List of Uncooperative Tax Havens. The Project Report for 2001 explained that in light of the progress made during the year and 'the number of ongoing discussions with jurisdictions on the conclusion of commitments' this extension was in accord with their aim for a 'cooperative process' (Organization for Economic Co-operation and Development, 2001a: p. 10). The extension was fairly successful, as it permitted 'intensive negotiations' that resulted in most of the identified jurisdictions making a commitment (Payne, 2004: p. 629). The initial List of Uncooperative Tax Havens, when it was finally published in April 2002, would contain only seven jurisdictions (Andorra, Liechtenstein, Liberia, Monaco, Marshall Islands, Nauru, and Vanuatu) (Owens, 2002: p. 2). Recall the earlier discussion about these commitment letters – many contain the explicit qualification that all conditions applicable to non-OECD jurisdictions must be equally applicable to the OECD member states.

The next significant activity with respect to the non-OECD jurisdictions was undertaken through an Informal Contact Group established under the oversight of the OECD's Global Forum. The Contact Group arranged a meeting in October 2003 to discuss the issue of a level playing field and it was attended by the representatives of forty OECD and non-OECD jurisdictions. The tone of discussions was set at the start of the meeting by the welcoming remarks of OECD Deputy Secretary General Hecklinger, who emphasized that it was about assuring compliance with international rules. 'This is not about one country acting as a tax collector for another: it's about international cooperation and good international relations between neighbours.' (OECD Global Forum on Taxation, 2003b: p. 1) The argument has already been made that from the perspective of small states, the 'international' rules must recognize that they too are sovereign entities, and not merely tax agents for the OECD member states.

The OECD's progress report in 2004 discussed the accomplishments of the subgroup's October meeting. 'Virtually all the participants reaffirmed their commitments to the principles underlying the exchange of information standard and acknowledged the need to continue their discussions to establish bi-lateral mechanisms for effective exchange of information.' (Organization for Economic Co-operation and Development, 2004a: p. 21) The use of the word 'virtually' in the progress report masks the forceful dissent of the representative from Antigua and Barbuda concerning the results of the meeting. In a statement reported by the Caribbean Media Corporation, the Prime Minister of Antigua and Barbuda urged other regional jurisdictions to withdraw from the OECD's Global Forum because 'his country remains very concerned that a level playing field still does not exist between OECD and non-OECD countries, which make up the Global Forum.' (Caribbean Media Corporation, 2003)[11]

Throughout this period, the Commonwealth Secretariat continued to exercise its 'good offices' to facilitate meetings and sponsor technical assistance for the non-OECD participants. One of these activities was mentioned in passing above, the Workshop on the International Financial Sector in Small Vulnerable Economies.[12] The participants at this gathering represented both the member jurisdictions of the ITIO and a number of interested non-member jurisdictions with international financial services sectors. Of particular note was the fact that the Commonwealth Secretariat organized a meeting for the members of another organization, though many are also members (or affiliated to a member) of the Commonwealth. The ITIO is the focus of the next section.

Beyond the Commonwealth

In March 2001, several offshore jurisdictions joined together and established the ITIO 'as a forum in which small and developing economies (SDEs) work on an equal basis and speak with a common voice.' (ITIO, 2003)[13] The choice of terms in this description is intentional, as the organization comprises both sovereign states and non-self governing territories.[14] The creation of the ITIO diversified the opportunities for collective action by small states specifically for the international finance domain and outside the structure of the Commonwealth, CARICOM and Pacific Islands Forum. Most international organizations involving the international financial sector are composed predominantly of the larger developed states. Establishing the ITIO as a forum for small and developing economies and one from which they could 'speak with a common voice' provides them with an alternative to these former institutions on the harmful tax competition issue and other similar financial sector initiatives (ITIO, 2003). Furthermore, the ITIO is not limited to sovereign states, opening its membership to any small and developing economy, including the non-self-governing territories. These latter jurisdictions are often left uninvited to the international conference table, simply because they are not fully sovereign entities. In part this is unfortunate because their limited sovereignty may include governance and legislation for finance and business, as for example the Cayman Islands. And in this circumstance, some of the largest actors in the offshore financial sector are non-self-governing territories. The Cayman Islands is frequently identified as a top world financial center, for example from the *Financial Times*, 'The Caymans' banking sector is the fifth-largest in the world and is a leading centre for hedge funds.' (Burton and Parker, 2003a: p. 1) With membership in the ITIO, the interested non-self-governing jurisdictions now have a forum in which to meet and discuss the issues of concern that are common to any small jurisdiction with a similarly structured economy.

The first major topic the ITIO addressed was not the harmful tax competition project, but instead involved a related OECD effort involving corporate governance. The OECD report, *Behind the Corporate Veil: Using Corporate Entities for Illicit Purposes*, approached the topic with an emphasis on those corporations registered in non-OECD member states, particularly in offshore jurisdictions. As with harmful tax competition, the OECD framed a very specific economic concern for its members as a global problem, and then proceeded to identify the source of the problem as lying substantially *outside* its membership. 'While the report examines both onshore and offshore jurisdictions, it places a greater focus on OFCs for three reasons.' The rationale given was that 1) the 'excessive' secrecy provided by some OFCs 'create a favourable environment for their misuse for illicit purposes'; 2) shell companies exist as a 'substantial proportion of the corporate vehicles established in some OFCs'; and 3) the 'specialised, sophisticated, and robust regimes' for information exchange in some OFCs should serve as a model for other jurisdictions (Organization for Economic Co-operation and Development, 2001b: pp. 7–8). It was this focus on OFCs that led the ITIO to prepare a report responding to it and in that rebuttal to defend the interests of the targeted offshore jurisdictions.

The ITIO teamed with an interested industry organization, the Society of Trust and Estate Practitioners (a 'professional body for the trust and estate profession worldwide'), to commission the international Canadian law firm of Stikeman Elliott to study the OECD's report and to prepare an analysis of it. In the foreword to their study, the Chairman of the Society of Trust and Estate Practitioners noted his organization's interest and concern with the OECD's report. The fact that the OECD had not found it necessary to consult with the industry affected by its proposals caused this professional community to be 'concerned with a process for change in which they are denied effective participation.' (Stikeman Elliott, 2002: p. 1)[15] In this concern, the professional community had common cause with the small jurisdictions as they too were not participants in drafting the report, an experience that echoed the development of the first OECD report on harmful tax competition.

The ITIO analysis of the OECD Report focused on three specific concerns, first with its emphasis on non-OECD international financial centers (IFCs), second with the regulatory burden that would be placed on the affected jurisdictions if the OECD's proposals were implemented, and finally on the erosion of the privacy of individual citizens.[16] Similar to *Harmful Tax Competition*, this OECD report identified a number of practices as an offshore problem that are equally problematic amongst OECD members. Secrecy is a feature of trusts and foundations in the United Kingdom and Austria for example, and the creation of shell (brass plate) companies is as much a commodity of Delaware (USA) as it is of the Channel Islands (Organization for Economic Co-operation and Development, 2001b:

pp. 25–28, 49, and 56). The point raised about financial secrecy is in fact neither unique nor specific to OFCs. The issue concerning the regulatory burden arises with every international standard or best practice to be implemented by the small state. In general, international standards are created with little or no participation from small jurisdictions and are likely to strain the limited resources of the small jurisdiction because of embedded assumptions with resource availability. The issue about the erosion of personal privacy with respect to private corporations is similar to the situation involving taxpayer data and information exchange as part of banking confidentiality laws. In this case, the privacy issue includes the specific feature that is sought by the use of corporations, trusts, foundations, and limited partnerships in their function as contractual vehicles for personal financial transactions – the desire to obscure beneficial ownership.[17] For *personal* privacy there may be solid ground for this concern within common law jurisdictions, but for *public corporations* recent business history reminds us this feature is far more problematic. The use of special purpose vehicles registered in offshore jurisdictions by Parmalat and Enron to obscure malfeasance underscores the OECD argument – not only that corporate vehicles are used for illicit purposes, but that the transnational nature of these activities requires a global response.

Any connection between the OECD documents on the Misuse of Corporate Vehicles and Harmful Tax Competition is not explicit, and illicit or harmful tax practices are only briefly mentioned in the Foreword and Introduction of *Behind the Corporate Veil*. However, a reading of the latter report does identify threads between these two OECD projects. The OECD report on Corporate Vehicles refers to 'illicit tax practices' while the phrase 'tax evasion' only appears in reference to a United States Internal Revenue Service observation concerning the 'proliferation in the use of OFC trusts and corporations in tax evasion schemes due to the difficulty in tracing their beneficial owners.' (Organization for Economic Co-operation and Development, 2001b: p. 36)[18] Consequently, the OECD has avoided the issues surrounding juridical definitions of tax evasion as outlined earlier. 'In this Report, conduct is "illicit" if it is illegal in the perpetrator's country of citizenship, domicile, or residence.' Thus, if illegal in some territory in which a 'perpetrator' has a nexus, the fact that it is *not* illegal at the location of the account or corporate registration (another jurisdiction, offshore or onshore) has become immaterial. This approach then is perhaps not an *extraterritorial* enforcement of state law, because the action deemed illicit occurred in the location where it was illegal, although the corporate vehicle may be registered in some other jurisdiction.

On the other hand, if the action was illegal in the state in which one is a citizen, but not illegal in the state where one is resident (or even where the event occurred) this could be seen as an extraterritorial enforcement of domestic law. One example would be in the legal perception of 'corruption' wherein a corporate executive, living in one state, makes a contribution which is categorized as illicit in the state of their citizenship, or corporate registration, but not in the state where payment was made.[19] The complexities of the Elf Aquitaine bribery and corruption case in France offer a ready example for the intricacies associated with transnational illicit conduct.[20] Many of the 37 defendants were French citizens, but also charged were a Turkish businessman, a German businessman, and an 'Iraqi-born British billionaire'. While Elf Aquitaine was a state-owned business during the period under investigation, the absence of any prominent French political figures from the indictment was noted in some media reports of the trial. The investigation produced a 1,045-page indictment with 44,000 pages of supporting documentation, the aftermath of what *The Guardian* (London) described as 'probably the biggest political and corporate sleaze scandal to hit a western democracy since the second world war.' (Henley, 2003; Tagliabue, 2003)

No longer would economic activity be considered in the context of its physical location. One objective of the OECD report on the misuse of corporate vehicles would be to establish conduct as illicit if a connection could be made between the perpetrator (individual or firm) and some territory in which the legal system has established it to be illicit conduct. Therefore, the fact that Enron used corporate vehicles registered in a Caribbean jurisdiction is inconsequential because ultimately they were implicated by authorities in the United States for illegal financial transactions involving the parent firm. Territorial jurisdiction was treated as immaterial to the pursuit of domestic justice.[21] The OECD's objective in their report investigating corporate vehicles and illegal conduct is to simplify access to information that *may* be evidence for some criminal activity. Note that this treatment of the illicit resonates with the solution to the level playing field proposed by the OECD's Global Forum. As noted above, in order to 'level the playing field' and achieve an effective exchange of information any domestic laws involving banking confidentiality and the legal requirement that the case in question involve conduct considered criminal in both jurisdictions (dual criminality) would no longer apply (Organization for Economic Co-operation and Development, 2001a: p. 11).

Concluding thoughts on collective action

Some authors have suggested that the effort for international tax harmonization (or at the very least tax-related information exchange) is simply one aspect of the larger process of globalization (Avi-Yonah, 2000; Deprez, 2003; Genschel, 2002). Increases in trade volume and the increased internationalization of manufacturing and services have created negative effects for public welfare according to the 'race to the bottom' thesis. Consequently, international coordination on taxation may be seen as part of a broader effort to reduce the negative impact of events and activities that spill over the territorial boundaries of one state into the territory of another state. The larger effort by developed economies to stabilize the international financial sector also includes international standards for bank capitalization and supervision (the Basel Capital Accord) and recommendations to combat money laundering and the financing of terrorism (the Financial Action Task Force (FATF)). A broad coordination of the efforts by a number of international financial agencies and institutions is managed through the Financial Stability Forum, which has prepared a compendium of relevant international standards.[22] Compliance costs for these activities are small within the context of a large developed economy, yet the impact for a small developing economy with limited resources looms large. The government of the Bahamas estimated it would cost US$45 million to implement the changed legislation enacted in 2000 by the Bahamas in an effort to address the issues raised by the FATF (Matthews, 2003a; Gray, 2002).

The Commonwealth has been effective in providing infrastructural support to small states to overcome the resource limitations. This support includes research work (such as vulnerability studies), aggregation of interests (such as with non-resident WTO representation), and the creation of model legislation (for example a model law on money laundering). Existing as a venue in which to consolidate small state interests and to promote small state interests with a larger voice is only one aspect of the Commonwealth's involvement, even if this is the aspect often suggested by the foreign policy literature. Another aspect of the Commonwealth role involves the limitations confronting the small state, those of resources, capacity and the capability to create, legislate, regulate, administer, audit and report for all the myriad 'best practices' increasingly promulgated in the international community (financial, legal, environmental, counter-terrorism, etc.). This aspect is reflected in the publication of *Combating Money Laundering and Terrorist Financing: A Model of Best Practice for the Financial Sector, the Professions and Other Designated Businesses* (2006) to help developing states comply with the international standards for anti-money laundering and combating the financing of terrorism. The Commonwealth was instrumental in facilitating a more inclusive discussion of tax competition, beyond the OECD club. The absence of some grand dramatic change in the treatment of OFCs does not mean this international governmental organization has not had a positive influence on behalf of its small state members.

In his analysis of 'weak-strong negotiations in the international economy' J. P. Singh observed that 'international organizations are usually storehouses of data/information during any negotiation' and may utilize this knowledge advantage to persuade other participants in the negotiations (Singh, 2000: p. 461). In this case, the OECD has been an established storehouse of economic data for decades and has collected and analyzed data on taxation throughout much of that time. The formation of the ITIO served to create an alternate viewpoint on these matters and specifically for the affected small jurisdictions. This alternative storehouse supplemented the support provided by the Commonwealth. When considered together the two OECD projects demonstrate a concerted effort towards controlling and regulating financial services beyond the direct legislative reach of OECD member states. Juxtaposing the ITIO analysis of the OECD report on corporate vehicles with the tax competition project suggests the existence of a wider agenda against international financial services in the offshore landscape.

The observation that the Commonwealth possesses a 'comparative advantage' for engaging with the international/multilateral concerns of small states overlooks the nature of the organization itself. The Commonwealth Secretary-General observed the fact that four Commonwealth members were also members of the OECD, and suggested that this situation provided the opportunity for dialogue. Beyond that circumstance, however, is the fact that the Commonwealth serves as a venue for this disparate collection of states to meet and discuss amongst themselves matters of international concern. In this environment the small state representatives have the opportunity to express their viewpoints on these matters, and to highlight those items that possess a particular concern for them, for example trade in agricultural products or the environment and climate change (Payne, 2004). They may both familiarize the other members' representatives to their concerns and lobby for their support when attending other international gatherings (for example the WTO and the EU). The shared history and common (for most members) legal tradition of the Commonwealth serve as a basis for mutual understanding and communication, or at least a starting position and common point of reference. To develop a sound and convincing argument, using the terms and concepts understood by larger states may be a case of small states 'using the weapons of the weak'. It is also the constructive problem solving approach touted by international institutions in order to reduce conflict and avoid violence in an anarchic international system. From this assessment of collective efforts to resist the harmful tax competition project, the next chapter looks at the individual activity of four Caribbean jurisdictions hosting an OFC.

6
Caribbean Offshore Finance Under Pressure

> Sometimes it seems as if small states were like small boats pushed out into a turbulent sea, free in one sense to traverse; but, without oars or provisions without compass or sails, free also to perish.
>
> – Shridath Ramphal[1]

The above epigram resonates with an analogy used by free market/free trade advocates, that a rising tide raises all boats. What is ignored by that analogy is the turbulence present in the tidal flow (which can vary based on other environmental factors), along with the turbulence created by the passage of larger ships in the global economic tidal basin as they move by the small boats of developing economies. As discussed in the previous chapter, the Commonwealth sought to assist its small state members in dealing with the additional turbulence generated by the Organization for Economic Co-operation and Development (OECD) and its project against harmful tax competition. In this chapter, the focus turns to several of the Caribbean jurisdictions themselves. There are sixteen offshore financial centers (OFCs) in the Caribbean, along with the North Atlantic island of Bermuda, which is often grouped together with the Caribbean OFCs in studies of global finance (Errico and Musalem, 1999: p. 11). Eight of these financial centers are sovereign states: Antigua and Barbuda, the Bahamas, Barbados, Dominica, Grenada, St. Kitts and Nevis, St. Lucia, and St. Vincent and the Grenadines. The remaining OFCs are located in non-self governing jurisdictions, six British (Anguilla, Bermuda, the British Virgin Islands, the Cayman Islands, Montserrat, and the Turks and Caicos Islands), two Dutch (the Netherlands Antilles and Aruba), and the United States-associated Commonwealth of Puerto Rico. Underscoring the observations of Shridath Ramphal (at the time, Commonwealth Secretary-General), there are a number of hazards in the waters surrounding these small ships of state, including natural disasters, transnational crime, and American foreign and economic policy for the Caribbean region. Accompanying the fear that a state might be 'captured' by the offshore business sector, there is also a potential for the state to be captured by external criminal elements.[2] In many cases, these islands support only one significant exportable cash crop, which is then subject to the vagaries of the global market place. Taken together, these obstacles to economic development and democratic freedom create an atmosphere of vulnerability affecting citizens and their governments.

Several research projects have attempted to quantify and understand the specific characteristics of small state vulnerability and the Commonwealth sponsored some of this work. The rationale of these research efforts and their conclusions are discussed in the next section. One aspect of small state vulnerability is the limited range of economic opportunities available to these small territories. The major economic sectors for many of the Caribbean islands are tourism, bananas, sugar and offshore business services. Data from several of them are presented in more detail in the second section of this chapter. The argument highlights the role and importance of the offshore financial business to these specific jurisdictions. The Central Bank of the Bahamas for example, has tracked the contribution of the financial services industry for their national economy over a number of years. By contrast, while Dominica and St. Vincent possess small OFCs, for these two small states it has been banana cultivation that historically was the major source of employment and export income. Finally, the British non-self-governing territory of the Cayman Islands is widely acknowledged as one of the largest financial centers in the world. For this small territory, banking and financial services has become a significant factor in the economy, originally as a means to overcome the vulnerable characteristics of agriculture and tourism. Ironically, offshore financial services are now themselves a source of vulnerability for the small developing economy.

The third section of this chapter provides a broader discussion of financial flows to and through the Commonwealth Caribbean. This analysis of international banking combines data from the Bank for International Settlements (BIS), the Eastern Caribbean Central Bank (ECCB), and several of the individual jurisdictions. It considers the impact of the various global initiatives to constrain, restrain, manage and control offshore finance, whether as an environment permitting criminal money laundering or facilitating civil tax avoidance. The impact of these measures on local employment and revenue is highlighted because it is one reason for resistance to the OECD project, in particular by the small Caribbean jurisdictions.

Quantifying vulnerability

Stephen Ambrose wrote that the intervention in Grenada by the United States in 1983 was a success for 'gunboat diplomacy' (Ambrose, 1986: p. 332). Outside of the US, however, it was heard as a wake-up klaxon directed at America's nominal allies within the Commonwealth. It represented a reminder that American perceptions of *its* national interests superseded other obligations. It is not a new message, reflecting as it does the history of US foreign policy in the Caribbean and Latin America. The Monroe Doctrine anchors the traditional American policy in the Western Hemisphere, and it was first announced in 1823 with the intention of keeping the European powers out. The fact that Grenada was a member of the Commonwealth was immaterial to the US decision to invade the island. 'The flagrant intervention into the internal affairs of a small (but still sovereign) state was apparently the last straw: this was the catalyst that led to a spate of treatises highlighting and exposing powerlessness and dependency.' (Baldacchino, 2000: p. 66) Godfrey Baldacchino's observation is an appropriate description for the range of research on small states sponsored by the Commonwealth in the 1980s.

The invasion was widely criticized by many observers located outside of the region, even though the governments of several other Caribbean states supported the US intervention, including Antigua, Barbados, Dominica, Jamaica, St. Lucia, and St. Vincent (Tyler and Hoffman, 1983: p. A1). The Commonwealth Secretariat, for example, convened a Consultative Group and tasked it to consider the consequences for small states indicated by the intervention in Grenada. This group's report was published in 1985 and emphasized security issues consonant with the Grenadian experience (Commonwealth Secretariat, 1985). With the end of the Cold War concerns shifted and a subsequent report from the Commonwealth Secretariat focused on the economic and development challenges facing small states (Commonwealth Advisory Group, 1997).

Studies of small state vulnerability and the effort to quantify it were one line of research begun following the 1985 Commonwealth report, specifically to quantify the vulnerability inherent to a small island economy (SIE) (Briguglio, 1995). A number of factors were studied, including natural disasters, economic dependence on a single export crop and environmental vulnerability. Global warning projections for example suggest that there could be an extensive melting of the polar ice caps and mountain glaciers. This melting would in turn raise sea levels and thereby inundate many low-lying islands, as well as low-lying continental coastal areas. Consequently, global warming is a vital concern for small islands, even though the impact would be substantially the same for any low-lying coastal areas.[3]

The validity of the methods and conclusions reached by the effort to demonstrate empirically a significant difference in the economic, political and social conditions of small states versus other states has been contested. Nonetheless, it serves to emphasize two points: first, that there exists a self-perception of difference among the residents of these societies and this perception is reproduced by the external institutions and individuals that study small states. The second point is the diversity of topics for which size and location are considered factors in the efficient operation of an economy, both in its utilization of resources and in its ability to provide for its citizens. The problem involves 'economies of scale' and some specific sectors are communication and transportation connections, as well as ready access to training and education resources.[4] Both points are part of the challenge facing the capacity and capability of a small state to participate in the global economy.

The Commonwealth report, *A Future for Small States*, referred to the 'pioneering work of Briguglio' demonstrating a correlation between size and economic vulnerability in small island developing states. The report also noted the intention of the Commonwealth Secretariat to 'refine the index with the example of the widely-used Human Development Index very much in mind.' (Commonwealth Advisory Group, 1997: p. 15) This in turn led to the creation of the

Commonwealth Vulnerability Index (CVI) (Atkins *et al.*, 2000). The factors used by the Index to derive the score for any particular state are: economic exposure, remoteness and insularity, susceptibility to environmental events, and other sources. The last factor was a catchall variable for the model as an attempt to capture and incorporate other, less quantifiable factors such as government stability and emigrant labor remittances. The results of the modeling exercise demonstrated that remoteness was not a necessary and sufficient cause for vulnerability. Reliance on a single commodity and susceptibility to natural disasters are also significant influences on any individual state's vulnerability index score.[5]

The significant conclusion reached by Christopher Easter was that because the primary factor influencing a small state's vulnerability differed from state to state, any attempt to address this vulnerability must necessarily also differ between individual states. In sum, there is no single solution that can be applied across the board for all small states. The conclusions made in the report's presentation of the vulnerability index emphasize a further point concerning the use of this evaluation. The CVI was 'designed as an indicator of vulnerability, not as a means to identify less developed countries (LDCs) or to indicate level of development status.' (Atkins *et al.*, 2000: p. 26) This last point is especially relevant when assessing any criticism to the Vulnerability Index project.

Contradicting these conclusions, two World Bank economists found that after controlling for a variety of variables, 'small states have on average higher income and productivity levels than large states'. (Easterly and Kraay, 2000: p. 2014) In their model, these authors considered per capita income, growth, openness and volatility, and opportunities for diversification. The broad conclusion from their analysis was that it is not necessary to create special measures in support of small states. Income rates in small states were similar to other states in their respective regions, and growth rates were not significantly different between small and large states. It was only in the area of trade volatility that smaller states suffered, 'but this is largely due to their greater trade openness – and the net benefits of openness on growth are positive.' (Easterly and Kraay, 2000: p. 2024) The authors acknowledged that small states have economic problems; nevertheless, they concluded that these problems were no different from any experienced in other poor economies.

These two models are operating at cross-purposes and evaluating different data in order to arrive at their differing conclusions. The CVI focused on those factors that distinguish the vulnerable aspects of an economy (and a small state as a society) not only in the present, but also for the future. The work of Easterly and Kraay on the other hand, analyzed discrete economic data for economic performance between 1960 and 1995. An argument that preferential treatment is not needed, based on past performance, should be treated cautiously given that the small developing economies of concern were operating with preferential trade regimes during the data period. Therefore, the recommendation that the CVI be used as a tool for evaluating vulnerability, rather than as a means to assess developmental status remains reasonable. This may not be sufficient to convince the World Trade Organization (WTO) that small states require special trade regime treatment, an objective for which vulnerability studies are often cited.[6] However, the results deserve consideration in any evaluation of the economic situation of a small state.

In addition to these small state vulnerability studies, there is the research program of Harvey Armstrong, Robert Read, and their colleagues. In addition to small developing states, they considered the economic status of the small state members of the European Union. The noteworthy aspect of their research conclusions for European small states is the similarity that they have to the economic development choices made by Caribbean small states. In the 1995 *World Development* article discussing EU small states and autonomous regions Armstrong and Read concluded,

> The most successful of the micro-states and autonomous regions are those with well-developed financial service sectors (the single most important variable), a valuable natural resource base (endowment) or a strong tourism sector (in this order of importance) – or some combination of these three factors. (Armstrong and Read, 1995: p. 1239)

This conclusion could just as readily have been applied to the more successful small Caribbean jurisdictions at that time (for example the Bahamas and the Cayman Islands). Subsequent research work however, concluded that the vulnerabilities inherent to remoteness and size that affect many small states are aggravated by efforts in the WTO and elsewhere to create a level playing field in the global economy (Armstrong and Read, 2002a). This conclusion reinforces the concern with vulnerability amongst many Commonwealth small states – the impact of size and distance upon their small economies. Of particular relevance here has been the change of attitude towards the use of financial services as a means for achieving economic development. The OECD's campaign against harmful tax competition represents this new attitude against offshore finance as an approach to economic development.

A further observation to be made about longitudinal economic analysis such as that applied in vulnerability studies is the limited recognition afforded to the historical trajectory of what are predominately former colonial societies. Present economic circumstances are the result of an accumulation of trade and agriculture decisions that may go back three hundred years in some instances. During its time as a colony, economic decisions would often be made within the context of the larger collectivity of the metropole state and its other colonies. In this context, the preferential treatment for the products of any individual subordinate colony was accepted practice. The practice of preferential treatment continued after independence, but in recent years has come to be challenged by the principles of free and open trade amongst all states promulgated by the WTO. Just as with location, size and the weather, history (in the form of past economic decisions) also makes these small jurisdictions vulnerable.

Notwithstanding the economic and quantitative analysis of small state vulnerability, in part vulnerability is a matter of perception. If investors perceive a location to be particularly vulnerable (whether due to government instability, prevailing weather patterns leading to frequent hurricanes, or a reliance on a single agricultural product) they will not necessarily invest in that location.[7] Correspondingly, if residents perceive themselves as living in a particularly vulnerable location, the perception encourages emigration, in addition to requests for special and differential treatment on trade and finance activity from international organizations. Perceptions are just as much a factor in the decision-making process as the use of econometric figures and other data. The perceptions surrounding small state vulnerability become judgements upon their political stability and a risk factor for financial and investment analysts (Johns, 1983: p. 191). Moreover, it is an unquantifiable component of reputation, and all financial centers seek to create a good reputation, whether or not they exist 'offshore', in order to retain current business and attract new business (Sharman, 2006; Sharman, 2007).

The imbalance between the OECD and any individual jurisdiction hosting an OFC inherently emphasizes the vulnerable position of the small state/territory. These studies suggest that perceptions of economic vulnerability should have induced the small states hosting an OFC to be extremely cooperative with the OECD project. As will be seen, the offshore business sector is a valuable source of revenue in these jurisdictions. It would appear to the outside observer that cooperation with the OECD (with an intention to reach a resolution that would maintain current levels of government revenue) is a reasonable decision. Instead, as discussed in the previous chapter, efforts were made to assemble a collective response among the affected jurisdictions, via the Commonwealth and with the creation of a purpose-built organization, the International Trade and Investment Organization (ITIO). But as will be seen below, even though these jurisdictions are vulnerable, and their business affected by the harmful tax competition project, the overall impact of the OECD project has not included a reduction in foreign deposits among the Caribbean OFCs.

Caribbean offshore financial centers

The origins of offshore finance within international finance were discussed in Chapter 1. While the OECD's Harmful Tax Competition Initiative (HTCI) with respect to small states is the case used in this study of state sovereignty, it is not the only international program addressing offshore finance and OFCs. The actions of the Financial Action Task Force (FATF) were discussed in Chapter 3 with specific reference to its use of a 'blacklist' to identify 'non-cooperative countries and territories' (in that instance, the experience of the Philippines was outlined). From the Caribbean the FATF blacklist contained Antigua and Barbuda, the Bahamas, Bermuda, the British Virgin Islands, the Cayman Islands, Dominica, St. Kitts and Nevis, St. Lucia, and St. Vincent and the Grenadines (Financial Action Task Force, 2000).[8]

This section considers four of the sixteen jurisdictions with OFCs in the Caribbean. The selection includes one state with a relatively large sector, the Bahamas, and two states with comparably small sectors, Dominica and St. Vincent and the Grenadines. The fourth example represents the non-self-governing jurisdictions of the Caribbean, the Cayman Islands, which is also a major actor in offshore finance. An OFC provides more than just banking services. In the Caribbean, various jurisdictions also specialize in providing international business company registrations, insurance company registrations, shipping registrars, and mutual (hedge) funds.

The emphasis in this review of offshore finance in the Caribbean is on the material economic contribution for the jurisdiction made by the OFC. As already highlighted in Chapter 1, for economic development in a small jurisdiction the OFC provides both employment and government revenue. Spillover effects for other local industries, including construction and tourism, also accompany these direct contributions. However, it will quickly become apparent that in most instances, the economic contribution of the OFC to the local economy has declined since 1998. At the same time, the following analysis of the flow of mobile capital through the Caribbean finds that the foreign assets reported on deposit in local institutions increased over the period in question.

The Bahamas

The Bahamas is a chain of islands lying close to Cuba and Florida, and it has been a significant global player in the offshore business sector for a number of years.[9] One author attributed the development of offshore banking in the Bahamas during the 1960s to banking regulation in the United States (Francis, 1985: pp. 92–93). Its economy is heavily dependent on tourism (mostly from North America) and on offshore business. A study of offshore banking in the Bahamas published in 1985 noted that offshore banks contribute to the local economy not only via the employment provided, but also through foreign exchange. In particular, this 'foreign exchange benefit arises from the fact that since the "pure" offshore banks have no Bahamian dollar income, all local expenses' would be satisfied with foreign currency converted to Bahamian dollars (Francis, 1985: pp. 98–99). During the period 1990–1998, the Bahamian services sector absorbed 80 per cent of the labour force, and in 2000 tourist receipts contributed 67 per cent of total export earnings. Tourist receipts amounted to a total of US$1,814 million in

2000, 38 per cent of GDP (US$4,800 million) (Commonwealth Secretariat, 2003c: pp. 111, 135). The global economic slowdown and decline in tourism after 2001 hit the Bahamian economy hard, and the offshore financial services sector also experienced a decline (Commonwealth Secretariat, 2003c: p. 9). The economic impact on offshore services was in part also a result of new legislation targeted at strengthening anti-money laundering enforcement in the Bahamas.

The action to strengthen the anti-money laundering laws was a necessary response to the listing of the Bahamas. The FATF report found that '[a]lthough the Bahamas has comprehensive anti-money laundering legislation, there are serious deficiencies in its system.' (Financial Action Task Force, 2000: p. 2) It also pointed out that new legislation was pending in the Bahamas to address the identified weak points. The revised legislation was enacted and subsequently the Bahamas was removed from the list of non-cooperative jurisdictions in 2001. From the perspective of the FATF and other organizations dealing with the problem of international money laundering, this case was represented as a success for blacklisting as a method to persuade states to implement FATF-approved standards. Within the Bahamas, the new legislation led to the closure of a number of institutions unable or unwilling to comply with some aspect of it.

The Central Bank of the Bahamas in its reports highlighted one specific change in the new licensing requirements. There is now a requirement for financial institutions to maintain 'an appropriate physical presence in the jurisdiction'. In March 2001, an analysis of the impact of the new regulation to offshore banking in the Bahamas predicted 'that approximately 60 banks will not be able to comply with the new physical requirements and will wind-up their managed operations' (The Central Bank of the Bahamas, 2001: p. 38). This analysis proved to be accurate, for the number of offshore banks and trusts licensed by the Bahamas declined from 395 in 1999 to 333 in 2001 and then down to 228 in 2005 (see Table 6.1). The decline in the number of institutions was accompanied by a decline in employment within the financial services sector. Later analysis from the Central Bank remained optimistic about the long-term effects of the changes in financial sector regulation. 'Ongoing efforts to strengthen the supervisory framework should enhance The Bahamas' reputation as a safe, well regulated jurisdiction.' (The Central Bank

Table 6.1 **The Bahamas, Offshore Entities and Employment**

	1996	1997	1998	1999	2000	2001	2002	2003	2004	2005	2006
Offshore banks & trusts (public and restricted)	n/a	n/a	398*	395	388	333	276	250	242	228	226
Bahamian employees	682	764	772	836	991	973†	962†	823†	967†	835†	9,869†
Non-Bahamian employees	124	128	130	142	195	242†	239†	222†	214†	192†	236†
Total employees	806	892	902	978	1,186	1,215†	1,201†	1,045†	1,181†	1,027†	1,105†
Registered offshore entities	n/a	n/a	n/a	n/a	n/a	27,896	16,115	15,147	18,601	19,231	19,231

Source: The Central Bank of the Bahamas, *Quarterly Economic Review*, March various years.
*estimated
n/a – not available
† These values were annotated with a 'p' indicating that the data was provisional in the *Quarterly Economic Review*, March 2007.

of the Bahamas, 2003: p. 43) The reason for this continued optimism is clear, for even with the decline in the number of licensed institutions, the government's estimate continued to put the contribution of the financial services sector at 15 to 20 per cent of GDP (see Table 6.2) (The Central Bank of the Bahamas, 2006: p. 32).

Dominica and St. Vincent

Dominica is a small island in the Lesser Antilles and together with Grenada, St. Lucia, and St. Vincent and the Grenadines it comprises the Windward Islands. The Central Intelligence Agency's *World Factbook* introduced its entry for the island with the observation that it was the last one to be colonized by Europeans 'due chiefly to the fierce resistance of the native Caribs' (Central Intelligence Agency, 2002). The island is described as rugged and mountainous with lush and varied flora and fauna. Consequently, its natural resources are timber, hydropower and agriculture. Agricultural land constitutes approximately 20 per cent of the island's 754 square kilometers of territory and is used primarily for bananas. In addition to the impact of hurricanes on the banana industry, banana exports were also affected by changes to the banana trade agreements for the Caribbean industry over the past decade. The contribution of agriculture to the island's economy as a result has declined, from 1988 when it comprised 28.8 per cent of GDP down to 18.2 per cent in 2005.[10] A lack of beaches on the island's rugged coastline and the absence of an international airport hamper Dominica's ability to diversify into the tourist sector. Consequently, Dominica turned to offshore financial services for economic development diversification. The legislation establishing the offshore sector was enacted in 1996 with the goal of positioning the jurisdiction as a low cost service provider (Feracho and Samuel, 1997: p. 250; Suss *et al.*, 2002: pp. 29–30).

The International Monetary Fund (IMF) report on *Caribbean Offshore Financial Centers*, included data for Dominica's offshore sector for the year 2001. In their report, the IMF listed five offshore banks, six gaming companies and 7,536 international business companies (IBCs); in addition to these entities, the report indicated that there were also two offshore insurance companies and five trust companies. By contrast in August 2004, Dominica reported that their offshore sector comprised one offshore bank, four Internet gaming

Table 6.2 The Bahamas, Offshore License Revenue (In thousands of Bahamian dollars)

Fiscal Year	1997/ 1998	1998/ 1999	1999/ 2000	2000/ 2001	2001/ 2002	2002/ 2003	2003/ 2004	2004/ 2005	2005/ 2006
Business and Professional License fees	33,678	58,504	55,061	54,661	55,778	53,776	56,334	60,558	74,289
includes Company fees and Registration	4,407	4,522	4,733	3,854	4,907	5,237	5,504	5,083	5,402
includes International Business Companies	8,010	17,381	17,247	13,290	18,000	16,604	15,835	15,055	14,855

Source: The Central Bank of the Bahamas, *Quarterly Statistical Digest*, August 2003 & 2004. (Table 7.2, Central Government: Current Revenue) and August 2006 & May 2007 (Table 5.2, Central Government: Current Revenue).
n.b. – all data values were annotated as provisional.

companies and approximately 1200 IBCs a significant decline in three years. As a contributor to Dominica's GDP, Banks and Insurance provided 10.4 per cent in 1988, had increased only to 12.9 per cent by 2001 and accounted for 14.7 per cent in 2005. This economic sector had failed to offset the decline in the banana industry over the period. Agriculture provided 28.8 per cent of GDP in 1988, dropping to 17.5 per cent in 2001 and recovered slightly by 2005 to provide 18.2 per cent of GDP.[11]

The small offshore sector of Dominica was identified by the FATF as a non-cooperative jurisdiction in their first list in 2000 and was removed from the blacklist in October 2002. The 2003 report identified Dominica as 'among the first to place its offshore banks under the direct supervision of the ECCB, in conjunction with the local supervisory authorities' (Financial Action Task Force, 2003c: p. 13). Other changes undertaken by Dominica were the establishment of a financial intelligence unit and new legislation strengthening anti-money laundering capabilities. By coordinating bank supervision with the ECCB, Dominica was able to overcome the FATF concern that their OFC appeared to be 'largely unregulated' (Financial Action Task Force, 2000: p. 5). At the same time, the assessment of the Eastern Caribbean Currency Union (ECCU) conducted by the IMF in 2003 recommended that supervisory and regulatory systems for offshore banking needed strengthening. It further recommended a realignment of the ECCB's supervisory role better to fit available resources and priorities (International Monetary Fund, 2004: p. 8).

The circumstances of the collection of islands and cays known as St. Vincent and the Grenadines are similar to Dominica. These islands are volcanic and mountainous, and their natural resources consist of hydropower and agriculture. Among these islands, 30 per cent of the land is used for agriculture (out of a total area of 389 square kilometers). The most important crop has been historically bananas for export, but again their contribution to the economy has declined. In 1988, agriculture provided 21.2 per cent of GDP for St. Vincent and the Grenadines, but by 2001 agricultural products had dropped to just 12 per cent of GDP and fell further to provide only 10 per cent in 2005. Concurrently, the contribution of the Banks and Insurance sector provided 7.4 per cent of GDP in 1988, increased slightly to provide 9 per cent in 2001 with a continued slow increase to 10.6 per cent by 2005.[12]

The offshore sector of St. Vincent and the Grenadines was established in 1976 to provide trust and international company registration services, but it did not perform as well as local officials had hoped (Feracho and Samuel, 1997: pp. 249–250). Because of the limited success with these services, the government of St. Vincent made a policy decision in 1996 to set the offshore financial services sector at 'the forefront of the national economy.' This policy required an extensive revision of existing legislation and the creation of additional legislation to define the limits and operation of their offshore financial services sector (International Financial Services Authority, 2004). The revisions did not find approval with the Financial Action Task Force when it came to the deterrence of financial crime. In particular, 'it was the strict secrecy afforded by the Confidentiality Act [1996] that brought St. Vincent and the Grenadines to the attention of the [FATF]' (Drayton, 2003: p. 170). As with Dominica, the FATF identified St. Vincent's small offshore financial sector as a non-cooperative jurisdiction in 2000. The list of specific shortcomings included the absence of anti-money laundering regulations for the offshore sector and the limited resources that were allocated to supervising offshore financial institutions (Financial Action Task Force, 2000: p. 10). The government of St. Vincent enacted a further series of legislative changes in response to the FATF assessment. Again, as with Dominica, one change was the provision for joint supervision of offshore banks between the ECCB and the International Financial Services Authority (IFSA) of St. Vincent (Drayton, 2003: pp. 172–173; Financial Action Task Force, 2003c: p. 6). The IFSA emphasized the fact that the ECCB brought 'a wealth of experience in banking supervision to the offshore sector.' (International Financial Services Authority, 2004)

The size of the offshore finance sector within St. Vincent and the Grenadines is similar to Dominica but with some key differences. Data provided for 2004 identified one offshore bank, five mutual funds and 1026 IBCs. There are a small number of international trusts, mutual funds and insurance firms, but no Internet gaming companies. These figures represent a decline in the size of St. Vincent's offshore sector over the previous seven years. From the data provided by the IFSA of St. Vincent and the Grenadines, the number of offshore banks peaked in 2000, when there were 13 in these islands. Similarly, the high point for IBCs was 1999, when they reported that there were 2,704. This pattern holds for the other offshore entities based in St. Vincent and the Grenadines. Even with some fluctuations between 1997 and 2006, in general there were fewer offshore entities in each category in 2006 (excepting IBCs and mutual funds) than in previous years (see Table 6.3).[13]

The varied experiences of the OFCs in the Bahamas, Dominica and St. Vincent reflect their historical circumstances. As mentioned, the Bahamas have operated a successful OFC for several decades. It has a long established reputation and an experienced workforce that is particularly focused on offshore banking and investment services. As a result, the Bahamas had the capacity to respond to international pressure effectively and, further, to establish a bilateral agreement with the US on the exchange of tax information (Spencer, 2002: p. 36). This agreement maintains a positive relationship with the OFCs' largest source of customers (Thompson, 2003; Matthews, 2003b). By contrast, both Dominica and St. Vincent were smaller centers and not as well established. They sought to establish and extend their presence by competing on cost and limited regulation, at least from the perspective of the FATF. As such, they represent a second generation of Caribbean OFCs believed explicitly to be pursuing hot money. They responded to the international pressure by both changing the legislation that governed their respective offshore sector and increased banking sector supervision with the assistance of the ECCB. Because these two smaller jurisdictions were no longer as amenable to hot money (licit and illicit) their offshore business sector shrank. The experience of the Cayman Islands was different from these three small states, as discussed in the next section.

British Overseas Territories

In 1997, the new British government initiated a review of Britain's relationship with its dependencies. One of the results of this review was the re-designation of these non-self-governing jurisdictions as the British Overseas Territories, replacing their previous identification as the Dependent Territories. Several of these Overseas Territories are located in the Caribbean, specifically Anguilla, the British Virgin Islands, the Cayman Islands, Montserrat, and the Turks and Caicos Islands. The British government White Paper published in 1999 identified four significant motivating factors for the review. These factors were the election of a new British government in 1997;

Table 6.3 St. Vincent and the Grenadines

Offshore Entity*	1997	1998	1999	2000	2001	2002	2003	2004	2005	2006
International Business Companies	1,188	1,540	2,704	2,175	1,438	858	742	1,026	1,398	1,381
International Trusts	19	210	236	251	124	37	12	10	7	17
Offshore Banks	2	10	11	13	6	0	0	1	1	0
Mutual Funds – Public & Private	0	0	1	3	3	3	0	5	5	10
Fund Manager/ Administrator	0	0	0	3	3	3	1	4	5	5
International Insurance & Insurance Manager/Broker	0	0	0	2	0	0	3	8	4	2

Source: International Financial Services Authority of St. Vincent and the Grenadines, August 2004 and June 2007.
*As categorized by the International Financial Services Authority of St. Vincent and the Grenadines. Note also that these figures do not necessarily reflect the number of entities in good standing in that year.

the increase of volcanic activity on Montserrat; an increased awareness of the economic problems facing these small jurisdictions (particularly St. Helena); and, most importantly for this discussion, 'the growing significance of the OFCs – in particular, Bermuda, the Cayman Islands, and the British Virgin Islands' (Secretary of State for Foreign and Commonwealth Affairs, 1999). Again, while the islands of Bermuda are actually located in the North Atlantic Ocean some distance from the Caribbean Sea, they are often grouped with the jurisdictions of the Caribbean with regards to offshore finance.

In general, the trends in offshore finance that are found in the sovereign small states are present also in these small non-self-governing jurisdictions. As OFCs, they range in size from Montserrat, suffering from the depredations of a number of volcanic eruptions since 1995, to the Cayman Islands, which is widely recognized as a global financial center. Indeed, the Financial Services Commission of Montserrat replied to a request for data on their offshore business sector by stressing the impact of the volcano upon the industry. Although they feel that the volcano has had far greater impact on Montserrat than any OECD initiatives, they nevertheless intend to revive their offshore industry.[14]

The Cayman Islands on the other hand serve as an exemplar for the small jurisdiction OFC and are frequently named in the media whenever offshore finance is mentioned. In 2006, the offshore sector in the Caymans included 274 banking trust firms (Category 'B' licenses), 732 captive insurance firms, 6,784 registered offshore mutual funds (also known as hedge funds), and 74,905 (figure reported for 2005) registered companies.[15] As the business most directly affected by the OECD harmful tax competition project, the number of banking trust firms has declined sharply from their high water mark in 1997 (see Table 6.4). Similar to the offshore financial sector of other jurisdictions, the downward trend has been in the number of firms operating in the international banking sector. The Cayman Islands Monetary Authority (CIMA), however, did not specifically point at increased regulation concerning taxation and financial crimes as the cause for the reduction in the number of licensed firms. Rather, the phrase most frequently used in their annual reports to explain the year to year fluctuation in the number of licenses was that changes resulted from 'mergers and acquisitions in the global financial market' (CIMA, various years).

The downward trend in licenses issued to offshore banking institutions was not reflected in other segments of the Cayman Islands'

Table 6.4 Cayman Islands Offshore Entities

	1996	1997	1998	1999	2000	2001	2002	2003	2004	2005	2006
Banking Trust Licenses Category 'A' *	28	30	30	31	31	31	30	27	23	21	19
Banking Trust Licenses Category 'B' **	471	475	417	430	433	396	353	322	299	284	269
Firms with a physical presence	107	108	114	112	117	113	128	n/a	n/a	n/a	n/a
Class 'B' (Captive) Insurance licenses	418	449	485	497	517	542	600	644	693	733	740
Registered mutual funds (Offshore hedge funds)	1,335	1,685	1,979	2,271	3,014	3,648	4,285	4,808	5,932	7,106	7,481
Trust Company Licenses	n/a	89	n/a	110	116	118	125	122	124	127	135
Registered companies	37,919	41,163	45,169	50,951	59,922	64,495	65,259	68,078	70,133	74,905	83,532

Source: The Cayman Islands Monetary Authority, *Annual Report*, various years; Economics and Statistics Office, *Annual Economic Report*, various years.
*A license to provide services to domestic and international markets.
**A license to provide services to international markets, and facilitate inter-bank transactions.
n/a – not available

offshore business sector. Licenses issued for captive insurance firms, offshore mutual funds and registered companies have all increased throughout the period 1996–2005. The number of captive insurance firms licensed in 1996 was 418 and increased to 733 in 2005 (see Table 6.4). These firms reported total assets of US$26.7 billion in 2005, up from the US$8.4 billion reported for 1997. Likewise, the number of registered mutual funds grew from 1,335 in 1996 to 7,106 in 2005, a figure noted by the *Annual Economic Report* as accounting for an estimated 80 per cent of all hedge funds globally (Economics and Statistics Office, 2006: p. 33). For the economy of the Cayman Islands, the fees collected on bank and trust licenses, insurance licenses, mutual funds administrators and company registrations generated between 18 and 28 per cent of all government revenues in the period 2000–2003. As a point of comparison, revenue collected from taxes on international trade ranged between 34 and 39 per cent during the same period (see Table 6.5).[16]

Arguably, the view of the CIMA to explain the decline in the number of banks licensed in the Cayman Islands is accurate. Mergers are a significant factor in the landscape of global business (Caulkin, 2005). Since most of the major international banking firms are represented in the Cayman Islands, the local business sector will feel and reflect global industry consolidation. In this instance, the decline in revenue from bank license fees has been substantially offset by revenue from license fees associated with mutual funds and captive insurance firms. The overall result for the Cayman Islands has been a more consistent contribution to government revenue from offshore licenses. A more interesting question about offshore finance in the Caribbean involves the quantity of capital that continues to transit through these financial centers, even while the number of banks handling these assets has declined.

Foreign assets 'offshore' in the Caribbean

If a major determinant of the flow of capital to and through OFCs is tax minimization (within an environment of banking confidentiality), then one should expect to find that these flows have declined since 1998 in anticipation of the imposition of an information exchange regime. Certainly, the establishment of a global information exchange regime anticipates the extension of the state's ability to collect taxes due from the interest accruing in offshore accounts. The information

Table 6.5 Cayman Islands Offshore License Fee Revenue (in millions of Cayman Island dollars)

	1996	1997	1998	1999	2000	2001	2002	2003
Banking & Trust Licenses	n/a	n/a	n/a	n/a	10.1	8.9	33.3	28.9
Insurance licenses	n/a	n/a	n/a	n/a	2.9	2.9	5.5	n.a.
Mutual Fund Administrators	n/a	n/a	n/a	n/a	3.2	3.7	11.8	12.5
Company fees	n/a	n/a	n/a	n/a	35.0	37.3	38.6	39.9
Sum of fee revenue	n/a	n/a	n/a	n/a	51.2	52.8	89.6	81.3†
Taxes on Domestic Goods & Services	n/a	n/a	n/a	n/a	104.8	113.1	150.8	153.4
Taxes on International Trade & Transactions*	n/a	n/a	n/a	n/a	110.0	106.2	106.7	117.6
Total revenue**	n/a	n/a	n/a	n/a	278.2	285.4	314.1	326.2
Fee revenue as percentage of total revenue	n/a	n/a	n/a	n/a	18.4%	18.5%	28.5%	24.9%†

Table 6.5 Cayman Islands Offshore License Fee Revenue (in millions of Cayman Island dollars) – *continued*

	1996	1997	1998	1999	2000	2001	2002	2003
International trade taxes as percentage of total revenue	n/a	n/a	n/a	n/a	39.5%	37.2%	34.0%	36.1%
Gross Domestic Product (GDP)	892.4	971.9	1275.2	1382.5	1444.9	1482.3	1546.0	1603.2
Fee revenue as percentage of GDP	n/a	n/a	n/a	n/a	3.5%	3.6%	5.8%	5.1%†

Source: The Cayman Islands Economics and Statistics Office, *Annual Economic Report*, various years.
*This includes travel & cruise ship tax and the Environmental Protection Fee imposed on all visitors as well as duties placed on imported goods.
**This includes items not listed here, property taxes, sales tax, etc.
†Incomplete data
n/a – not available

sharing component of the EU Savings Tax Directive was expected by some either to 'bring capital home' or to force it beyond the reach of its fundamentally European information exchange regime (Burton and Parker, 2003b). The experience from the first full year of implementation for the Directive demonstrated significant displacement of capital from reporting locations to non-reporting locations, especially Hong Kong and Singapore (Bilefsky, 2006). When this particular EU Directive was in negotiation, the European Commission provided the funding for an empirical research project to look into the question 'Are international deposits tax-driven?' The published version of the paper declared that its purpose was to determine the extent that international banking flows were influenced by tax policy and its enforcement (Huizinga and Nicodème, 2004: p. 1094). The authors concluded that 'non-bank external liabilities [those deposits not owed to another bank] have been positively related to interest income taxes and to the presence of domestic bank interest reporting.' They take this to be 'evidence that international deposits are in part intended to facilitate tax evasion.' (Huizinga and Nicodème, 2004: p. 1115) The states studied by Harry Huizinga and Gaëtan Nicodème were limited to a subset of the states that report data on external deposits and liabilities to the Bank of International Settlements. Crucially, their methodology contained only a few OFCs (the Bahamas, Bahrain, Cayman Islands, Hong Kong and Singapore), while the remaining states analyzed were OECD members (Huizinga and Nicodème, 2004: p. 1097).

Huizinga and Nicodème found that between 1983 and 1992 the relationship between external deposits and interest income was statistically significant, but that the relationship changed during the period 1992–1999. They offered two possible explanations to account for why the tax burden became 'almost insignificant' relative to patterns of external bank deposits. The first possible explanation was the decline in the rate of tax imposed on deposit interest across the OECD member states (Huizinga and Nicodème, 2004: Figure 1, p. 1102).[17] If it was the tax on interest that motivated citizens to deposit their funds offshore, then as the tax rate declined it was no longer a strong motivator for tax avoidance. Statistically, there was a relationship between external deposits and the tax burden when the interest on deposits was taxed. However, as the rate of tax declined, this statistical relationship also declined. At the same time, the quantity of non-bank external deposits did not decline. This development led to the second explanation proposed by Huizinga and Nicodème, which was that there was a decline in the 'relative importance of individual tax evaders, as holders of non-bank external liabilities' (Huizinga and Nicodème, 2004: p. 1112). This explanation implied that there was not a decline in tax evasion by citizens, but rather that there was an increase in the proportion of total external deposits held by actors that would not be responsive to changes in personal income tax rates – corporations, mutual funds or insurance firms. The implication of these explanations is that because tax evasion could not be directly measured, these authors assumed that it continued at the same rate, even though the motivating force (the tax rate) was no longer present.

The BIS introduced the sectoral and geographical breakdown of banking statistics in the early 1970s in order 'to provide information on the development and growth of the eurocurrency markets' (Monetary and Economic Department, 2003: p. 1). The first chart (Figure 6.1) provides an historical overview for the period from 1977 to 2006 (see Table 6.6 for the membership of each data set). It shows not only an increase in the foreign assets on deposit in offshore banks, but also the much greater increase in foreign deposits held within OECD members. The line for the OECD substantiates an observation frequently made concerning the nature of globalization, that most FDI (and international financial flows in general) involves financial exchange amongst developed states, and not between developed states and developing states (Held *et al.*, 1999: Chapter 5). The most recent ten-year period for the same data is presented in Figure 6.2. This graph shows the trend amongst OECD member states, the BIS-designated offshore centers, and Commonwealth Caribbean states. The BIS locational banking statistics consolidate data reported by all banking offices resident in those reporting jurisdictions. Specifically, the data used are reported assets on deposit from Table 6a of the June 2007 *Quarterly Review* published by the BIS. This table contained the external positions of the banks reporting quarterly balance sheet data to the BIS, with respect to the identified individual jurisdictions. Thus, it reflected the assets and liabilities of all reporting banks with respect to financial institutions located in another jurisdiction. The table contained for example, the assets and liabilities of all reporting jurisdictions that are held by a financial institution located in the Bahamas.

The two non-OECD categories depicted in these graphs overlap in part because of the criteria used to determine membership in the

Figure 6.1 Foreign assets on deposit, OECD and OFCs

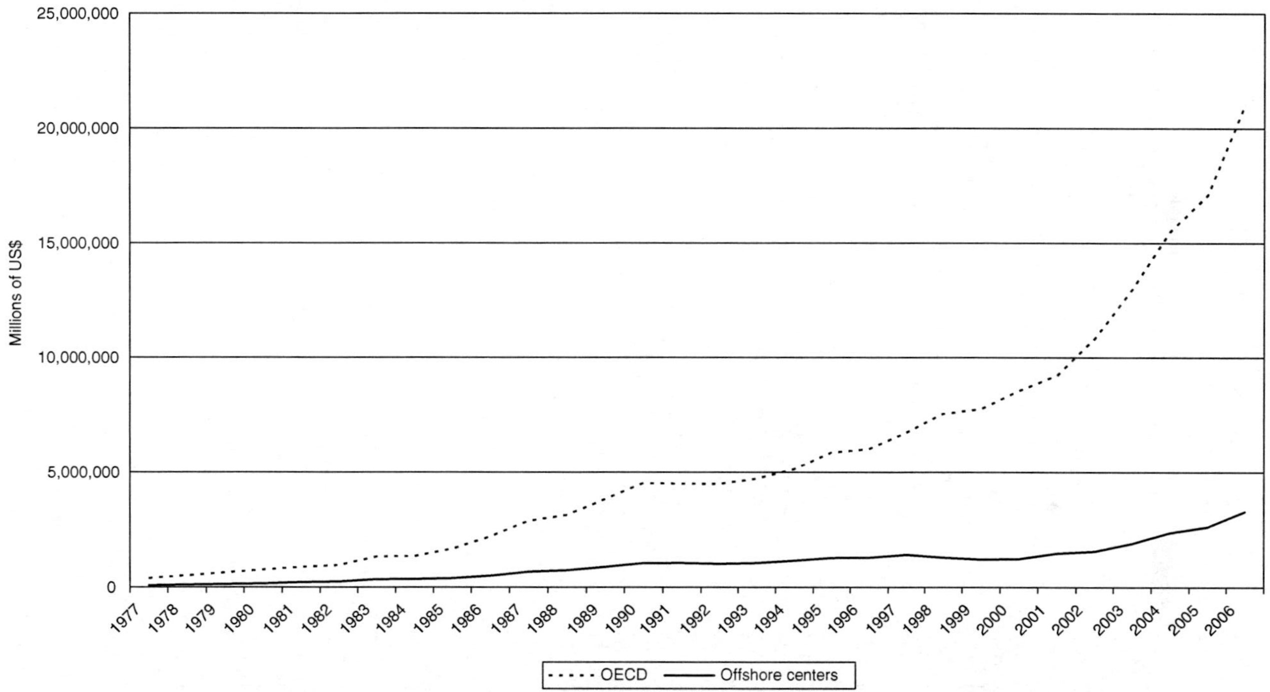

Source: Bank for International Settlements, *Quarterly Review*, June 2007, available at <http://www.bis.org/> [accessed 24 June 2007].

Table 6.6 BIS Data Sets

OECD Member States	Offshore financial centers*	Commonwealth Caribbean
Australia	Aruba	Antigua and Barbuda†
Austria	Bahamas	Bahamas
Belgium	Bahrain	Barbados
Canada	Barbados	Dominica
Czech Republic	Bermuda	Grenada
Denmark	Cayman Islands	Jamaica
Finland	Gibraltar	St. Kitts and Nevis†
France	Guernsey	St. Lucia
Germany	Hong Kong SAR	St. Vincent and the Grenadines
Greece	Isle of Man	Trinidad and Tobago
Hungary	Jersey	
Iceland	Lebanon	
Ireland	Macau SAR	
Italy	Mauritius	
Japan	Netherlands Antilles	
Korea	Panama	
Luxembourg	Samoa	
Mexico	Singapore	
Netherlands	Vanuatu	
New Zealand	West Indies UK†	
Norway		
Poland		
Portugal		
Slovak Republic		
Spain		
Sweden		
Switzerland		
Turkey		
United Kingdom		
United States		

Source: Table 6a – *BIS Quarterly Review*, June 2007 – International banking and financial market developments, p. A21 (Bank for International Settlements, June 2007).
*Offshore centers – An expression used to describe countries with banking sectors dealing primarily with non-residents and/or in foreign currency on a scale out of proportion to the size of the host economy (Monetary and Economic Department, 2003: 76).
†West Indies UK is a synthetic jurisdiction used by the BIS to aggregate data from a number of small Caribbean financial centers. It comprises Anguilla, Antigua and Barbuda, the British Virgin Islands, Montserrat, and St. Kitts and Nevis (Bank of England, 2001: 107).

Figure 6.2 Foreign assets on deposit, OECD, OFCs and Commonwealth Caribbean

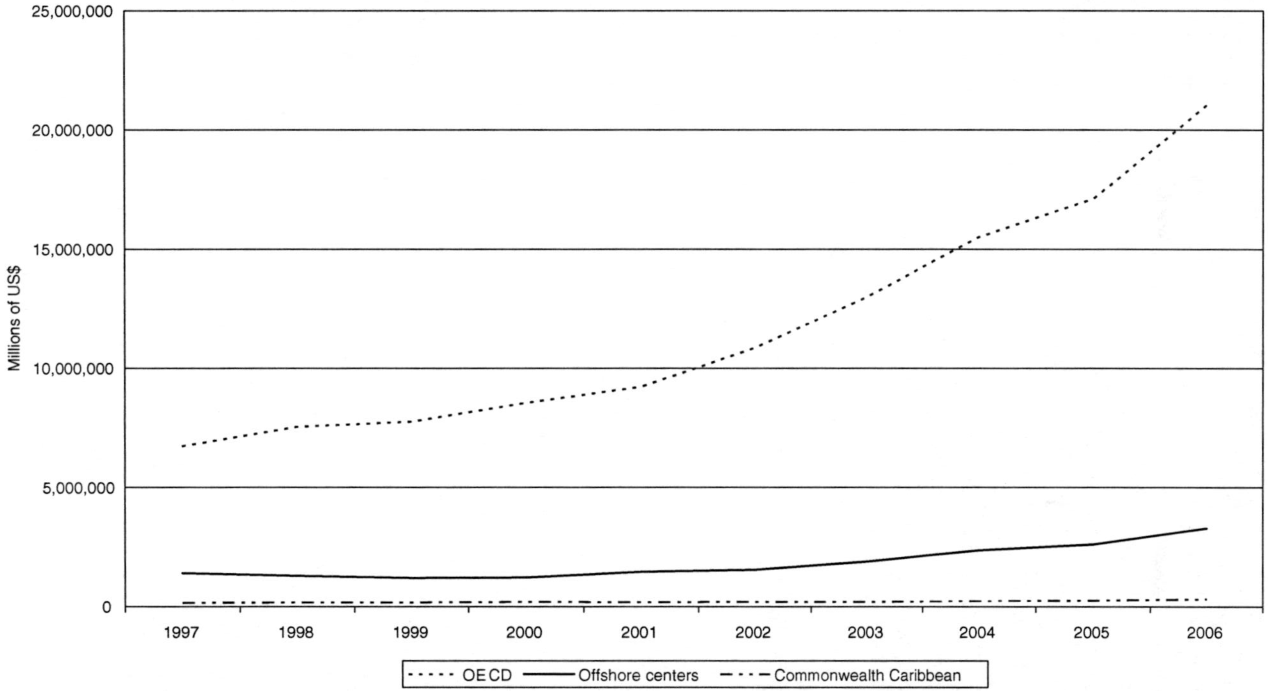

Source: Bank for International Settlements, *Quarterly Review*, June 2007, available at <http://www.bis.org/> [accessed 24 June 2007].

group. The first category consists of those jurisdictions that have been designated by the BIS as an offshore center. The BIS classified a jurisdiction as an offshore center if its banking sector dealt predominately 'with non-residents and/or in foreign currency on a scale out of proportion to the size of the host economy.' (Monetary and Economic Department, 2006: p. 60) This classification methodology excludes some of the jurisdictions identified by other organizations (such as the International Monetary Fund) as an OFC. The criteria used by the BIS considers the banking business of the jurisdiction and its relative size as part of the domestic economy, rather than the attention given to tax rates or banking confidentiality laws that are among the evaluation criteria used for similar lists of offshore centers. The second non-OECD category of data displayed in the chart consists of the Commonwealth Caribbean states reported in the BIS data. The overlap between these two categories results from the fact that the Bahamas, Barbados and a jurisdiction identified as 'West Indies UK' are designated by the BIS as OFCs in their data set. The West Indies UK is a synthetic jurisdiction in which the BIS aggregates data from Anguilla, Antigua and Barbuda, the British Virgin Islands, Montserrat, and St. Kitts and Nevis. (Dixon, 2001: 107)[18]

Even though assets on deposit increased, data from several Caribbean jurisdictions demonstrate that there has been a marked decline in the number of financial institutions registered in the Caribbean OFCs. The growth of offshore financial flows, even though they are utilizing fewer institutions, indicates that global finance has not been impacted by the OECD's harmful tax competition project. On the other hand, the Caribbean economies themselves have been affected just as predicted by some representatives of the affected small Caribbean states. Employment and non-tax revenues from offshore banking within these small economies have declined. Fewer institutions employ fewer citizens and pay less in licensing and other fees. At the same time, any expectations that publicity about the OECD campaign by itself would reduce the use of OFCs (and thereby tax avoidance) have not been met. Mobile capital continues to flow to OFCs, in the Caribbean and elsewhere, before being recycled to return as investments in OECD states and elsewhere.

In sum, the *market* response to OECD efforts to reduce international tax competition and harmful tax practices argues that their efforts are a minor concern to financial markets. Similar to data from the BIS,

Figure 6.3 Commercial banks' total non-resident deposits (ECCU)

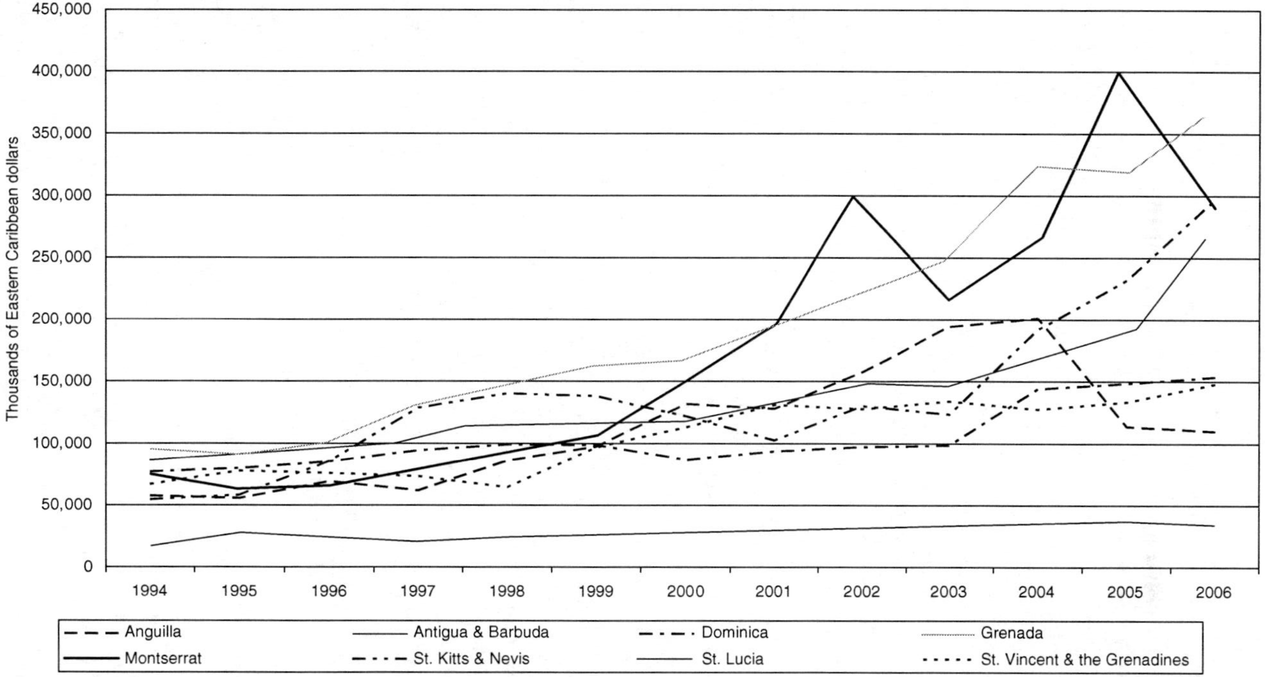

Source: Eastern Caribbean Central Bank, *Statistics*, available at <http://www.eccb-centralbank.org/Statistics/index.asp> [accessed 16 July 2007].

charting data available from the ECCB finds that the outstanding assets on deposit fluctuated in these small jurisdictions between 1994 and 2006 (Figure 6.3). But again, the aggregate values for offshore centers maintained a continuing upward trend (increasing deposits).[19] Among those factors influencing global financial flows to, and through, offshore centers, tax minimization behind a veil of banking confidentiality does not possess the weight attributed to it. The analysis of Huizinga and Nicodème found that the relationship between external deposits and the tax burden declined as the tax rate itself declined. Yet, the OECD viewpoint argues that with transparency and information exchange, the account holder information required to collect taxes from citizens' foreign accounts would be available. The availability of account data makes tax enforcement a more credible threat. Yet expectations for the implementation of the regime, accompanied by sanctions against those jurisdictions that failed to comply with it, are not reflected in this data on deposits within Caribbean OFCs. Other factors and other concerns motivate the actions of depositors. The continued trend of increasing deposits demonstrated a perception by market participants that the impact of the OECD measures against tax competition remained a distant future event, if they are ever implemented. In this case, deposits may reflect near-term strategies, and so the amounts on deposit would decline in the event an information exchange regime is agreed upon and an implementation schedule publicized.[20] From the perspective of the FATF, this institutional reduction in the offshore banking sector advanced the global effort to reduce financial crime and promoted the international regime against money laundering. Yet at the same time, the regime against money laundering also has had little impact on this trend of increasing foreign bank deposits in the Caribbean and among OFCs more generally (Financial Action Task Force, 2003c: pp. 6, 13).

Conclusions

The experience of Caribbean OFCs with respect to outside agencies demonstrates that the vulnerabilities of small open economies extend beyond security, trade preferences, and the environment. Externally mandated initiatives, whether from the FATF, the OECD or the IMF, strain the limited human and financial resources of these jurisdictions. Often, the limited resources applied to regulation enforcement and countering financial crime were criticized by the FATF and IMF. Yet failing to cooperate with these initiatives raises the threat of retaliatory measures that could isolate the jurisdiction within the structures of global finance. This isolation could effect not only the operation of financial institutions, but also all transnational money transfers – by the government, by businesses and by individual citizens sending money to family and friends.

The data collected by the BIS documents inter-bank activity rather than deposits by individuals seeking to avoid taxation of bank interest payments. It must therefore be emphasized that this data on global financial flows does not indicate the extent to which it contains the deposits of individuals. Recall that citizens avoiding taxes do not volunteer this information and as a result are the indirect target of the OECD project, for it is their avoidance of tax that motivated the project and its information exchange regime. Nonetheless, to limit one's conclusions about the OECD project to census figures tracking a declining number of offshore banks, offshore trusts, IBCs, etc. in these small jurisdictions would suggest that the *threat* of reprisals against them succeeded. However, expanding the analysis to data on the assets and liabilities managed by the reduced number of financial institutions produces a contradiction with respect to global financial flows. The individual small state offshore finance sector may have experienced a decline in funds on deposit between 2000 and 2003, as was the situation for the Bahamas. Nevertheless, the assets reported on deposit in the Bahamas for 2003 still exceeded those reported for any of the years between 1994 and 1999 and continued to increase through 2006. As already discussed, the Bahamas underwent an extensive effort to comply with international anti-money laundering standards, leading to a reduced number of offshore banks in this small state. The decline seen in the size of foreign assets on deposit in the Bahamas in 2001 may also have resulted from the economic recession in the United States, rather than the operation of fewer banks. The decline experienced in the Bahamas was subsumed within the aggregate data for all Caribbean OFCs, or amongst the group of jurisdictions designated by the BIS as an OFC. In the broader context of Caribbean OFCs as a group (and the offshore world more generally), this means that in 2003 there were fewer financial institutions servicing a greater quantity of offshore assets and liabilities than was the situation prior to the publication of *Harmful Tax Competition: An Emerging Global*

Issue in 1998. As shown in Figures 6.2 and 6.3 the situation in 2006 continued to be very much the same.

In the specific case of the OECD's harmful tax competition project and small Caribbean states, it could be characterized as a 'lose-lose' situation. The flow of capital through these OFCs continued to increase, while the implementation schedule for the information exchange regime desired by the OECD had been repeatedly postponed. Essentially, this latter aspect of the situation represents a 'lose' for the OECD. Capital it assumed to conceal tax evasion flowed through the OFCs in ever-greater amounts, while the information exchange methods intended to identify incidents of tax avoidance remain to be established. The economic benefits that were provided by a successful offshore business sector have shrunk during the period explored here for small Caribbean states. Levels of employment and the revenue from associated licensing fees for the offshore banking industry declined along with the number of registered bank and trust firms. As predicted, the Harmful Tax Competition project resulted in a 'lose' for the economic development of these small states. The experience of the Cayman Islands suggests that it is beneficial for one's offshore sector to be diversified. For this non-self-governing jurisdiction, revenues from licensing non-bank businesses continued to grow even though revenue from bank and trust licensing fees declined. This strategy is reflected in the data for St. Vincent with increased licenses for mutual funds and IBCs to offset the decline in offshore banks (Table 6.3).[21]

In response to a request for data, an Assistant Regulator with the Nevis Financial Services Department emphasized the provision of 'risk management' as a value-added feature offered by the offshore industry.

> The increased emphasis being placed on risk management, has caused many service providers to realise that there is much more business out there than the typical fiduciary (company/trust management) business that we have all grown accustomed to over the years.[22]

Combined with the enhanced regulatory regimes implemented in response to FATF initiatives, the emphasis on risk management has led to an improvement in the quality of the industry in the Caribbean. The perception of quality may be yet another explanation for the observation that while the number of institutions have declined, the overall size of financial flows through the Caribbean continues to increase. An awareness for emerging trends in both financial services and financial regulation will enhance any prospect to maintain an OFC in these small Caribbean jurisdictions. The drive and desire for economic development, as a sovereign jurisdiction, remains strong in both governments and citizens (Oberg, 2003: p. 157).

7
A Future for Sovereignty at the Margins

> The end may justify the means as long as there is something that justifies the end.
>
> – Leon Trotsky[1]

Within this research on small state sovereignty, the controversial nature of the case study itself should be very apparent. Taxation is a domestic issue exciting great emotion on the part of taxpayers and tax administrators alike. In this instance then, a domestic policy concern intersected with relations between states, over the actions of their citizens and resident firms in relation to decisions made about who, what, and how much to tax. Global tax minimization is not however, an intersection represented by a singular point; it is rather a collection of points variously representing individuals, firms, and the cross-section of state actors, large and small. Moreover, it is facilitated, and opposed, by an extensive network of lawyers, accountants, bankers and financial advisors (Sikka and Hampton, 2005; Weil, 2005).

The first section of this chapter summarizes a number of salient points from the preceding chapters about state sovereignty, small states, and taxation. After the refresher on these three variables (sovereignty, size and money), the next section considers the impact of the offshore taxation issue upon small states, for their efforts to maintain sovereignty, construct sovereignty, and, where necessary, share sovereignty. The final section tackles the overarching question of what this case study about offshore finance indicates for the future of small state sovereignty, and the continued presence of the 'offshore' in international society.

A summation

In order to present an analysis that is focused on the sovereignty of small states, a number of preliminary topics were explored and an argument for their relevance made. A common understanding for both sovereignty and size was established for use within the context of the study. A definition of the 'small' state was identified and justified in the first chapter; the one used here is the same as that used by the Commonwealth, a multinational organization with a significant number of small states among its members. Moreover, the definition emerges from a literature extending back a number of decades and efforts made to understand and incorporate the proliferation of small states in the international system following decolonization. For this study, a small state was one possessing less than 1.5 million residents, and on this criterion 18 Commonwealth members were identified as small states. These states are also developing economies, explaining in part the efforts made by the Commonwealth to assist them in a variety of ways on development matters.

The next topic discussed was *sovereignty*, with an implicit acceptance that states exist and are sovereign in terms of independence of action and (relative) freedom from outside interference. The inside/outside dichotomy inherent in accepting the state as given simply acknowledges the social nature of the situation as an organizing method for groups of people to interact with other, similar groups of people. Either one is a member of a group, or one is not a member of that group. This is a constant circumstance, whether the group is a schoolyard clique, one's co-workers within a large corporation, a political party, or the citizenry of some bounded territory.

The discussion then turned to features of the specific controversy over tax competition, which has been used by a number of developed states to dispute the sovereign decisions of a number of small states. The characteristics of offshore financial centers (OFCs) placed into historical and geopolitical context in the first chapter, were then used to frame an understanding of the nature of the threat posed to their sovereignty by the Organization for Economic Co-operation and Development (OECD) project on harmful tax competition. The project, as described by OECD publications, is contingent upon creating a perception that offshore finance does not meet the regulatory standards of onshore jurisdictions, and that offshore financial services exist solely to serve the interests and needs of money launderers, tax avoiders and drug traffickers. Offshore jurisdictions are viewed as somehow existing outside the system of sovereign states, and continuing in the pirate traditions of their ancestors by poaching the tax revenues of developed states. Through the provision of offshore finance, small states facilitate the efforts of citizens to operate as free-riders on the public goods of their state of residence by not contributing towards their maintenance.

The OECD perspective confronts the very nature of *fiscal* sovereignty – the right of a sovereign state to determine what, and how much, tax to impose on its residents and citizens[2] The topic of fiscal sovereignty is a fundamental point of contention with respect to the OECD project, and a source of the tension embedded within the OECD declaration that tax competition is a form of global harm. On the one hand, their documents clearly stated that this effort was not intended to negate the fiscal sovereignty of any sovereign state. On the other hand, they also declared that because of different national approaches to taxation (such as choosing not to have an income tax), this diversity is itself the source of harmful tax competition. The study by Ramon Jeffery, *The Impact of State Sovereignty on Global Trade and International Taxation*, argued that long-held concepts of sovereignty are impeding the efforts of states to enforce their own tax laws. Efforts to enforce domestic tax law upon residents have been impeded by a lack of information concerning any foreign assets or investments they may own. This information has not been forthcoming from most foreign states because sovereign independence means that no state is obligated to function as the tax agent for any other sovereign state. A similar argument could be made about any number of issues impacted by globalization (*qua* interdependence) due to differences in state legal structures and regulations, for example labor standards (Chan and Ross, 2003). However, in order to satisfy the desires and concerns for the provision of public goods, the state requires sovereignty (the independence to act) over its fiscal activity, for both the collection of revenue and the allocation and distribution of that revenue. This situation is just as relevant to the small state hosting the OFC as it is to the large state with an extensive public welfare apparatus. It is simply a matter of scale between the two extremes.

Fundamental differences exist between states in this area, and domestic perceptions about taxes shape both the presentation of harmful tax competition emerging from the OECD, and reactions to the project. Consequently, a vital factor for the success of the harmful tax competition project is cooperation among all sovereign states to support and enforce its objectives. Without universal cooperation, the means and opportunity to circumvent any information exchange structure resulting from the OECD project is likely to remain available. Indeed, this is explicitly recognized by the inclusion of a process to name and shame non-cooperative jurisdictions into acquiescing to the OECD's demands, and of proposals to impose defensive reprisals should blacklisting prove insufficient to force cooperation. Here again, global cooperation is essential to impose and maintain an effective reprisal regime. Without it, a space would exist which could permit the uncooperative jurisdiction to circumvent the regime and continue to serve the financial services needs of its customers, beyond the oversight of an OECD-mandated information exchange regime.

Rather than disrupting this need for cooperation, small states focused instead on several very specific aspects of the OECD project that directly impede their sovereign independence to regulate and manage the financial services sector of their economies. The first aspect of the OECD project that small states found problematic was the imposition of these changes upon them, without their involvement in the policy formulation process. Fundamentally, the changes expected by the OECD are in conflict with existing laws concerning confidentiality and privacy in financial services. The next aspect addressed was the contention that the OECD is not the appropriate forum in which to negotiate the solution to an ostensibly global problem. The small states identified by the OECD as harmful competitors are not members of the club, while members of the OECD club appear to receive different (preferential) treatment concerning their financial sectors and tax administrations. This second point leads quite naturally into the third aspect of the critique presented concerning the OECD project, which is the expectation that efforts to counter harmful tax competition embody common standards and rules for all jurisdictions. Some small states submitted conditional agreements to cooperate with the OECD, subject to the condition that all states operating financial service centers be treated the same – whether or not the state in question is a member of the OECD club.

In response to these concerns, OECD representatives emphasized the establishment of the Global Forum on Taxation, which includes representation from non-OECD states. Moreover, they insisted that the OECD is the correct multilateral organization to tackle the issue of tax competition and that one standard of conduct applied, whether or not a state is a member of the OECD. The discussion then went beyond small states to include the small non-self-governing territories that host an OFC. These territories are identified as independent from their administering state on the list of non-cooperative jurisdictions, yet they are treated as an extension of that state for the purposes of compliance. Furthermore, dependencies of the United Kingdom and the Netherlands are under pressure to comply with the requirements of the EU Savings Tax Directive.

As part of the effort to contest the rationale behind the harmful tax competition project, and to counter-balance the OECD, some small states looked to the Commonwealth as a site for collective action. This international organization may have originated as a club for the United Kingdom and its former colonies, but it has transformed itself into a vocal advocate for small states since the early 1980s on a variety of international issues. The Commonwealth served as a collective voice for its small members on the issue of tax competition, and the Secretariat facilitated and mediated meetings between small states and the OECD. At the same time, there was an effort to overcome the lack of international representation for the non-self-governing jurisdictions with an OFC by inviting them to become members of the International Trade and Investment Organization (ITIO). Again, this is an international non-governmental organization intended to serve 'as a forum in which small and developing economies (SDEs) work on an equal basis and speak with a common voice' irrespective of their sovereign status (ITIO, 2003).

As discussed earlier, the flow of mobile capital through the offshore world has not declined since the publication of the OECD's initial report in 1998 and the sums involved are immense. As noted in particular with the Cayman Islands, but relevant to the Caribbean as a whole, these sums include the vast financial assets of captive insurance firms, offshore hedge funds, and special purpose vehicles (such as the international business companies formed by Enron and Parmalat).[3] While it must be agreed that estimates of tax avoidance are as nebulous as estimates of money laundering, nonetheless these offshore assets will contain some measure that are hiding from state revenue authorities. Yet the economies of these small Caribbean states are vulnerable to the implied threat of the OECD project. Consequently, the number of financial institutions registered in their OFCs has declined; reducing in tandem the employment of local residents and the revenue collected from licenses. At the same time, it must be acknowledged that factors other than the OECD may be responsible for the decline, including a recession in the US economy, the anti-money laundering efforts of the Financial Action Task Force (FATF), and the on-going consolidation of large multinational financial firms.

Sovereignty for small states

The focus of this study is on small states, as they strive to deal with the consequences of the actions taken by large developed states both in global politics and the global economy. In 2003, Peter Katzenstein had an opportunity to reflect on the continued relevance of his 1985 text, *Small States in World Markets*. He commented upon the experience of the European small states, possessing open economies and following flexible economic policies, for dealing with economic change.

> Whether we call it internationalisation or globalisation, the underlying condition, however, is here to stay and will force important change in how large states exercise their reconstituted sovereign powers. (Katzenstein, 2003: p. 27)

Yet, a large state may strive to resist any change encouraged by this interdependence and continue to maintain its existing economic policies. It may also seek to coerce its economic partners to cooperate in its efforts in order to maintain the economic *status quo*. In the instance of competitive tax regimes, the OECD states are resisting the pressure from a liberalized financial system to adjust to the competition introduced by the offshore financial sector as one part of the liberalized global system. Rather, they seek to establish a global information exchange regime to overcome the tax arbitrage possibilities provided by state sovereignty and facilitated by capital mobility. Sovereignty alone is not enough; the end of capital controls in most developed economies was also a factor. The approach of the OECD would compel coordination among states, as a means to maintain the current level of income taxation in OECD member states. Consequently, large economies are continuing to follow the policy approach described by Katzenstein in *Small States in World Markets*. 'Large industrial states tend to export the costs of change while the small European states tend to live with them.' (Katzenstein, 1985: p. 59) The conclusion from Katzenstein's research was that small open economies handle increased interdependence (globalization) better than the larger economies, in the sense that they are more adaptive.

Within the larger realm of *state sovereignty*, the point is that the independence of action conferred by sovereignty is, has been, and will remain important for the state as part of international society. At issue here is more than just an intervention into the domestic activities of a politically defined entity (a state). It is also the concern for the freedom of choice available to citizens for them to best determine the distribution of social/public goods. In answering the question of 'who gets what' the relative independence of the territory to choose, and to be able to act on that choice, is important.[4] The problem for large states is that they have residents who desire the public goods available to them while at the same time they do not wish themselves to actually pay for these public goods.

Irrespective of how the offshore world emerged in the global economy, the fundamental aspect remains the same. Whether it involves shipping registries, financial services or corporate residency, it is the intentional use of sovereignty that is at the core of the activity in question. It is sovereignty and the ability not only to establish the law for a bounded territory, but to be able to fashion the law free of undesired external influence, that facilitates the presence of the offshore in a global financial landscape. This is the problem that the OECD has to address, not that there is tax competition, harmful or otherwise, but that state sovereignty as a constituent element of the international system has been manipulated to serve as a barrier to the flow of information and thereby creates a space of privacy (secrecy) no longer available to citizens living within the borders of the state itself.

Maintaining sovereignty

Fiscal sovereignty, as an aspect of state sovereignty, prevents the OECD from forcing the low/no tax jurisdictions to raise their rate of tax, which would remove tax avoidance as a motivation to maintain a foreign bank account. An attempt to do so could open for debate a complex issue within the OECD concerning member states' preferential tax regimes and relative tax rates on income and capital. The complex and arcane structures of developed state municipal tax law result from the competing interests and desires of domestic politics. Tax rates, tax credits, deductions and exclusions are all part of the tax code in order to encourage, or discourage, certain behaviors or developments, to support targeted activities, to reward faithful constituents, *ad infinitum*. The very nature of these structures discourages debate over a 'global tax regime' because of the many vested interests contained within each domestic community. The situation, again, involves the right to choose the distribution of public goods within the defined territory of the state and the use of tax legislation to control conduct in society.

The resistance of small states, in the Caribbean and elsewhere, to the OECD initiative is an explicit effort to maintain their independence of action, their sovereignty. The decision to create and sustain an offshore regime, whether in banking, shipping, Internet domains, or satellite parking orbits, was made in pursuit of economic development for the small jurisdiction and the welfare of its residents (van Fossen, 1999). As demonstrated above with respect to several Caribbean jurisdictions, the OFC can be a significant contributor to the local economy. For a number of small states, particularly the 'late' entrants to this industry, the OFC was an alternative to the declining economic contribution made by their agricultural sector. The options for economic diversification in a small state are limited, and the OECD project has produced yet another constraint on diversification activity.

Constructing sovereignty

The desire for self-determination is a desire for sovereignty, as a space in which a group of people is able to establish its own structure of laws and regulations for public goods and collective welfare. It is accepted that sovereignty is a basket of rights and privileges guiding the conduct of independent, territorially-bound societies, but the socially constructed nature of society provides some room for variation among practitioners in the discourse encompassing small states and the offshore financial landscape.

In an article exploring globalization and 'offshoreness' for a geopolitical economy, for example, Alan Hudson did not use the generally accepted understanding of *fiscal* sovereignty as used in this study. In that instance, sovereignty was treated as a bundle of capabilities, and 'by choosing to maintain a low or zero tax rate, the OFCs in effect surrender some of their sovereignty-derived regulatory powers.' (Hudson, 2000: p. 272) The implied assumption behind this assertion would be that the only proper exercise of fiscal sovereignty is to impose taxes, rather than understanding it as the right and freedom to choose whether, what, and how much to tax. As was noted earlier, because small jurisdictions have proportionately small government revenue requirements, they may find revenue sources other than individual and corporate income tax satisfy their needs. Yet, the assumption that fiscal sovereignty means taxation was a prerequisite to Hudson's case for an 'offshore unbundling of sovereignty' and the argument that this produces a post-modern geo-political economy. This assumption is also implicit in the criteria used by the OECD to determine a harmful versus a preferential tax regime. The difference between the two is predicated upon the collection of 'significant revenue' from the taxation of income by the state with a preferential tax regime (Organization for Economic Co-operation and Development, 1998: pp. 19–20).

Similar to this discussion of offshore finance and income taxes are the arguments made concerning Internet-based commerce and consumption taxes. One such argument is 'if taxation of Internet based transactions becomes problematic, the ability of governments to provide essential services could be compromised.' (Kobrin, 2001: p. 689) This situation would be due to the fact, as discussed earlier, that any given state is not responsible to become the tax collector for any other state's tax administration. As with Jeffery's argument that state sovereignty hinders the requisite collection of tax in the face of globalization, so too has the increased incidence of commercial transactions via the Internet hindered the collection of consumption taxes. 'Electronic commerce breaks down the necessary and clear connection between territory and commerce, and makes this type of information more difficult to obtain, thus complicating the task of taxing income based on source or residence.' (Paris, 2003: p. 162) The problem of tax collection from Internet transactions (and control of other illegal and illicit Internet activity) may be overstated. A case for the 'abiding significance of territorial sovereignty' emphasized the point that something somewhere retained a physical presence in a sovereign territory.

Consequently, appropriate legal and legislative action could be taken in that territory against Internet-based activity (Goldsmith, 1998).[5] This approach is reflected by the action taken by France to ensure that Yahoo (an American firm) complied with French law concerning the sale of Nazi memorabilia within its territory (Kobrin, 2001: pp. 691–692).

The point for this discussion of an Internet-based 'offshore' landscape is to emphasize once again that sovereignty is about choice without interference from superior (outside) authority. Globalization is only in part the cultural homogenization decried by an anti-globalization movement against (predominantly American) multinational corporations. As a process, it is also leading to the imposition of Western ideals via the international institutionalization of 'best practices'. These best practices, standards and codes are intended to supersede local choice of action regarding finance, legislation, transparency, social provision, etc. The presumption is that because they work in developed states they are actually *better*, and not simply the result of a hegemonic influence of Western practices of governance (corporate and political). The formulation of these standards is problematic in that they tend to follow an 'Anglo-American' business model, which conflicts with the business practices of both continental Europe and East Asia (Soederberg, 2003). These standards and procedures have also been promoted as leading to a level playing field, which again will only result in facilitating the continued dominance of developed states' businesses. Therefore, to incorporate these standards and practices locally entails accepting a curtailment of sovereignty, in that it constrains local freedom of choice and action concerning the regulation of the economy. The constraints produced by placing developed states' practices upon developing states' economies lead to social tensions that threaten political elites and local conceptualizations of sovereign statehood.[6] More recently, the UN Security Council passed Resolution 1617 (2005), which 'Strongly urges all Member States to implement the comprehensive, international standards embodied in the FATF's Forty Recommendations on Money Laundering and the FATF Nine Special Recommendations on Terrorist Financing' (United Nations Security Council, 2005). Consequently, while the discussion here has focused on the sovereignty of *small* states, the challenge to state sovereignty in the financial domain is not limited to these small jurisdictions.

Sharing sovereignty

There are areas of international governance that operate without the conflict noted above, and foster cooperative conduct amongst groups of states. As discussed in Chapter 2 the Schengen Agreement among European states established standards for passport control, visas and a separation between those approved for access to the Schengen zone, and those not approved. In acceding to this agreement, the participating states yield a portion of their sovereignty (border controls of the defined territory), with an explicit understanding that the other member states continue to exercise control of mutually external borders up to acceptable standards. Thus, the other member states provided passport control at external borders (the periphery of the Schengen zone) on their behalf. In presenting the Schengen Agreement as an example, the emphasis is placed on the matter of shared sovereignty amongst a variety of states. Moreover, not all signatories of the Schengen Agreement belong to the European Union, nor do all members of the EU participate in the Schengen Agreement. In this fashion, it provides an example for the cession of fiscal sovereignty amongst a variety of states that do not otherwise cooperate extensively on other matters. In the latter case involving extensive cooperation, the EU (or its predecessors) serves as a better example for yielding state sovereignty to a multinational organization.

To recover tax revenue from income that had 'escaped' national controls, OECD states are endeavoring to establish standards for interstate information exchange, in order to track and pursue recalcitrant (reluctant) taxpayers.[7] However, a sense of common objectives and shared community amongst the jurisdictions expected to participate in this process is absent. This absence represents a significant difference from the example of shared sovereignty offered by the Schengen Agreement. Moreover, there is not a sense of shared benefit from participation in the process. With the Schengen Agreement, the participating governments no longer maintain internal border controls amongst themselves, thereby reducing government expenditures. With the OECD project, small states would have increased costs due to the compliance requirements, while at the same time they will collect fewer licensing fees as the financial sector shrinks when mobile capital moves along to other locations. The exclusion of small states from the process makes it all the more difficult to create a sense of common purpose. The result was acrimonious meetings and the subsequent postponement of OECD deadlines for cooperation.

The abiding significance of the state

The debates surrounding sovereignty and the retreat of the state as an actor in global politics were outlined in Chapter 2. As noted at the beginning, the practice of sovereignty by small states (demonstrated by their resistance to the OECD project) represents the continued salience of the state as an institution. The OECD itself recognized this fact from the beginning of their campaign against tax competition.

> The Committee concludes that there is a strong case for intensifying international co-operation when formulating a response to the problem of harmful tax competition, although the counter-acting measures themselves will continue to be primarily taken at the national, rather than at the multilateral level. (Organization for Economic Co-operation and Development, 1998: p. 38)

The desired objectives and proposed methods to achieve these objectives may be the product of an international organization (OECD or FATF), but the changes are implemented by *states*. Legislation must be changed or introduced by *state* governments and acted upon by *state* agencies. The collection and exchange of taxpayer information are performed by *state* tax administrations. Just as sovereignty creates the space in which a small state can produce a tax-friendly financial regime, sovereignty also creates the borders through which a large state can control the passage of international transactions. This latter aspect of sovereignty was demonstrated for example by the imposition of 'counter-measures' (including increased surveillance of all transactions) against Nauru in 2001 because of its non-compliance with FATF anti-money laundering recommendations (Financial Action Task Force, 2002; Her Majesty's Treasury, 2001). Notwithstanding the existence of international standards (for example the Basel Capital Accord), the regulation, de-regulation, and re-regulation of finance within a specific territory remains a responsibility of the *state* and not of the collection of financial institutions operating within that jurisdiction.

The FATF's identification of Nauru as a non-cooperative country is an example of the increased role of international standards in the structure of a state. This case is representative for an increased re-regulation of international finance through the promulgation of international standards and best practices. The action of the FATF was in response to the failure of one small state to be fully compliant with its Forty Recommendations against money laundering. These Recommendations, along with the Basel Capital Accord are perhaps the best-known examples of international standards for state regulation and supervision of financial institutions. They exemplify the quiet growth over the past couple of decades of a global financial regulatory regime. These standards and practices are intended for implementation by all jurisdictions participating in global finance, yet select groups representing a limited number of states created them. The extent of their influence is apparent from the fact that since 2000 the IMF has conducted financial sector assessments that measure compliance against standards produced by the Basel Committee on Banking Supervision, International Association of Insurance Advisors, and the International Organization of Securities Commissions, as well as the FATF's Forty Recommendations (Monetary and Financial Systems Department, 2005). As discussed previously, the extent and range of these standards and practices increased the cost burden for small states to administer and supervise an OFC. Moreover, they strain the capacity of the limited personnel resources of these jurisdictions to monitor and enforce compliance with financial regulation, a specific point of concern for the FATF with regard to anti-money laundering efforts. The results from this use of non-treaty instruments to manage and regulate the global political economy have been analyzed by a number of authors, including Susanne Soederberg (2004), A. Claire Cutler (2003) and Rodney Bruce Hall and Thomas J. Biersteker, eds (2002).

Thoughts on the US presence in the tax competition debate

The transition from support to ambivalence by the United States in 2001 presented a problem for those members of the OECD promoting the information exchange element of the OECD project. The characterization of the US as the world's largest offshore tax haven was noted and emphasized the OECD's need for the full cooperation and participation of the US in its project. Even with low interest rates in the United States, the ability to collect interest without taxation (for non-resident non-citizens) remains attractive as an alternative to possessing an account in a place deducting income taxes. Yet the OECD has not explicitly and publicly confronted this opportunity for tax avoidance. Similarly, the OECD did not consider Singapore as a potential tax haven when it began the project (Zagaris, 2004). As a result, the OECD has never listed this small island state as an uncooperative jurisdiction, nor was it identified as a location required to exchange taxpayer data with the EU. Subsequently, Singapore was touted as a potential safe haven, 'and is welcoming European private banks that want to develop their wealth management operations.' (Burton and Parker, 2003b: p. 17) Certainly, the response following the implementation of the EU Savings Tax Directive demonstrated such a pattern. Significantly, the US also remains outside the functional parameters of the project when the only activity identified as a preferential tax regime was the same Foreign Sales Corporations regime that was subject to a WTO challenge (Organization for Economic Co-operation and Development, 2000: p. 14; Organization for Economic Co-operation and Development, 2004a: p. 9).[8]

The US is in the position that it does not require global cooperation on taxation or information exchange. With the aggressive pursuit of abusive tax schemes by the US Internal Revenue Service (IRS) and its development of an extensive web of bilateral agreements, the US is able to threaten, if not achieve, a significant level of interdiction against tax evasion by its citizens.[9] The pursuit of international corporate tax minimization is rather more complex. That is a multi-player game involving the firm, the US, and every other state in which the firm has some presence and where it surrenders a measure of tax revenue. Within this game are such additional factors as tax holidays and tax abatements to attract foreign direct investment (FDI), the use of transfer pricing and thin capitalization by the firm to transfer profits to lower tax jurisdictions, and the existence of jurisdictions that do not tax capital in which to establish corporate accounts (for example a holding company in the Cayman Islands). Nevertheless, some research shows that revenue from corporate tax has not declined, though it also perhaps has not increased in line with overall economic growth in some sectors (Hobson, 2003). Yet, we stand at a point in time where economic figures, calculations and estimates are suspect. Models built on data from the 1990s reflect the economic growth and new economy boom of that decade. More recent data (since the recession of 2001) is not yet available in quantity for analysis. Certainly, all tax revenue declined at the beginning of the twenty-first century, which only seems reasonable since profits, interest and dividends also declined (Organization for Economic Co-operation and Development, 2003).

Where does this leave us? Small states in the twenty-first century

It seems appropriate to return to the topic of offshore in some of its various dimensions, to open this reflection on what the future may hold for small states. The economic (as opposed to the political) nature of offshore is frequently referenced in business media in connection with moving jobs and/or production facilities to another country. So we have the experience of shoes manufactured in Indonesia, shirts assembled in Costa Rica, and the call center for our bank operating from India.

The point behind raising the business use of the concept of the offshore is to emphasize the fact that the offshore is more than a simple construction of the modern states system (Cameron and Palan, 2004). Offshore has become, in the parlance of some political thinkers, the Other. It is now a threat to respectable society, extending beyond global finance and taxation to incorporate other practices that are deemed illegal, illegitimate or illicit in an onshore jurisdiction. The offshore world is more than financial centers and corporate holding companies, for it now involves the relocation of white-collar service jobs beyond the sea to some exotic location. Similar to the OECD concern with losing potential tax revenue to OFCs, here the concern with the offshore has expanded to include the loss of jobs and an attendent reduction of the tax base itself. In a liberalized (globalized) world economy it appears that practically anything can be moved 'offshore' with a related loss to the domestic economy.

The transfer of jobs to India is the dominant form of 'offshore' presented in the US media and starting point for the book, *The World is Flat: A Brief History of the Twenty-first Century* (Friedman, 2005). While India is not a small state, nevertheless small states are also attempting to profit from offshore economic development opportunities other than banking services. Many of these opportunities are facilitated by the same telecommunications links that support offshore finance. Thus we should see the OFC as but one facet of the larger phenomenon of the offshore world. On the one hand, these concerns engender the unease felt by some and attributed by them to globalization. However, the term also is being used to name their sense of a loss of power. Decisions that previously were contained within the local community are no longer limited in scope, or even made locally. Yet a firm's *economic* choice to improve its competitiveness, whether by lowering labor costs or by pursuing a strategy of tax minimization, ultimately impacts the lives of local citizens. At the same time, this movement of service jobs behind the earlier movement of manufacturing jobs represents the operation of economic principles like comparative advantage. In order to remain competitive in an open, global marketplace, firms large and small are seeking ways to keep their costs down in order to offer their products and services at a competitive price.

In global financial services, small jurisdictions used their fiscal sovereignty to take advantage of their ability to legislate a space for regulatory arbitrage. These opportunities attract firms and mobile capital to the OFC, which then contributes to the local economy through license fees and employment. The difficulty experienced by the OECD's harmful tax competition initiative to change this situation suggests that there is a space in the global economy for small states to maneuver. This space is created whenever there is not a broad-based consensus amongst the major national economies for a global regime. Historically, this may be reflected by the failure to establish a New International Economic Order or more recently the failure to enact a Multilateral Agreement on Investment. In some sense, the WTO serves as a venue for the production of a global consensus on topics of trade, services, and intellectual property. Failing the production of a consensus, the alternative function of the WTO is to provide a legal arbitration mechanism to promote compliance with already existing standards of economic conduct. The small jurisdictions of the Caribbean and elsewhere are able to participate in the WTO and other multilateral governmental organizations. This membership affords them a voice, however small it may appear, that is a *sovereign* equal to that of any other member. The difficulty lies in first achieving membership in the WTO, and then navigating the intricacies of the rules and policies required before utilizing the arbitration mechanism. In this latter aspect the Commonwealth and its trade facility in Geneva has provided the additional knowledge and guidance necessary for small state members to benefit more fully from WTO membership.

The use of the WTO dispute mechanism by Antigua and Barbuda against the United States highlights the potential of an equal opportunity for the small state as represented by membership in a multilateral organization. In that case, the small Caribbean state of Antigua and Barbuda protested a US law criminalizing the use of offshore, Internet-based casinos. The WTO Appellate Body agreed with Antigua and Barbuda that the US law was discriminatory and in contradiction with WTO obligations with trade in services (BBC News, 2005).[10] Clearly, other research work has shown that membership in multilateral organizations enhances the limited international influence of a small state. At the same time however, politics continue to exist within their organizational structure. The very basic activity of setting and maintaining the agenda of an organization constricts the individual initiative(s) of a state. In this, the relative power (within the confines of the organization as much as in the world at large) of a member state affects the extent of their influence on the agenda-setting process. Moreover, it is at this point that the knowledge, skills and abilities of the individual representatives contribute to each state's relative position, with individual powers of persuasion influencing the agenda construction and their success in negotiation (Arter, 2000).

The formation of the ITIO in March 2001 is a sign of the recognition of this predicament and serves as a route towards overcoming it. The fact that the ITIO is especially focused on the domain of global finance determines the nature of their agenda. Additionally, because of the targeted nature of its membership (for and by small jurisdictions) the ITIO serves to provide a means to project a collective voice for these small jurisdictions. At the same time, this small IGO (with its limited remit) possesses a smaller voice within the global cacophony of international relations. So, even though it is focused on very specific areas of concern, the viewpoint expressed by the ITIO is overshadowed in the media by any pronouncements emanating from the OECD, IMF or World Bank.

The formation of an issue-focused organization such as the ITIO emphasizes the exclusionary nature of the OECD, FATF and other similar international organizations. In fact, at least one author has argued that the limited membership and control of the agenda of these latter organizations are benefits. 'Coalitions of the willing can successfully influence and enforce international standards, especially if the coalition partners have a predominant interest in and influence over the subject at hand.' (Wechsler, 2001: p. 53) William Wechsler had most recently been Special Advisor to the Secretary of the Treasury in the Clinton Administration when this article was published in 2001. For critical security questions this may be a valid point, best represented by the work of the United Nations Security Council. The broad-spectrum application of international standards produced by a club with limited membership, however, is not a consensual approach and so it will encounter resistance from the excluded. Wechsler concluded from the experience with the anti-money laundering 'name & shame' exercise that 'the initiative showed that US leadership was essential even in a multilateral setting.' (Wechsler, 2001: p. 53)

This leads us back to the role and influence of the United States within global finance, and in particular within this very specific OECD project concerning harmful tax competition. From one perspective, it appears that the withdrawal of the United States from the OECD project has limited the likelihood of any implementation of sanctions. Without sanctions, efforts to force/encourage compliance become more difficult. Here the research work of Daniel Drezner is particularly apt. He has outlined a model for global regulatory coordination, that considers the interplay of regulatory efforts by great powers (in this case Drezner takes them to be the United States, Japan and the European Union), developing states, IGOs and NGOs. Within this theoretical framework, Drezner finds that 'The effectiveness of both NGOs and IGOs clearly depends on state power and preferences.' (Drezner, 2002: p. 35) This assessment includes an IGO such as the OECD, and a regulatory coordination effort like the harmful tax competition initiative.

> Most important, this theory makes it clear that great powers are the key actors in determining the pattern of global regulatory regimes. If they can agree among themselves, coordination will occur regardless of NGO, IGO, or peripheral state preferences. Opposition from these actors only affects the means of regulatory coordination, not the ultimate end. (Drezner, 2002: p. 36)

Drezner's theoretical work explains the empirical experience described by Wechsler. Consequently, the best efforts of the non-OECD states to effect a change in the regulatory structure of the OECD project were quite likely to fail, had the 'great powers' agreed upon the structure and sanctions of the project. However, with the withdrawal of explicit support for the project by the United States, clearly one of the key actors for this regulatory regime, the OECD initiative has effectively stalled. The result of this disagreement between the large states is that a space has been left in which the small states and their OFCs may continue to operate.

Thus, in the end, the conclusion to be reached about small states' ability to enforce their sovereign independence is that it will rely upon a combination of factors. For this specific study, these factors included the resistance and intransigence of some small states towards the efforts of the OECD, the support of the Commonwealth (and in particular the Commonwealth Secretariat) on the behalf of small states by hosting joint meetings and funding research as part of an effort to ensure that they receive *equitable* treatment from the OECD, and the absence of any strong *national interest* on the part of the United States to support a European campaign to reduce tax *avoidance*. The Commonwealth Secretariat remains active in this issue area, for example by sponsoring a research report analyzing the OECD's report in 2006 that assessed the structures permitting the exchange of tax-related information in 'over 80 economies.' (Stoll-Davey, 2007)

Part of the puzzle surrounding the OECD project is the fact that in the main the similar effort of the FATF to create a global anti-money laundering regime has succeeded. This may be seen as a reflection of a global consensus against this form of financial crime (and the various predicate crimes subsumed within money laundering charges, such as drug trafficking). It may also result from determined American action to promote and institutionalize anti-money laundering policies. The circumstances surrounding the Harmful Tax Competition Initiative (HTCI) are not the same. There is not a global consensus on tax competition as harmful in the first instance, or of tax avoidance/evasion as 'criminal' in the second instance. Within the OECD itself, the lack of a consensus was apparent from the beginning with the abstention of Switzerland and Luxembourg from the 1998 report.

There are several lessons to take forward from this experience. First, the support of an intervening international organization, such as the Commonwealth, against the efforts of another IGO affords a space in which the collective voice of small states may be coordinated and synchronized.[11] Second, lobbying one of the major actors to shift, or at least moderate, their position can lead to a change in the position of the group of large states. In this instance, it was a case of predominately domestic lobbying in the US that contextualized the issue as a potential domestic problem (threat). Thus, the US became the moderating influence upon a predominately European initiative, but this could also work in the other direction. Some might, for example, make an effort to convince the EU to moderate American initiatives to expand the data collection and surveillance of individuals (travelers) that is increasingly part of the war on terror (Levi and Wall, 2004).

I take the point that 'sovereignty and its meaning have become a battleground' with respect to the role and position of the state within international relations (Hill, 2003: p. 30). For the leaders and citizens of small states, however, the debate is superfluous and it is far more important to guard their self-perception of sovereign independence from the world at large, because for them to be sovereign is to have the freedom to choose. Any number of factors and influences may constrict the space within which they are free to act, as highlighted by Krasner and others (Krasner, 2001; Krasner, 1999; Strange, 1996). These restrictions do not reduce the value held by small states for their sovereign independence. The multifaceted nature of sovereignty was underscored once again by R. J. B. Walker in a more recent analysis.

> Sovereignty, we have come to remember, can be understood simultaneously as a principle, an institution, and a practice, and, indeed, has to be understood historically as a complex site/event in which it is quite difficult, and perhaps necessarily impossible, to distinguish with much analytical clarity between principle, institution, and practice. We now speak about sovereignty less like an it, a thing, or achieved condition than as an act that works by producing a presence, a state of being, exactly where there is and can be no such thing. (Walker, 2004: p. 242)

It is exactly this need to reproduce themselves as independent sovereign territories that helps to motivate the leaders and involved citizens of the small Caribbean states to resist the efforts of the

OECD. To resist serves to demonstrate the capacity to act, and forces the representatives of international organizations and their constituent member states to *acknowledge* the participation of small states as sovereign actors.

Global financial flows suggest that markets are ignoring the efforts of the OECD. The withdrawal of US support for the harmful tax competition project delayed any implementation of an information exchange regime. At the same time, OECD member states went forward with reducing/eliminating the preferential tax structures identified by the project (Organization for Economic Co-operation and Development, 2004a). The fact remains, however, that small states stood their ground and in the main insisted upon recognition of their sovereignty. The governing leadership teams of these Caribbean jurisdictions continued to pursue an economic development agenda for their citizens and societies that includes offshore finance.

Notes

Chapter 1 International Norms and the Practice of Sovereignty

1 (Kindleberger, 1987: p. 87).
2 See for example the work of Carolyn Nordstrom (Nordstrom, 2000; Nordstrom, 2003; Nordstrom, 2004).
3 For example, the case made against the Seychelles in 1995, when they passed legislation for an economic development act offering citizenship to anyone, with a provision providing immunity from criminal prosecution, if they had an investment greater than $10 million. Under intense international pressure, the legislation was rescinded (Glynn *et al.*, 1997: pp. 24–25).
4 This perspective does not take into account another significant reason for capital mobility – return on investment. Even with equivalent taxes, some locations will continue to offer a higher rate of return on investments, and capital will seek that return.
5 See below, Tables 1.2 through 1.5 for specific data.
6 Immigration moreover possesses its own version of 'non-tariff' barriers, for example training and education prerequisites (transferral of accreditation) and licensing requirements.
7 (Baines, 2002: 344, citing Ron Martin, 'Stateless Monies, Global Financial Integration and National Economic Autonomy: The End of Geography?' in S. Corbridge, R. Martin and N. Thrift (eds), *Money, Power and Space* (Oxford: Blackwell, 1994)).
8 This practice helps to explain the substantial number of international business companies registered in such places as the Cayman Islands, the Bahamas, and the British Virgin Islands.
9 (United Kingdom. Public Record Office, 1974: folio 67) These communications involved the development of a letter (dated 30 August 1974) from the British Prime Minister in reply to a letter from the Australian Prime Minister (23 July 1974) expressing the concerns of Australian Revenue authorities with their residents' use of New Hebrides as a 'tax haven'.
10 For a consideration of tax competition from this perspective, see (Bjorvatn and Schjelderup, 2002) And with regard to related anti-money laundering initiatives, see (Tsingou, 2005).
11 See for example (United Kingdom. Public Record Office, 1963).

Chapter 2 Sovereignty and Taxation

1 (Ruggie, 1993: p. 162) Ruggie is citing (Wight, 1977: p. 135).
2 F. H. Hinsley, *Power and the Pursuit of Peace: Theory and Practice in the History of Relations between States* (Cambridge: Cambridge University Press, 1963), especially Chapter 1.

3 For a discussion of the Taiwan case, and its position as a state in the Westphalian sense, but not in the international legal sense see (Madsen, 2001).
4 Hans Blix, *Sovereignty, Aggression, and Neutrality* (Stockholm: Almquist & Wiksell, 1970), p. 10, as cited in (Fowler and Bunck, 1995: p. 71).
5 Such a 'collective concept' has been refined into the term 'meme' and a field of study known as 'memetics.' For one view of this phenomenon of the transfer of a cultural practice or idea from one mind to another, see (Blackmore, 1999).
6 This matter of decertification would lead to the loss of US foreign aid and a US veto on any loans and loan guarantees by international financial institutions.
7 However tax-payer activity was suggested by Lorz when analyzing the effects of tax competition for interest group lobbying; and also by Sørensen when he analyzed the impact of tax coordination relative to income (re)distribution. See (Lorz, 1998; Sørensen, 2000).
8 For a review of the tax compliance literature see (Andreoni *et al.*, 1998).
9 Similar efforts are made with respect to determining the size of the money laundering problem, see (Walker, 1999).
10 Two Norwegian economists reached a different conclusion. In their paper they demonstrate 'that international spillovers from public goods reduce tax competition. In fact, in the case of purely international public goods, there will be no tax competition at all. Underprovision of public goods will however prevail due to the free-rider problem.' (Bjorvatn and Schjelderup, 2002: p. 119)
11 While a 'benevolent maximizer' state is not necessarily also a 'welfare' state, the challenge to increase (or even to maintain) tax revenue in the face of tax competition is felt to confront the welfare state more urgently, see (Tanzi, 2002).
12 There is a more fundamental question present in Alesina and Angeletos' paper concerning public perceptions of state social welfare support. These perceptions about the level of need and quantity of state welfare provision obviously have a direct impact on levels of taxation. For this latter question on social preferences, see also (Alesina *et al.*, 2001). For a discussion of the incorporation of morals and social aspects in economic research, see the review article by (Andreoni *et al.*, 1998).
13 As explained by Kay and King, residence is the state where one lived in a particular tax year; ordinary residence is the state where one usually lives; and domicile is the state with which one 'has the strongest associations'. While for many of us these are all the same, there are a number of UK citizens where it is not the case, thus the benefit of offshore banking.
14 As a starting point on this debate, see (Collison and Tiley, 2003: pp. 1197–1203). Naturally, as with all discussions of individual income tax, this comes with the standard disclaimer to consult with one's tax professional on one's individual circumstances.
15 While this approach reduces tax obligations to a state, it does increase the value of the firm to its owners/share holders (who are presumably

taxed in some jurisdiction). This tactic also intersects with the question of fairness and redistribution, as it benefits the few (owners/share holders) without redistribution of income to the many (public or public goods). Though if it is a publicly traded firm, it is possible those shareholders include mutual funds and pension plans, increasing the number of citizens that compose the 'few'. Furthermore, in a fashion similar to individuals renouncing citizenship, firms may undertake a 'corporate inversion', in which the firm 'sells' itself to an offshore affiliate for the purpose of transferring corporate residence (citizenship) in order to reduce its corporate taxes. This strategy became a political issue in the US in 2002, initiated after the announcement by Stanley Works of its intention to 'relocate' to Bermuda (Walker, 2002; Kun, 2004; Desai and Hines, 2002).

16 At issue is the legality of enforcement beyond the borders of the state in which the law has been enacted, particularly when in this case tax evasion is not consistently considered a crime in all jurisdictions. Nevertheless, Jeffery felt that 'To say that enforcement jurisdiction is the prime regulator in international law is to confuse theory with practice. Just because a law cannot in practice be enforced does not in any way relate to its legality or otherwise.' (p. 117)

Chapter 3 Global Financial Governance and Tax Competition

1 As discussed in the previous chapter, this is the argument made by Jeffery concerning the impact of globalization. As will be seen below, the OECD identifies globalization as a concern with respect to taxation as well.

2 In general see the work of Susan Strange and Philip Cerny.

3 See for example (Razin and Sadka, 1991; Avi-Yonah, 2000).

4 Prior to this, it was simply part of the underlying (predicate) crime that it helped serve to conceal, see (US Congress Office of Technology Assessment, 1995: p. 3).

5 However a caution is offered by Michael Levi, '...it is not clear how much Russian money was related, respectively, to drugs, to organized crime, or to capital flight searching for an economically and politically safer home.' (Levi, 2002: p. 189)

6 For more on the subject of money laundering and efforts to suppress it, see (Reuter and Truman, 2004; Gilmore, 2004; Cuéllar, 2003; Levi, 2002).

7 The argument that the OECD project is merely an extension of the long struggle within the EU to achieve tax harmonization may be overstated. Certainly, Japan and the Clinton Administration in the US were strong supporters for the project inside the OECD. For example, 'It is therefore not surprising that Japan, the most rapidly ageing OECD country, instigated the OECD work against tax havens and tax competition in 1995.' (Dwyer, 2002: p. 1) Further, it could be that government officials in Japan were concerned with the potential for increased tax avoidance by

citizens in response to several iterations of new tax legislation imposed during the 1990s (Seabrooke, 2006: Chapter 6, 'The Financial Reform Nexus in Japan'). Regardless, the confluence of the EU initiative with the OECD project would be too fortuitous simply to be coincidence; and the current state of play for the EU Savings Tax Directive reinforces the need for a global information exchange regime. See for example (Sharman, 2006: p. 31).

8 For an analysis of their calculations (which develops an argument that they are inflated as a result of the assumptions made in the analysis), see (Mitchell, 2001a).

9 Rajiv Biswas, a Senior Economist in the Commonwealth Secretariat has suggested that the OECD 'ring-fenced' out of the definition of harmful economic practices such things as agricultural subsidies (for instance the Common Agricultural Policy of the European Union) (Biswas, 2001). The absence of FDI however may not be critical, as discussed in Chapter 1 some research suggests that tax competition among states and sub-state entities for FDI has limited influence on business decisions. Much more important to businesses are matters of infrastructure, local workforce education and skills, political environment, etc. (a decision-making approach which has also been self-reported by major multinational corporations), see (Oman, 2000).

10 Recall the definition of avoidance – minimizing tax owed, *within the letter of the law*. This observation generally follows the hyperglobalist thesis as sketched out in (Held *et al.*, 1999: pp. 3–5).

11 This aspect of offshore finance is explored in more detail for several Caribbean jurisdictions in Chapter 6.

12 Doggart identified the US and UK as having deductions for corporate insurance premiums. However, this was something the US was also aggressively seeking to eliminate as a tax avoidance method. Captive insurance firms are not limited to corporations. Cooperative groups of US medical doctors also use them for malpractice insurance, a high-cost, high-risk aspect to practising medicine in a very litigious society.

13 Bermuda was highlighted in this report, as the destination of 'more than $2.5 billion' from Australia. For a perspective on the issue from the media in Bermuda, see (Ausenda, 2003a).

14 This could change if the supposition was confirmed that mobile capital will still escape from high-tax jurisdictions for lower-tax jurisdictions with sufficient power to avoid reporting the income gained by the citizens of the high-tax jurisdictions. In 2002, the US fell into this category of state.

15 There is a literature concerning the 'race to the bottom' thesis in both economics and regulation (environmental regulation in particular). John Hobson has argued that in the case of taxation it should more accurately be described as a 'race to the middle', see (Hobson, 2003).

16 However, 'Jersey, the other Channel Islands and many other low-tax or no-tax jurisdictions have stuck to tax systems installed up to 60 years ago. These systems were not designed to lure foreign investors and tax

avoiders but to raise sufficient revenue for domestic public expenditure needs.' (Doggart, 2002: p. 6) Thus, low domestic requirements resulted in low domestic tax collection receipts, and again, it is a matter of social preferences.

17 The sole exception made is for the accounts of Canadian citizens.

18 The assertion here that the United States possessed a preferential tax regime for the deposits of non-resident aliens is mine. As Langer (2002) reported, the US issued proposed regulations in 2001 requiring the collation of data on payments to non-resident aliens. Internal Revenue Service requirements on income tax withholding for non-resident aliens are contained in IRS Publication 545, 'Withholding of Tax on Nonresident Aliens and Foreign Entities' (Rev. April 2007) and available from http://www.irs.gov/. The only US preferential tax regime identified in the OECD reports was the Foreign Sales Corporation. See (Organization for Economic Co-operation and Development, 2000: p. 14; Organization for Economic Co-operation and Development, 2004a: p. 9).

19 Palan (2002, pp. 157–58) cites Robert Z. Aliber, *The International Money Game*, 2nd ed. London: Macmillan, 1976, p. 182.

20 In the case of Belgium this position is a change from an earlier approach to tax competition. Genschel and Plümper describe Belgium's efforts to limit tax competition in the early 1990s, first through the IMF, 'arguing that tax competition was a truly global problem.' When that initiative failed to gain purchase, Belgium turned to the European Community to pursue its goal to limit tax competition. (Genschel and Plümper, 1997: p. 632)

Chapter 4 Resistance and Withdrawal

1 (Strange, 1996: p. 93).

2 Experience has shown that courts, particularly American courts, did not agree with this perspective. Antoine discussed this problem in depth in (Antoine, 2002: pp. 282–292).

3 Hudson cited *US vs. Field*, US Court of Appeal, *Congressional Record*, 25 June 1976. Note that US actions are an example of the resolution desired by Jeffery, as discussed above in Chapter 3.

4 Sir Ronald Sanders was the Antigua and Barbuda's High Commissioner in London and Chief Negotiator on International Financial Services at the time.

5 Bishnodat Persaud is former Director of the Economic Affairs Division of the Commonwealth Secretariat, and an Honorary Professor of the University of the West Indies.

6 Among the participants in this outreach program, the only states previously identified as possessing an offshore financial center were Malaysia, Philippines, Singapore, and Thailand. China also participated, but whether this meant the interests of the Hong Kong and Macao SARs were represented is not clear.

7 Moreover, reviewing the list of 'cooperative tax havens' listed on the OECD's 'Tax Haven Update' webpage also shows that none of the six jurisdictions that provided a commitment to cooperate prior to publication of this report attended. See http://www.oecd.org/document/19/0,2340,en_2649_33745_1903251_1_1_1_1, 00.html [accessed 11 June 2003].

8 As an example, the relevant paragraphs from the Antigua and Barbuda commitment letter were:

The commitment is offered on the basis that:

> Antigua and Barbuda is not included on the OECD list of un-cooperative tax havens nor subject to any framework of co-ordinated defensive measures;
>
> Antigua and Barbuda is determined to protect its economic interests and fiscal autonomy in any future negotiations with OECD. The issue of a level playing field is critical to those interests.
>
> Those jurisdictions, including OECD Member countries and other countries and jurisdictions yet to be identified, that fail to make equivalent commitments or to satisfy the standards of the 1998 Tax Competition Report, will be subject of a framework of co-ordinated defensive measures; and
>
> Antigua and Barbuda is invited to participate fully on an equal basis with all committed jurisdictions and OECD countries in any discussion in the Global Forum on the design of internationally-accepted standards for the implementation of these and any similar commitments.
>
> (Office of the Prime Minister, 2002)

9 This statement was later contradicted by the definition produced by the OECD's 'Sub-Group on Level Playing Field Issues' in 2004, which emphasizes this it is 'fundamentally about fairness to which all parties in the Global Forum are committed.' (Global Forum on Taxation, 2004: p. 2)

10 The limitations inherent to this approach are recognized by the OECD's Committee on Fiscal Affairs. The 2004 project report declared 'that there are limits to the usefulness of unilateral and bilateral measures to respond to a problem that is inherently global in nature. Thus, the Committee has examined ways in which defensive measures may be co-ordinated to more effectively neutralize the deleterious effects of harmful tax practices.' (Organization for Economic Co-operation and Development, 2004a: p. 14)

11 In the document Jeffrey Owens was identified as Head, Fiscal Affairs, OECD.

12 See the frontispiece of any major OECD document for the membership list (and date of accession) current at the time of publication. A cynic could suggest that the *economic co-operation and development* aspects of the organization are limited to those states already developed, and extensively cooperating with each other.

13 It should be noted that the US was not the only OECD member to raise this concern, similar remarks came from Australia and New Zealand on

behalf of the Pacific island states with OFCs (Agence France Presse, 2002; Bingham and Andrews, 2001).

Chapter 5 Working Together – Small States in the Commonwealth and Elsewhere

1 See the *Festschrift* issue for Peter Lyon, *The Round Table*, No. 376, September 2004.
2 This statement has been made also about the Caribbean Regional Negotiating Machinery (RNM) by Bulmer-Thomas (2001, p. 367). For an example with respect to the EU see (Armstrong and Read, 2002a: p. 78).
3 See the Commonwealth Secretariat website at www.thecommonwealth.org/smallstates.
4 The historical origins of the Vanuatu offshore financial center were outlined in Chapter 1.
5 The Commonwealth jurisdictions listed were: Antigua and Barbuda, the Bahamas, Barbados, Belize, Dominica, Grenada, the Maldives, Nauru, Samoa, the Seychelles, St. Kitts and Nevis, St. Lucia, St. Vincent and the Grenadines, Tonga, and Vanuatu. The British Dependencies and Overseas Territories included were: Anguilla, the British Virgin Islands, Gibraltar, Guernsey, the Isle of Man, Jersey, Montserrat, and the Turks and Caicos Islands. Additionally, the New Zealand affiliated territories of the Cook Islands and Niue were identified as tax havens by the OECD.
6 These jurisdictions were: Bermuda, the Cayman Islands, Cyprus, Malta, Mauritius, and San Marino (all affiliated with the Commonwealth in some fashion with the exception of San Marino). See (OECD, 2003).
7 Participants at the meeting of Senior Commonwealth Law Officials in November 2001 remarked upon the fact that the representation to these meetings usually consisted of tax and finance officials. 'Other Senior Officials emphasised that taxation was a legal issue as well as an economic issue and therefore there was a need to be careful not to limit taxation to a mere economic concept.' (Commonwealth Secretariat, 2001h: p. 16) This point reflects the legislative necessities of the tax administration and legal differences between states discussed in earlier.
8 This news release was issued jointly by the Commonwealth Secretariat and the OECD Secretariat.
9 For example, the difference of opinion amongst Commonwealth members on how to respond to the unilateral declaration of independence by Rhodesia in 1965 was a crisis that overshadowed all other Commonwealth issues in the 1960s. See (McIntyre, 2001: pp. 31–37).
10 This demonstrates the changes that have occurred within the process of international negotiations since the end of the Cold War. Negotiations are no longer subject only to the distribution of power amongst participants existing in the previous environment of global insecurity. International negotiations are facilitated now by negotiation tactics that give 'weak actors' more influence. See (Singh, 2000).

11 A report in *The Financial Times* (London) stated that two Caribbean countries, including Antigua and Barbuda were 'suspending their commitments'. See (Warn, 2003).
12 The papers tabled and debated by the workshop participants were published by the Commonwealth Secretariat, see (Antoniou, 2004).
13 The organization was later rebranded as the International Trade and Investment Organization, see <http://www.itio.org/>.
14 Anguilla, Antigua and Barbuda, The Bahamas, Barbados, Belize, British Virgin Islands, Cayman Islands, Cook Islands, Malaysia, St. Kitts & Nevis, St. Lucia, Turks & Caicos Islands and Vanuatu; with the Commonwealth Secretariat, Pacific Islands Forum Secretariat, CARICOM Secretariat, Caribbean Development Bank and Eastern Caribbean Development Bank participating as formal observers.
15 Certainly, the case could be made that this particular 'professional community' was not the relevant epistemic community, and that in fact it included some of the elements that the OECD report sought to constrain.
16 It is interesting to note that this ITIO report *vigorously* avoided the use of the term 'offshore' – except in those circumstances where it was used by others, at which point it took exception to the term. This is perhaps an effort to incorporate non-self-governing territories into the responsible state (an OECD member), or simply because the connotation of 'offshore' implies a small island economy, which ignores the non-resident financial business conducted in a number of OECD member states. See (Stikeman Elliott, 2002: p. 10 and the associated citation to the Financial Stability Forum, Report of the Working Group on Offshore Centers, 2000).
17 The concern with privacy is an important yet possibly losing proposition in light of the efforts to increase surveillance, including all monetary/financial transactions, as part of the burgeoning 'war on terrorism.' See for example (Vlcek, 2008; Vlcek, 2007; Ball and Webster, 2003).
18 The preferential tax status of a corporation in US tax statutes is left unexplored, by both the OECD and the IRS in this context. However, the lower rate of tax on a corporation, versus individual income tax rates would suggest incorporation as a benefit for high net worth individuals, over and above the secrecy aspect.
19 Consequently, the campaign to outlaw corrupt practices globally, such as the United Nations Convention Against Corruption.
20 The relationship between France and its former African colonies were described by one author as 'fundamentally corrupt.' The Elf-Aquitaine affair is merely symptomatic of the complex economic nature of these circumstances (Médard, 1997: p. 23).
21 A similar concern involves changes made to US banking laws following the 2001 terrorist attacks, which also was raised in the Commonwealth Law Ministers meeting in 2002. 'Ministers noted that the provisions of the US legislation have the potential to circumvent mutual legal assistance treaties between member countries and the United States.'

(Commonwealth Secretariat, 2002: p. xiii) For more on the USA PATRIOT Act, see (Vlcek, forthcoming; Roberts, 2004).

22 See http://www.fsforum.org/compendium/about.html.

Chapter 6 Caribbean Offshore Finance Under Pressure

1 (Ramphal, 1984: 369).

2 For the argument that an offshore business sector has 'captured' the state apparatus, see (Hampton and Christensen, 1999; Hampton and Christensen, 2002). Similar to this is the concept of a 'shadow government', which one author identified as a problem in Belize. See (Duffy, 2000).

3 Another organization, the Alliance of Small Island States (AOSIS), addresses the common concerns and challenges facing island and low-lying coastal microstates (AOSIS is associated with SIDSnet – Small Island Developing States Network, the Global Network for the Barbados Programme of Action).

4 The effect of economies of scale on transportation services for example involves the number and frequency of airline flights and freighter visits, see (Titchener, 1992).

5 For example, consider the extensive evacuation and devastation of the Caribbean island of Montserrat, following the resumption of volcanic activity.

6 Paul Sutton, for example, felt that the effort to quantify vulnerability was unlikely to convince sceptics due to the 'multidimensional' nature of vulnerability (Sutton, 2002: p. 101).

7 Similar to this perspective is the business case used to explain foreign direct investment in manufacturing facilities. Recall the explanation offered for the decision by Intel to place a global facility in Costa Rica, which included political stability, infrastructure, and quality of life. See Chapter 1.

8 The other jurisdictions identified on this first blacklist included Belize, the Cook Islands, Cyprus, Gibraltar, Guernsey, the Isle of Man, Jersey, Israel, Lebanon, Liechtenstein, Malta, the Marshall Islands, Mauritius, Monaco, Nauru, Niue, Panama, Philippines, Russia, and Samoa.

9 In 1983, Richard Johns identified five major offshore financial centers in the Caribbean basin – Bermuda, the Bahamas, the Cayman Islands, the Netherlands Antilles, and Panama (Johns, 1983: p. 191).

10 Percentages calculated by the author from Eastern Caribbean Central Bank data on GDP by Economic Activity at Factor Cost, in Constant Prices (Research Department (Statistics Unit), 2004).

11 Percentages calculated by the author from Eastern Caribbean Central Bank data on GDP by Economic Activity at Factor Cost, in Constant Prices (Research Department (Statistics Unit), 2004). Total GDP in 1988 was 351.7 million Eastern Caribbean dollars, and grew to 415 million (constant prices) by 2003.

12 Percentages calculated by the author from Eastern Caribbean Central Bank data on GDP by Economic Activity at Factor Cost, in Constant Prices.
13 The data provided by the International Financial Services Authority of St. Vincent and the Grenadines.
14 Personal correspondence, 12 August 2004.
15 The Category 'B' Banking and Trust license is issued specifically to firms providing services to international markets and performing inter-bank transactions.
16 The taxes on international trade included travel & cruise ship tax and the Environmental Protection Fee imposed on all visitors as well as duties placed on imported goods.
17 This accords with the 'race to the bottom' thesis, see for example (Drezner, 2001). For the case of corporate income taxes, the thesis has been very effectively rebutted by John Hobson in (Hobson, 2003).
18 The membership of this synthetic entity remained the same as of July 2007, as verified in personal correspondence with the Bank for International Settlements.
19 In the case of the Cayman Islands, these international financial flows cannot be interpreted as simply an increase in non-resident funds on deposit in fewer banks. The large numbers of captive insurance firms and offshore hedge funds have vast financial assets that are also flowing through the Cayman Islands.
20 Near-term investment strategies have short time horizons. Huizinga and Nicodème looked for a lagged response to their policy variables, but found that 'there is no evidence that depositor response policy change is stretched out over more than a year.' (Huizinga and Nicodème, 2004: p. 1113)
21 But this does not guarantee continued success for the Cayman Islands, British Virgin Islands and other locations specializing in the registration of International Business Companies (IBCs). As discussed in the previous chapter, the OECD is engaged in a separate campaign to counter the use of 'corporate vehicles for illicit purposes'. Given the use of corporate entities registered in the Cayman Islands in both the ENRON and Parmalat corporate scandals, this topic will remain an issue of concern. See (Organization for Economic Co-operation and Development, 2001b).
22 Personal correspondence, 15 October 2004.

Chapter 7 A Future for Sovereignty at the Margins

1 Quoted in (Pozzolini, 1970: p. 21).
2 Again, the distinction between *residents* and *citizens* is important. Most states impose some measure of income taxation upon all residents, whether or not they are citizens of that state. In addition to this tax, some states have chosen to tax the global income of their *citizens* irrespective of where they reside.

3 In 2005, hedge funds received an increasing level of interest, both from investors and regulators. See for example (Zuckerman, 2005; Financial Services Authority, 2005).
4 Alternatively, as phrased by Alan James – 'It asks, who rules – or, who is sovereign? In so doing, it echoes a famous definition of politics as the business of deciding "who gets what, when, how". This issue is, of course, always of supreme importance to those who are engaged in the domestic political conflict.' (James, 1999: p. 458) James noted – 'This was the title of a famous book by H. D. Lasswell, *Politics: Who Gets What, When, How* (New York, Whittlesey House, 1936).'
5 Goldsmith recognizes the continuing hazard of spillover, where an action deemed legal in one jurisdiction causes harm in another jurisdiction. This spillover problem 'can be diminished through international harmonization. But they can only be eliminated by abolishing national (as opposed to international) lawmaking entities altogether, or by eliminating transnational activity.' (p. 488) This observation encapsulates the problem the OECD is attempting to identify and resolve with the harmful tax competition initiative.
6 For a critical view of the impact of this international financial architecture on developing economies, see (Soederberg, 2004).
7 The exchange of taxpayer information was incorporated in a 2004 revision of the OECD Model Income Tax Treaty. For a treatment of this change see Spencer (2005a; 2005b).
8 As the 2004 Report correctly noted, the Foreign Sales Corporation regime was abolished. At the same time, however, the relevant legislation also created 'extraterritorial income exclusion provisions' in US tax law. These new features for corporate tax preferences have also been challenged. For details on the current status of WTO Dispute Case DS108, 'United States – Tax Treatment for "Foreign Sales Corporations",' see <http://www.wto.org/english/tratop_e/dispu_e/cases_e/ds108_e.htm>.
9 For an analysis of the US Tax Information Exchange Agreements with the Bahamas and the Cayman Islands in the context of the OECD harmful tax competition project, see (Spencer, 2002: pp. 35–36).
10 Further details on Dispute DS 285, 'United States – Measures Affecting the Cross-Border Supply of Gambling and Betting Services', are available on the WTO's website, see <http://www.wto.org/english/tratop_e/dispu_e/cases_e/ds285_e.htm>.
11 Drezner noted a related phenomenon in his work, when states engage in 'forum-shopping' in pursuit of the international forum most amenable to national goals and objectives. See (Drezner, 2002: p. 35).

References

Andrews, R., Biggs, M. and Seidel, M., *et al.* (eds) (1996) *The Columbia World of Quotations*. New York, Columbia University Press.

Anonymous (8 Nov 2000) *General Assembly Commemorates 40th Anniversary of Decolonization Declaration, Declares 2001–2010 Second Decade for Elimination of Colonialism*. Press Release GA/9844, New York, United Nations.

Anonymous (2001a) Can't we all just get along? *International Money Marketing,* 12 April, 14.

Anonymous (2001b) Fur flies at OECD talks. *International Money Marketing,* 12 April, 1.

ABS-CBN NEWS (2003) *FATF accepts anti-money laundering changes*. Reuters/abs-cbnNEWS.com, 2003, last revised 4 March, available at <http://www.abs-cbnnews.com/abs_news_body.asp?section=Business&oid=17329>.

Agence France Presse (2002) Australia calls for OECD leniency for Pacific tax offenders. (Sydney) 1 March.

Albin, C. (2003) Negotiating international cooperation: global public goods and fairness. *Review of International Studies,* 29, no. 3: 365–385.

Alesina, A. & Angeletos, G.-M. (2003) *Fairness and Redistribution: U.S. versus Europe*. Working Paper, No. 9502. Cambridge, MA: National Bureau of Economic Research, Available: http://www.nber.org/papers/w9502.

Alesina, A., Glaeser, E. & Sacerdote, B. (2001) Why Doesn't the United States Have a European-Style Welfare State? *Brookings Papers on Economic Activity,* no. 2: 187–277.

Ambrose, S. E. (1986) *Rise to Globalism: American Foreign Policy Since 1938*. fourth revised ed. New York, Penguin.

Andreoni, J., Erard, B. & Feinstein, J. (1998) Tax Compliance. *Journal of Economic Literature,* 36, no. 2: 818–860.

Angara, E. J. (2003) *Lifting 48-year bank secrecy will scare away depositors, cause peso to depreciate, against economy & people*. The Manila Bulletin ONLINE, 2003, last revised 27 February, available at <http://www.mb.com.ph/news.php?art=28460&sect=1&fname=MN03022728460o.txt>.

Antoine, R. (2001) The Offshore Financial Services Sector: Legal Policy Issues on the Path to Development: A Legal Defence. *Journal of Eastern Caribbean Studies,* 26, no. 4: 1–27.

Antoine, R.-M. B. (1999) *Commonwealth Caribbean Law and Legal Systems*. London, Cavendish Publishing Limited.

—— (2002) *Confidentiality in Offshore Financial Law*. Oxford, Oxford University Press.

Antoniou, A. (ed.) (2004) *International Financial Services Sectors in Small Vulnerable Economies: Challenges and Prospects*. London, Commonwealth Secretariat.

Armstrong, H. & Read, R. (1995) Western European Micro-States and EU Autonomous Regions: The Advantages of Size and Sovereignty. *World Development,* 23, no. 7: 1229–1245.

Armstrong, H. W. & Read, R. (2002a) The importance of being unimportant: The political economy of trade and growth in small states. In Murshed, S. M. (ed.) *Issues in Positive Political Economy*. London, Routledge.

—— (2002b) Small States and the European Union: Issues in the Political Economy of International Integration. *Current Politics and Economics of Europe,* 11, no. 1: 31–47.

Arter, D. (2000) Small State Influence Within the EU: The Case of Finland's 'Northern Dimension Initiative'. *Journal of Common Market Studies,* 38, no. 5: 677–697.

Atkins, J. P., Mazzi, S. & Easter, C. D. (2000) *A Commonwealth Vulnerability Index for Developing Countries: The Position of Small States*. London, Commonwealth Secretariat.

Ausenda, B. (2003a) Bermuda – a magnet for Australian tax dollars. *The Royal Gazette* (Hamilton, Bermuda) 7 January.

—— (2003b) EU tax directive signed. *The Royal Gazette* (Hamilton, Bermuda) 11 March.

Avi-Yonah, R. S. (2000) Globalization, Tax Competition, and the Fiscal Crisis of the Welfare State. *Harvard Law Review,* 113, no. 7: 1575–1676.

Bacchetta, P. & Espinosa, M. P. (1995) Information sharing and tax competition among governments. *Journal of International Economics,* 39, no. 1–2: 103–121.

Baines, A. (2002) Capital mobility and European financial and monetary integration: a structural analysis. *Review of International Studies,* 28, no. 2: 337–357.

Baldacchino, G. (2000) The Challenge of Hypothermia: A Six-proposition Manifesto for Small Island Territories. *The Round Table: The Commonwealth Journal of International Affairs,* no. 353: 65–79.

Ball, K. & Webster, F. (eds) (2003) *The Intensification of Surveillance: Crime, Terrorism and Warfare in the Information Age.* London, Pluto Press.

Bank For International Settlements (June 2007) *BIS Quarterly Review: International banking and financial market developments.* Basel, Bank for International Settlements.

BBC News (2001) *US eases stance on 'tax havens'.* BBC News Business ed., BBC, 2002, last revised 20 July, available at <http://news.bbc.co.uk/1/hi/business/1446603.stm>.

—— (2005) *US and Antigua dispute WTO ruling.* BBC News, 2005, last revised 7 April, available at <http://news.bbc.co.uk/go/pr/fr/-/2/hi/business/4422457.stm>.

Biersteker, T. J. (2004) The Return of the State: Financial Reregulation in the Pursuit of National Security After September 11. In Tirman, J. (ed.) *The Maze of Fear: Security and Migration After 9/11.* New York & London, The New Press.

Bilefsky, D. (2006) EU looks to Asian havens for taxes on savings. *International Herald Tribune* 4 September.

Bingham, E. & Andrews, J. (2001) Islands face dirty-money backlash. *The New Zealand Herald* 3 March.

Bird, R. M. & Wilkie, J. S. (2000) Source- vs. residence-based taxation in the European Union: the wrong question? In Cnossen, S. (ed.) *Taxing Capital*

Income in the European Union: Issues and Options for Reform. Oxford, Oxford University Press.

Biswas, R. (2001) The Outlook for the Global Offshore Financial Services Industry. *International Capital Markets, Quarterly Review,* 21, no. 2/3: 58–66.

Bjorvatn, K. & Schjelderup, G. (2002) Tax Competition and International Public Goods. *International Tax and Public Finance,* 9: 111–120.

Blackmore, S. (1999) *The Meme Machine*. Oxford, Oxford University Press.

Briguglio, L. (1995) Small island developing states and their economic vulnerabilities. *World Development,* 23, no. 9: 1615–1632.

Buffini, F. (2003) ATO talks tough on tax havens. *Australian Financial Review* (Sydney) 7 January. sec. News: 3.

Bulmer-Thomas, V. (2001) Regional Integration in Latin America and the Caribbean. *Bulletin of Latin American Research,* 20, no. 3: 360–369.

Burn, G. (1999) The state, the City and the Euromarkets. *Review of International Political Economy,* 6, no. 2: 225–261.

Burton, J. & Parker, A. (2003a) Ultimatum to Caymans on EU tax directive: Caribbean territory urged to comply in crackdown on evasion. *The Financial Times* (London) 1 December, 1.

—— (2003b) Is the global crackdown on tax evasion 'slowing to the speed of the last ship in the convoy'? *The Financial Times* (London) 1 December. sec. Comment & Analysis: 17.

Cadacio, J. (2003) *U.S.-funded lobbying behind BIR reform, solons claim*. Today newspaper, 2003, last revised 18 February, available at <http://uw2.abs-cbnnews.com/abs_news_body.asp?section=Headlines&oid=16284>.

Cameron, A. & Palan, R. (2004) *The Imagined Economies of Globalization*. London, Sage Publications.

Cappelen, A. W. (2001) The Moral Rationale for International Fiscal Law. *Ethics and International Affairs,* 15, no. 1: 97–110.

Caribbean Media Corporation (2003) *Antigua Calls on Regional Countries to Withdraw From OECD Global Tax Forum*. BBC Monitoring International Reports, 2003, last revised 24 October, available at <Lexis-Nexis>.

Carroll, A. (2001) US ambivalence grows towards OECD initiative. *Private Banker International,* 14 May, 1.

Casayuran, M. B. (2003) *Senators decry FATF 'unfairness, bias' vs Philippines*. The Manila Bulletin ONLINE, 2003, last revised 15 February, available at <http://www.mb.com.ph/news.php?art=27761&sect=1&fname=MN03021527761o.txt>.

Caulkin, S. (2005) What's the big deal? *The Observer* (London) 31 July. sec. Business.

Cayman Islands Monetary Authority (1998) *Annual Report 1997*.

—— (1999) *Annual Report 1998*.

—— (2000) *Annual Report 1999*.

—— (2002) *Annual Report 2001*.

—— (2003) *Annual Report 2002*.

—— (2004) *Annual Report 2003–2004*.

—— (2005) *Annual Report 2004–2005*.

—— (2006) *Annual Report 2005–2006*.

Central Intelligence Agency (2002) *World Fact Book*. Central Intelligence Agency, 2003, last revised 1 January, available at <http://www.cia.gov/cia/download.html>.

— (2004) *World Fact Book*. Central Intelligence Agency, 2004, last revised 11 May, available at <http://www.cia.gov/cia/publications/factbook/index.html>.

Centre For Tax Policy And Administration *Centre for Tax Policy and Administration Brochure*. Committee on Fiscal Affairs, 2002, last revised 31 August 2001, available at <http://www.oecd.org/dataoecd/38/17/1909369.pdf>.

Chan, A. & Ross, R. J. S. (2003) Racing to the bottom: international trade without a social clause. *Third World Quarterly*, 24, no. 6: 1011–1028.

Clegg, P. (2006) The UK Caribbean Overseas Territories, New Labour, and the Strengthening of Metropolitan Control. *Caribbean Studies*, 34, no. 1: 131–161.

Cobb, S. C. (1998) Global Finance and the Growth of Offshore Financial Centers: The Manx Experience. *Geoforum*, 29, no. 1: 7–21.

Collison, D. & Tiley, J. (2003) *Simon's Tiley and Collison UK Tax Guide 2003–04*. 21st ed. London, LexisNexus UK.

Committee on Governmental Affairs (2001) *Testimony of Robert M. Morgenthau before the United States Senate, Permanent Subcommittee on Investigations*. U.S. Senate, last revised 18 July, available at <http://www.senate.gov/~gov_affairs/071801_psimorgenthau.htm [accessed 22 July 2002]>.

Commonwealth Advisory Group (1997) *A Future for Small States: Overcoming Vulnerability*. London, Commonwealth Secretariat.

Commonwealth Ministerial Group on Small States (2002) *Chairperson's Report to CHOGM*. 2002, last revised 1 March, available at <http://www.chogm2002.org/pub/reports/smallstates.html>.

Commonwealth News and Information Service (2000) *eNews for the Commonwealth*. Announcement for 'High-level Consultations on Harmful Tax Practices' to be held in Barbados 8–9 January 2001, London, Commonwealth Secretariat, last revised 23 November.

Commonwealth Secretariat (1985) *Vulnerability: Small States in the Global Society*. London, Commonwealth Secretariat.

— (1997) *Money Laundering: Key Issues and Possible Action*. London, Commonwealth Secretariat.

— (2000a) *Combating Money Laundering: A Model of Best Practice for the Financial Sector*. London, Commonwealth Secretariat.

— (2000b) *The Implications of the OECD Harmful Tax Competition Initiative for Offshore Financial Centres*. FMM(00)(O)4. London: Commonwealth Secretariat, Available: http://www.thecommonwealth.org/papers/oecd/FMM(00)(0)4.doc (7 October 2002).

— (2000c) *Commonwealth Finance Ministers Meeting St Julians, Malta, 19–21 September 2000 – COMMUNIQUÉ*. London, Commonwealth Secretariat, 2005, available at <http://www.thecommonwealth.org/Templates/Internal. asp?NodeID=141664>.

— (2001a) *Law in Cyberspace*. London, Commonwealth Secretariat.

— (2001b) *Commonwealth and OECD Countries to hold high-level consultations on 'harmful tax competition'*. Information & Public Affairs Division, 2005,

last revised 3 January, available at <http://www.thecommonwealth.org/Templates/Internal.asp?NodeID=34634>.
— (2001c) *OECD, Commonwealth Agree to Work Towards Global Cooperation on Harmful Tax Practices*. Information & Public Affairs Division, 2005, last revised 10 January, available at <http://www.thecommonwealth.org/Templates/ Internal.asp?NodeID=34633>.
— (2001d) *OECD-Commonwealth Working Group Continues Discussions on Tax Co-operation*. Information & Public Affairs Division, 2005, last revised 28 January, available at <http://www.thecommonwealth.org/Templates/Internal. asp?NodeID=34649>.
— (2001e) *OECD-Commonwealth Joint Working Group Concludes Meeting in Paris*. Information & Public Affairs Division, 2005, last revised 5 March, available at <http://www.thecommonwealth.org/Templates/Internal.asp?NodeID=34656>.
— (2001f) *Statement by Commonwealth Secretary-General on Document Related to Tax Talks*. Information & Public Affairs Division, 2005, last revised 28 February, available at <http://www.thecommonwealth.org/Templates/Internal.asp?NodeID=34653>.
— (2001g) *Joint Commonwealth-OECD Working Group on Harmful Tax Competition to Meet in London*. Information & Public Affairs Division, 2005, last revised 24 January, available at <http://www.thecommonwealth.org/Templates/ Internal.asp?NodeID=34632>.
— (2001h) 'Summary Record of Discussions for the *Meeting of Senior Officials of Commonwealth Law Ministries*.' London, 6–9 November.
— (2002) 'Minutes and Memoranda for the *2002 Meeting of Commonwealth Law Ministers and Senior Officials*.' Kingston, St. Vincent and the Grenadines, 18–21 November.
— (2003a) *Report of a Workshop on the International Financial Sector in Small Vulnerable Economies*. FMM(03)(INF)2. London: Commonwealth Secretariat, Available: http://www.thecommonwealth.org/papers/fmm/docs/FMM(O3)(INF)2.doc [accessed 8 September 2003].
— (2003b) *Small States: Meeting the Challenges in the Global Economy*. FMM(03)10. London: Commonwealth Secretariat, Available: http://www.thecommonwealth.org/papers/fmm/docs/FMM(03)10.doc [accessed 8 September 2003].
— (2003c) *Small States: Economic Review and Basic Statistics*. London, Commonwealth Secretariat.
— (2006) *Combating Money Laundering and Terrorist Financing: A Model of Best Practice for the Financial Sector, the Professions and Other Designated Businesses*. 2nd ed. London, Commonwealth Secretariat.
Cooper, G. S. (1997) Conflicts, Challenges and Choices – The Rule of Law and Anti-Avoidance Rules. In Cooper, G. S. (ed.) *Tax Avoidance and the Rule of Law*. Amsterdam, IBFD Publications BV in co-operation with the Australian Tax Research Foundation.
Cornwell, R. (2001) Commonwealth clashes with rich nations over tax haven clampdown. *The Independent* (London) 2 April. sec. Business: 17.

Council of Europe (1980) *Measures Against the Transfer and Safekeeping of Funds of Criminal Origin: Recommendation and Explanatory Memorandum.* Rec(80)10E, last revised 27 June.

Crawford, J. (1989) Islands as Sovereign Nations. *International and Comparative Law Quarterly,* 38: 277–298.

Cuéllar, M.-F. (2003) The Tenuous Relationship between the Fight against Money Laundering and the Disruption of Criminal Finance. *The Journal of Criminal Law & Criminology,* 93, no. 2–3: 311–466.

Cutler, A. C. (2003) *Private Power and Global Authority: Transnational Merchant Law in the Global Political Economy.* Cambridge, Cambridge University Press.

Delaney, J. K. F. (2003) Uneven Ground: The unlevel playing field for the world's financial centres. *The Nassau Guardian* (Bahamas) 12 February.

Deprez, J. (2003) International tax policy: recent changes and dynamics under globalization. *Journal of Post Keynesian Economics,* 25, no. 3: 367–384.

Desai, M. A. & Hines, J. R., Jr. (2002) Expectations and Expatriations: Tracing the Causes and Consequences of Corporate Inversions. *National Tax Journal,* LV, no. 3: 409–440.

Dixon, L. (2001) Financial flows via offshore financial centres as part of the international financial system. *Financial Stability Review,* no. 10: 105–116.

Doggart, C. (2002) *Tax havens and their uses.* 10th ed. London, Economist Intelligence Unit.

Drayton, F.-R. (2003) Anti-Money Laundering Legislation in St Vincent and the Grenadines. *Journal of Money Laundering Control,* 7, no. 2: 170–174.

Drezner, D. W. (2001) Globalization and Policy Convergence. *International Studies Review,* 3, no. 1: 53–78.

—— (2002) 'Who Rules? The Regulation of Globalization.' Paper presented at the Annual Meeting of the American Political Science Association, Boston

Duffy, R. (2000) Shadow players: ecotourism development, corruption and state politics in Belize. *Third World Quarterly,* 21, no. 3: 549–565.

Dwyer, T. (2002) 'Information exchange and global economic regulation – for whose benefit?' Paper presented at the fourth meeting of the International Tax and Investment Organization (ITIO), Port Vila, Vanuatu, 4–6 February.

Eastern Caribbean Central Bank, *Statistics,* available at <http://www.eccb-centralbank.org/Statistics/index.asp>.

Easterly, W. & Kraay, A. (2000) Small States, Small Problems? Income, Growth, and Volatility in Small States. *World Development,* 28, no. 11: 2013–2027.

Economics and Statistics Office (2006) *Annual Economic Report 2005.* George Town, Grand Cayman, Available: http://www.eso.ky [accessed 21 June 2007].

Edwards, J. & Keen, M. (1996) Tax competition and Leviathan. *European Economic Review,* 40: 113–134.

Eggert, W. (2001) Capital tax competition with socially wasteful government consumption. *European Journal of Political Economy,* 17, no. 3: 517–529.

Errico, L. & Musalem, A. (1999) *Offshore Banking: An Analysis of Micro- and Macro-Prudential Issues.* Working Paper of the International Monetary Fund, WP/99/5. Washington, D.C.: International Monetary Fund.

Faith, N. (1982) *Safety in Numbers: The Mysterious World of Swiss Banking.* London, Hamish Hamilton.

Feld, L. P. & Frey, B. S. (2002a) *Trust Breeds Trust: How Taxpayers Are Treated.* Working Paper No. 98, Zurich: Institute for Empirical Research in Economics, Available: http://www.iew.unizh.ch/wp/ [accessed 19 August 2004].

—— (2002b) *Deterrence and Morale in Taxation: An Empirical Analysis.* CESifo Working Paper No. 760, Munich: Ifo Institute for Economic Research, Available: http://www.CESifo.de (19 August 2004).

Feracho, J. & Samuel, W. A. (1997) Regulation and Financial Services Development in the ECCB Area. *Social and Economic Studies,* 46, no. 2 & 3: 231–270.

Financial Action Task Force (1990) *Financial Action Task Force on Money Laundering Report.* English ed., 2002, available at <www.oecd.org/fatf/pdf/AR1990_en.pdf>.

—— (2000) *Review to Identify Non-Cooperative Countries or Territories: Increasing the World-Wide Effectiveness of Anti-Money Laundering Measures.* English ed., 2002, last revised 22 June, available at <http://www.fatf-gafi.org/pdf/NCCT2000_en.pdf>.

—— (2002) *Review to Identify Non-Cooperative Countries or Territories: Increasing the World-Wide Effectiveness of Anti-Money Laundering Measures.* English ed., 2002, last revised 21 June, available at <http://www.fatf-gafi.org/pdf/NCCT2002_en.pdf>.

—— (2003a) *Press Release – FATF decides not to impose counter-measures on the Philippines.* English ed., 2003, last revised 13 March, available at <http://www1.oecd.org/fatf/pdf/PR-20030313_en.PDF>.

—— (2003b) *The Forty Recommendations (2003).* English ed., Paris, 2003, last revised 20 June 2003, available at <http://www.fatf-gafi.org/dataoecd/38/47/34030579.PDF>.

—— (2003c) *Annual Review of Non-Cooperative Countries or Territories.* English ed., 2003, last revised 20 June, available at <http://www.fatf-gafi.org/pdf/NCCT2003_en.pdf>.

—— (2005) *Annual Review of Non-Cooperative Countries or Territories.* English ed., 2005, last revised 10 June, available at <http://www.fatf-gafi.org/dataoecd/41/26/34988035.pdf>.

Financial Services Authority (2005) *Hedge funds: A discussion of risk and regulatory engagement.* Discussion Paper, 05/4. London, Available: http://www.fsa.gov.uk [accessed 22 August 2005].

Financial Stability Forum (2000) *Report of the Working Group on Offshore Centres.* Basel, Financial Stability Forum.

Fowler, M. R. & Bunck, J. M. (1995) *Law, Power, and the Sovereign State: The Evolution and Application of the Concept of Sovereignty.* University Park, Pennsylvania, The Pennsylvania University Press.

Francis, C. Y. (1985) The Offshore Banking Sector in the Bahamas. *Social and Economic Studies,* 34, no. 4: 91–110.

Friedman, T. L. (2005) *The World is Flat: A Brief History of the Twenty-first Century.* New York, Farrar, Straus and Giroux.

Fuest, C. & Huber, B. (2001) Why is there so little tax coordination? The role of majority voting and international tax evasion. *Regional Science and Urban Economics,* 31, no. 2–3: 299–317.

Genschel, P. (2002) Globalization, Tax Competition, and the Welfare State. *Politics and Society,* 30, no. 2: 245–275.
Genschel, P. & Plümper, T. (1997) Regulatory competition and international co-operation. *Journal of European Public Policy,* 4, no. 4: 626–642.
Gilmore, W. C. (2004) *Dirty Money: The evolution of international measures to counter money laundering and the financing of terrorism.* Third ed. Strasbourg, Council of Europe Publishing.
Global Forum on Taxation (2004) *A Process for Achieving a Global Level Playing Field.* Organisation for Economic Co-operation and Development, Available: http://www.oecd.org/dataoecd/13/0/31967501.pdf (12 June 2004).
Glynn, P., Kobrin, S. J. & Naim, M. (1997) The Globalization of Corruption. In Elliot, K. A. (ed.) *Corruption and the Global Economy.* Washington, D.C., Institute for International Economics.
Goldsmith, J. L. (1998) The Internet and the Abiding Significance of Territorial Sovereignty. *Indiana Journal of Global Legal Studies,* 5, no. 2: 475–491.
Goodman, J. B. & Pauly, L. W. (1993) The Obsolescence of Capital Controls? Economic Management in an Age of Global Markets. *World Politics,* 46, no. 1: 50–82.
Gordon, R. A. (1981) *Tax Havens and Their Use by United States Taxpayers – An Overview.* Washington, D.C., United States Government Printing Office.
Graham, E. M. (1996) *Global Corporations and National Governments.* Washington, D.C., Institute for International Economics.
Gray, S. (2002) Dust settles after general election upset. *International Money Marketing,* August, 29.
Griffin, C. E. (2000) Democracy and Political Economy in the Caribbean. In Griffith, I. L. (ed.) *The Political Economy of Drugs in the Caribbean.* Basingstoke, Macmillan Press Ltd.
Hall, R. B. & Biersteker, T. J. (eds) (2002) *The Emergence of Private Authority in Global Governance.* Cambridge, Cambridge University Press.
Hampton, M. P. (1994) Treasure Islands or Fool's Gold: Can and Should Small Island Economies Copy Jersey? *World Development,* 22, no. 2: 237–250.
— (1996) *The Offshore Interface: Tax Havens in the Global Economy.* London, Macmillan Press Ltd.
Hampton, M. P. & Christensen, J. (1999) *Treasure Island* revisited. Jersey's offshore finance centre crisis: implications for other small island economies. *Environment and Planning A,* 31: 1619–1637.
— (2002) Offshore Pariahs? Small Island Economies, Tax Havens, and the Re-configuration of Global Finance. *World Development,* 30, no. 9: 1657–1673.
Held, D., McGrew, A., Goldblatt, D. & Perraton, J. (1999) *Global Transformations: Politics, Economics and Culture.* Stanford, California, Stanford University Press.
Henke, H. (1998) Drugs in the Caribbean: The 'Shiprider' Controversy and the Question of Sovereignty. *European Review of Latin American and Caribbean Studies,* no. 64: 27–47.
Henley, J. (2003) Gigantic sleaze scandal winds up as former Elf oil chiefs are jailed. *The Guardian* (London) 15 November. sec. Foreign Pages: 15.
Her Majesty's Treasury (2001) *HM Treasury Acts Against Money Laundering Risks in Nauru.* Her Majesty's Treasury, 2005, last revised 14 December,

available at <http://www.hm-treasury.gov.uk./newsroom_and_speeches/press/2001/press_145_01.cfm>.

Hey, J. A. K. (ed.) (2003a) *Small States in World Politics: Explaining Foreign Policy Behavior*. Boulder and London, Lynne Rienner Publishers.

— (2003b) Introducing Small State Foreign Policy. In Hey, J. A. K. (ed.) *Small States in World Politics: Explaining Foreign Policy Behavior*. Boulder and London, Lynne Rienner Publishers.

Hill, C. (2003) *The Changing Politics of Foreign Policy*. Basingstoke, Hampshire, Palgrave.

Hinsley, F. H. (1963) *Power and the Pursuit of Peace: Theory and Practice in the History of Relations between States*. Cambridge, Cambridge University Press.

Hinsley, F. H. (1986) *Sovereignty*. 2nd ed. Cambridge, Cambridge University Press.

Hobson, J. M. (2003) Disappearing taxes or the 'race to the middle'? Fiscal policy in the OECD. In Weiss, L. (ed.) *States in the Global Economy: Bringing Domestic Institutions Back In*. Cambridge, Cambridge University Press.

Hochstetler, K., Clark, A. M. & Friedman, E. J. (2000) Sovereignty in the Balance: Claims and Bargains at the UN Conferences on the Environment, Human Rights, and Women. *International Studies Quarterly*, 44: 591–614.

Holzinger, K. (2005) Tax Competition and Tax Co-Operation in the EU: The Case of Savings Taxation. *Rationality and Society*, 17, no. 4: 475–510.

Hudson, A. (2000) Offshoreness, globalization and sovereignty: a postmodern geo-political economy? *Transactions of the Institute of British Geographers*, 25, no. 3: 269–283.

Hudson, A. C. (1998) Reshaping the regulatory landscape: border skirmishes around the Bahamas and Cayman offshore financial centres. *Review of International Political Economy*, 5, no. 3: 534–564.

Huizinga, H. & Nicodème, G. (2004) Are international deposits tax-driven. *Journal of Public Economics*, 88: 1093–1118.

Huizinga, H. & Nielsen, S. B. (2002a) The coordination of capital income and profit taxation with cross-ownership of firms. *Regional Science and Urban Economics*, 32, no. 1: 1–26.

— (2002b) Withholding taxes or information exchange: the taxation of international interest flows. *Journal of Public Economics*, 87, no. 1: 39–72.

International Financial Services Authority (2004) *Tracing the Development of St. Vincent and the Grenadines as an International Financial Centre*. 2004, last revised September, available at <http://www.stvincentoffshore.com/offshore_indus.htm>.

International Monetary Fund (2004) *Eastern Caribbean Currency Union: Financial System Stability Assessment, including Report on the Observance of Standards and Codes on Banking Supervision*. IMF Country Report No. 04/293. Washington, D.C.: International Monetary Fund.

ITIO (2003) *About the ITIO*. International Tax and Investment Organisation, 2003, available at <http://www.itio.org/about.htm>.

Jackson, R. H. (1990) *Quasi-states: Sovereignty, International Relations and the Third World*. Cambridge, Cambridge University Press.

James, A. (1999) The Practice of Sovereign Statehood in Contemporary International Society. *Political Studies,* XLVII: 457–473.

Jeffery, R. J. (1999) *The Impact of State Sovereignty on Global Trade and International Taxation.* The Hague, Kluwer Law International.

Johns, R. A. (1983) *Tax Havens and Offshore Finance: A Study of Transnational Economic Development.* London, Frances Pinter.

Johnston, D. J. (2001) *Commitment Reply Letter to the Minister of Finance, Aruba.* OECD, 2003, last revised 29 June, available at <http://www.oecd.org/dataoecd/12/56/1903656.pdf>.

Katzenstein, P. J. (1985) *Small States in World Markets: Industrial Policy in Europe.* Ithaca and London, Cornell University Press.

— (2003) *Small States* and Small States Revisited. *New Political Economy,* 8, No. 1: 9–30.

Kay, J. A. & King, M. A. (1990) *The British Tax System.* 5th ed. Oxford, Oxford University Press.

Keen, M. (1997) Peculiar institutions: a British perspective on tax policy in the United States. *Fiscal studies,* 18, no. 4: 371–400.

Kindleberger, C. P. (1987) *International Capital Movements.* Cambridge, Cambridge University Press.

Kobrin, S. J. (2001) Territoriality and the Governance of Cyberspace. *Journal of International Business Studies,* 32, no. 4: 687–704.

Kochan, N. (2005) *The Washing Machine: How Money Laundering and Terrorist Financing Soils Us.* Mason, Ohio, Texere.

Komisar, L. (2001) After dirty air, dirty money. *The Nation,* 18 June, 16–19.

Kondo, S. (2002) *Ending Tax Haven Abuse.* OECD, 2002, available at <http://www.oecd.org/pdf/M00028000/M00028566.pdf>.

Krasner, S. D. (1999) *Sovereignty: Organized Hypocrisy.* Princeton, Princeton University Press.

— (ed.) (2001) *Problematic Sovereignty: Contested Rules and Political Possibilities.* New York, Columbia University Press.

Kun, O. (2004) Corporate Inversions: The Interplay of Tax, Corporate, and Economic Implications. *Delaware Journal of Corporate Law,* 29: 313–375.

Langer, M. J. (2002) New EU, U.K., and U.S. Reporting Rules on Bank Deposit Interest Paid to Nonresidents. *Tax Notes International,* 28 January, 403–411.

Lasswell, H. D. (1936) *Politics: Who Gets What, When, How.* New York, Whittlesey House.

Levi, M. (2002) Money laundering and its regulation. *Annals of the American Academy of Political and Social Science,* no. 582: 181–194.

Levi, M. & Wall, D. S. (2004) Technologies, Security, and Privacy in the Post-9/11 European Information Society. *Journal of Law and Society,* 31, No. 2: 194–220.

Lewis, P. (2000) A Future for Windward Islands' Bananas? Challenge and Prospect. *Commonwealth & Comparative Politics,* 38, no. 2: 51–72.

— (2005) Unequal Negotiations: Small States in the New Global Economy. *Journal of Eastern Caribbean Studies,* 30, no. 1: 54–107.

Lorz, O. (1998) Capital mobility, tax competition, and lobbying for redistributive capital taxation. *European Journal of Political Economy,* 14, no. 2: 265–279.

Lucas, D. L. (2003) FATF: Meet the enforcer. *The Manila Times* 23 January.

Lyne, J. & Venable, T. (1994) Speed, Growth Drive Intel's Pick of Arizona for US$1.3 Billion Plant. *Site Selection,* 39, no. 6: 1006–1009.

Lyon, P. (1996) Small States Reconsidered. *The Round Table: The Commonwealth Journal of International Affairs,* no. 340: 399–405.

Madsen, R. A. (2001) The Struggle for Sovereignty Between China and Taiwan. In Krasner, S. D. (ed.) *Problematic Sovereignty: Contested Rules and Political Possibilities.* New York, Columbia University Press.

Martin, S. (2003) Bad money law sinks loan. *The Manila Times* 18 February.

Matthews, M. (2003a) Globalisation's 'dark side'. *The Nassau Guardian* (Bahamas) 16 September. sec. Business.

—— (2003b) TIEA will 'boost tourism'. *The Nassau Guardian* (Bahamas) 11 December. sec. Business.

McCarthy, I. (1979) Offshore banking centers: benefits and costs. *Finance and Development,* 16, no. 4: 45–48.

McIntyre, W. D. (2001) *A Guide to the Contemporary Commonwealth.* Basingstoke, Hampshire, Palgrave.

Médard, J.-F. (1997) France-Africa: Within the Family. In Della Porta, D. & Mény, Y. (eds) *Democracy and Corruption in Europe.* London and Washington, Pinter.

Mellish, M. (2003) ATO under pressure on tax havens. *Australian Financial Review* (Sydney) 6 January. sec. News: 1.

Menéndez, A. J. (2001) *Justifying Taxes: Some Elements for a General Theory of Democratic Tax Law.* Dordrecht, Kluwer Academic Publishers.

Minority Staff of the Permanent Subcommittee on Investigations (2001) *Report on Correspondent Banking: A Gateway For Money Laundering.* Washington, D. C.: U.S. Senate Committee on Government Affairs, Available: http://www.senate.gov/~gov_affairs/020501_psi_minority_report.htm [accessed 17 July 2002].

Mitchell, D. J. (2001a) *Oxfam's Shoddy Attack on Low-Tax Jurisdictions. Prosperitas* (Vol I, Issue I), A Publication of the Center for Freedom and Prosperity Foundation, 2002, available at <http://www.freedomandprosperity.org/Papers/oxfam/oxfam.shtml>.

—— (2001b) *The Adverse Impact of Tax Harmonization and Information Exchange on the U.S. Economy. Prosperitas* (Vol. I, Issue IV), A Publication of the Center for Freedom and Prosperity Foundation, 2002, last revised November, available at <http://www.freedomandprosperity.org/Papers/taxharm/taxharm.shtml>.

Monetary and Economic Department (2003) *Guide to the international banking statistics.* BIS Papers, No 16. Basel: Bank for International Settlements, Available: www.bis.org [accessed 30 July 2004].

—— (2006) *Guidelines to the international locational banking statistics.* Basel, Bank for International Settlements.

Monetary and Financial Systems Department (2005) *Offshore Financial Centers: The Assessment Program – A Progress Report.* Washington, D.C.: International Monetary Fund, Available: http://www.imf.org/external/np/pp/eng/2005/022505.htm [accessed 12 March 2005].

Morisset, J. & Pirnia, N. (2000) *How Tax Policy and Incentives Affect Foreign Direct Investment: A Review*. Washington, D.C.: The World Bank and International Finance Corporation Foreign Investment Advisory Service, Available: wvww.worldbank.org/research/workingpapers.

Morris, G. N. M. O. (2001) The Loss of Sovereignty, the United Nations, and Offshore Financial Centres. *Tax Notes International,* 23: 1297–1298.

Munroe, T. (2000) Cooperation and Conflict in the US-Caribbean Drug Connection. In Griffith, I. L. (ed.) *The Political Economy of Drugs in the Caribbean*. Basingstoke, Macmillan Press Ltd.

Nguyen, E. L. (2003) The International Investment Position of the United States at Yearend 2002. *Survey of Current Business,* 83, no. 7: 12–21.

Nordstrom, C. (2000) Shadows and Sovereigns. *Theory, Culture & Society,* 17, no. 4: 35–55.

— (2003) ICT and the World of Smuggling. In Latham, R. (ed.) *Bombs and Bandwidth: The Emerging Relationship Between Information Technology and Security*. New York & London, The New Press.

— (2004) *Shadows of War: Violence, power, and international profiteering in the twenty-first century*. Berkeley, California and London, University of California Press.

Oberg, C. (2003) A Balancing Act: Offshore Financial Centre Strategy and the Global Anti-Money Laundering Movement. *Journal of Money Laundering Control,* 7, no. 2: 153–157.

OECD (2003) *Tax Haven Update*. Organization for Economic Co-operation and Development, 2003, available at <http://www.oecd.org/document/19/0,2340,en_2649_33745_1903251_1_1_1_1,00.html>.

OECD Global Forum on Taxation (2003a) *OECD Global Forum on Taxation, Ottawa, 14–15 October. Closing Statement by the Co-Chairs*. OECD, 2003, last revised 16 October, available at <http://www.oecd.org/document/0/0,2340,en_2649_34897_16643264_1_1_1_1,00.html>.

— (2003b) *Welcoming Speech by Deputy Secretary General Hecklinger, OECD*. OECD, 2003, available at <http://www.oecd.org/dataoecd/13/20/16647699.pdf>.

OED (2002) *OED online*. 2nd edition (1989) ed., Oxford University Press, 2002, available at <http://athens.oed.com/>.

Office of the Prime Minister (2002) *Commitment of Antigua and Barbuda*. OECD, 2003, last revised 20 February, available at <http://www.oecd.org/dataoecd/0/6/2066005.pdf>.

Oman, C. (2000) *Policy Competition for Foreign Direct Investment: A Study of Competition among Governments to Attract FDI*. Paris, Development Centre of the Organisation for Economic Co-operation and Development.

O'Neill, P. (2001a) *Treasury Secretary O'Neill Statement on OECD Tax Havens*. PO-366 ed., Office of Public Affairs, 2003, last revised 10 May, available at <http://www.treas.gov/press/releases/po366.htm>.

— (2001b) *Statement of Paul H. O'Neill before the Senate Committee on Governmental Affairs, Permanent Subcommittee on Investigations, OECD Harmful Tax Practices Initiative*. PO-486 ed., Office of Public Affairs, 2003, last revised 18 July, available at <http://www.treas.gov/press/releases/po486.htm>.

Organization For Economic Co-operation and Development (1998) *Harmful Tax Competition: An Emerging Global Issue.* Paris, OECD Publications.

— (2000) *Towards Global Tax Co-operation: Progress in Identifying and Eliminating Harmful Tax Practices.* Paris, OECD Publications.

— (2001a) *The OECD's Project on Harmful Tax Practices: The 2001 Progress Report.* Paris, OECD Publications.

— (2001b) *Behind the Corporate Veil: Using Corporate Entities for Illicit Purposes.* Paris, OECD Publications.

— (2002) *Access for Tax Authorities to Information Gathered by Anti-Money Laundering Authorities.* Country Practices, Paris: OECD, Available: http://www.oecd.org/pdf/M00036000/M00036918.pdf [accessed 8 December 2002].

— (2003) *Revenue Statistics, 1965–2002.* Paris, OECD Publications.

— (2004a) *The OECD's Project on Harmful Tax Practices: The 2004 Progress Report.* Paris, OECD Publications.

— (2004b) *International Investment Perspectives.* Paris, OECD Publications.

— (2006) *Tax Co-operation – towards a level playing field.* Paris, OECD Publications.

Owens, J. (2001) *Promoting Fair Tax Competition.* Organisation for Economic Co-operation and Development, 2002, last revised 6 March, available at <http://www.oecd.org/dataoecd/63/11/1915964.pdf>.

— (2002) *The OECD work on Tax Havens.* Presented at the conference on 'Money Laundering and Tax Havens – The Hidden Billions for Development' held in New York on 8–9 July 2002 ed., OECD Centre for Tax Policy and Administration, 2003, available at <http://www.oecd.org/dataoecd/51/19/1940467.pdf>.

Oxfam (2000) *Tax Havens: Releasing the Hidden Billions for Poverty Eradication.* London, Oxfam GB, 2002, last revised June, available at <http://www.oxfam.org.uk/policy/papers/taxhvn/tax3.htm>.

Palan, R. (2002) Tax Havens and the Commercialization of State Sovereignty. *International Organization,* 56, no. 1: 151–176.

— (2003) *The Offshore World: Sovereign Markets, Virtual Places, and Nomad Millionaires.* Ithaca and London, Cornell University Press.

Palan, R., Abbott, J. P. & Deans, P. (1999) *State Strategies in the Global Political Economy.* Revised ed. London and New York, Pinter.

Paris, R. (2003) The Globalization of Taxation? Electronic Commerce and the Transformation of the State. *International Studies Quarterly,* 47, no. 2: 153–182.

Payne, A. (2004) Small States in the Global Politics of Development. *The Round Table: The Commonwealth Journal of International Affairs,* 93, no. 376: 623–635.

Peretz, D., Faruqi, R. & Kisanga, E. J. (eds) (2001) *Small States in the Global Economy.* London, Commonwealth Secretariat.

Perroni, C. & Scharf, K. A. (2001) Tiebout with Politics: Capital Tax Competition and Constitutional Choices. *Review of Economic Studies,* 68: 133–154.

Persaud, B. (2001) OECD Curbs on Offshore Financial Centres: A Major Issue for Small States. *The Round Table: The Commonwealth Journal of International Affairs,* no. 359: 199–212.

Picciotto, S. (1999) Offshore: The State as Legal Fiction. In Hampton, M. P. & Abbott, J. P. (eds) *Offshore Finance Centres and Tax Havens: The Rise of Global Capital.* London, Macmillan Press Ltd.

— (2007) Constructing Compliance: Game Playing, Tax Law, and the Regulatory State. *Law & Policy,* 29, no. 1: 11–30.

Pieth, M. (2002) Financing of Terrorism: Following the Money. *European Journal of Law Reform,* 4, no. 2: 365–376.

Pozzolini, A. (1970) *Antonio Gramsci: An introduction to his thought.* London, Pluto Press.

Ramphal, S. (1984) Small is Beautiful But Vulnerable. *The Round Table: The Commonwealth Journal of International Affairs,* no. 292: 367–371.

Ratner, S. R. (1996) Drawing a Better Line: *Uti Possidetis* and the Borders of New States. *American Journal of International Law,* 90, no. 4: 590–624.

Razin, A. & Sadka, E. (1991) International tax competition and gains from tax harmonization. *Economics Letters,* 37, no. 1: 69–76.

Report of a Commonwealth Working Group (1997) *Promoting Private Capital Flows and Handling Volatility: Role of National and International Policies.* London, Commonwealth Secretariat.

Research Department (Statistics Unit) (2004) *Statistics.* Eastern Caribbean Central Bank, 2004, available at <http://www.eccb-centralbank.org/Statistics/index.asp>.

Reuter, P. & Truman, E. M. (2004) *Chasing Dirty Money: The Fight Against Money Laundering.* Washington, D.C., Institute for International Economics.

Roberts, M. (2004) Big Brother Isn't Just Watching You, He's Also Wasting Your Tax Payer Dollars: An Analysis of the Anti-Money Laundering Provisions of the USA Patriot Act. *Rutgers Law Review,* 56, no. 2: 573–602.

Roberts, S. M. (1995) Small Place, Big Money: The Cayman Islands and the International Financial System. *Economic Geography,* 71, no. 3: 237–256.

Rodríguez-Clare, A. (2001) Costa Rica's Development Strategy based on Human Capital and Technology: how it got there, the impact of Intel, and lessons for other countries. *Journal of Human Development,* 2, no. 2: 311–324.

Rosenberg, J. (2005) Globalization Theory: A Post Mortem. *International Politics,* 42, no. 1: 2–74.

Royle, S. A. (2001) *A Geography of Islands: Small island insularity.* London, Routledge.

Ruggie, J. G. (1993) Territoriality and Beyond: Problematizing Modernity in International Relations. *International Organization,* 47, no. 1: 139–174.

Samuelson, P. A. (1954) The Pure Theory of Public Expenditure. *The Review of Economics and Statistics,* 36, no. 4: 387–389.

Sanders, R. M. (2002) The Fight Against Fiscal Colonialism: The OECD and Small Jurisdictions. *The Round Table: The Commonwealth Journal of International Affairs,* no. 365: 325–348.

Savona, E. U. (1999) 'The nexus between corruption and offshore financial centres: an introduction.' Paper presented at the Programme of action against corruption, 4th European Conference on services specialised in the fight against corruption, Limassol (Cyprus), 20–22 October.

Schulze, G. G. & Ursprung, H. W. (1999) Globalisation of the Economy and the Nation State. *The World Economy,* 22, no. 3: 295–352.

Scott, C. (24 April 2001) *OECD 'Harmful' Tax Competition Move May Violate WTO Obligations, Expert Says.* Center for Freedom and Prosperity, 2002, available at <http://www.freedomandprosperity.org/Articles/tni04-25-01/tni04-25-01.shtml>.

Seabrooke, L. (2006) *The Social Sources of Financial Power: Domestic Legitimacy and International Financial Orders.* Ithaca and London, Cornell University Press.

Secretary of State for Foreign and Commonwealth Affairs (1999) *Partnership for Progress and Prosperity: Britain and the Overseas Territories.* London, Her Majesty's Stationery Office.

Sharman, J. (2003) 'Small States and Weapons of the Weak in the Global Governance of Tax and Financial Services.' Paper presented at the Australasian Political Studies Association, University of Tasmania, Hobart, 29 September–1 October.

Sharman, J. C. (2005) South Pacific tax havens: From leaders in the race to the bottom to laggards in the race to the top? *Accounting Forum,* 29, no. 3: 311–323.

— (2006) *Havens in a Storm: The Struggle for Global Tax Regulation.* Ithaca and London, Cornell University Press.

— (2007) Rationalist and Constructivist Perspectives on Reputation. *Political Studies,* 55, no. 1: 20–37.

Sikka, P. & Hampton, M. P. (2005) The role of accountancy firms in tax avoidance: Some evidence and issues. *Accounting Forum,* 29, no. 3: 325–343.

Singh, J. P. (2000) Weak Powers and Globalism: The Impact of Plurality on Weak-Strong Negotiations in the International Economy. *International Negotiation,* 5: 449–484.

Skinner, Q. (2002) A Third Concept of Liberty. *Proceedings of the British Academy,* 117: 237–268.

Small States Task Force (2002) *Background Information: Progress on the Small States Task Force Report Agenda.* Washington, DC: International Monetary Fund – World Bank Group, Available: http://wbln0018.worldbank.org/html/smallstates.nsf/(attachmentweb)/2002SSFBckgrndDocENGLISH/$FILE/2002SSFBckgrndDocENGLISH.pdf [accessed 4 August 2003].

Soederberg, S. (2003) The promotion of 'Anglo-American' corporate governance in the South: who benefits from the new international standard? *Third World Quarterly,* 24, no. 1: 7–27.

— (2004) *The Politics of the New International Financial Architecture: Reimposing Neoliberal Domination in the Global South.* London & New York, Zed Books.

Solly, M. (1994) *Government and Law in the Isle of Man.* Castletown, Isle of Man, Parallel Books.

Sørensen, G. (1999) Rethinking Sovereignty and Development. *Journal of International Relations and Development,* 2, no. 4: 391–402.

Sørensen, P. B. (2000) The case for international tax co-ordination reconsidered. *Economics Policy,* 15, no. 31: 429–472.

Spencer, D. (2002) OECD Project on Tax Havens and Harmful Tax Practices: An Update (Part 2). *Journal of International Taxation,* 13, no. 5: 32–46.
— (2005a) Tax Information Exchange and Bank Secrecy (Part 1). *Journal of International Taxation,* 16, no. 2.
— (2005b) Tax Information Exchange and Bank Secrecy (Part 2). *Journal of International Taxation,* 16, no. 3.
Stikeman, E. (2002) *Towards A Level Playing Field: Regulating Corporate Vehicles in Cross-Border Transactions.* International Tax and Investment Organisation and The Society of Trust and Estate Practitioners, Available: http:// www.step.org/showarticle.pl?id=363&n=&toparticle=363 (7 October 2002).
Stoll-Davey, C. (2007) *Assessing the Playing Field: International Cooperation in Tax Information Exchange.* London, Commonwealth Secretariat.
Strange, S. (1996) *The Retreat of the State: The Diffusion of Power in the World Economy.* Cambridge, Cambridge University Press.
— (1998) *Mad Money.* Manchester, Manchester University Press.
Summers, L. H. (2000a) *Treasury Welcomes OECD Report on Harmful Tax Competition Havens.* LS-735 ed., Office of Public Affairs, 2004, last revised 26 June, available at <http://www.ustreas.gov/press/releases/ls735.htm>.
— (2000b) *Tax Administration in a Global Era.* LS-759 ed., Office of Public Affairs, 2004, last revised 10 July, available at <http://www.ustreas.gov/press/releases/ls759.htm>.
Suss, E. C., Williams, O. H. & Mendis, C. (2002) *Caribbean Offshore Financial Centers: Past, Present, and Possibilities for the Future.* Working Paper of the International Monetary Fund, WP/02/88. Washington, D.C.: International Monetary Fund.
Sutton, P. (2001) Small States and the Commonwealth. *Commonwealth & Comparative Politics,* 39, no. 3: 75–94.
— (2002) On Small States in the Global System: Some Issues for the Caribbean (with particular reference to financial flows and aid effectiveness). In Ramsaran, R. (ed.) *Caribbean Survival and the Global Challenge.* Kingston, Jamaica, Ian Randle Publishers.
Tagliabue, J. (2003) 3 Elf executives convicted of graft. *International Herald Tribune* 14 November. sec. News: 9.
Tanzi, V. (1995) *Taxation in an Integrating World.* Washington, D.C., The Brookings Institution.
— (2002) Globalization and the Future of Social Protection. *Scottish Journal of Political Economy,* 49, no. 1: 116–127.
The Cayman Islands Economics and Statistics Office (2001) *Annual Economic Report.*
— (2002) *Annual Economic Report.*
— (2003) *Annual Economic Report.*
— (2004) *Annual Economic Report.*
— (2005) *Annual Economic Report.*
The Central Bank of the Bahamas (2001) *Quarterly Economic Review,* 10, no. 1.
— (2003) *Quarterly Economic Review,* 12, no. 1.
— (2006) *Quarterly Economic Review,* 15, no. 1.

— (2007) *Quarterly Economic Review,* 16, no. 1. Nassau, The Central Bank of the Bahamas.
— (2003) *Quarterly Statistical Digest,* 12, no. 3. Nassau, The Central Bank of the Bahamas.
—(2004) *Quarterly Statistical Digest,* 13, no. 3 (Nassau, The Central Bank of the Bahamas).
— (2006) *Quarterly Statistical Digest,* 15, no. 3 (Nassau, The Central Bank of the Bahamas).
— (2007) *Quarterly Statistical Digest,* 16, no. 2 (Nassau, The Central Bank of the Bahamas).
Thompson, L. (2003) Clients' job to provide credit card data to U.S. IRS. *The Nassau Guardian* (Bahamas) 18 March.
Thorhallsson, B. (2000) *The Role of Small States in the European Union.* Aldershot, Ashgate.
Tiebout, C. M. (1956) A Pure Theory of Local Expenditures. *The Journal of Political Economy,* 64, no. 5: 416–424.
Titchener, G. (1992) The Role of Transportation in the Trade Patterns of the Lesser Antilles. In Hintjens, H. M. & Newitt, M. D. D. (eds) *The Political Economy of Small Tropical Islands: The Importance of Being Small.* Exeter, University of Exeter Press.
Tsingou, E. (2005) Targeting Money Laundering: Global Approach or Diffusion of Authority? In Krahmann, E. (ed.) *New Threats and New Actors in International Security.* Basingstoke, Palgrave Macmillan.
Tyler, P. E. & Hoffman, D. (1983) U.S. Invades Grenada, Fights Cubans. *The Washington Post* 26 October. sec. A: 1.
U.S. Congress Office of Technology Assessment (1995) *Information Technologies for Control of Money Laundering.* Washington, D.C., U.S. Government Printing Office.
United Kingdom. Public Record Office (1963) *Proposals for Establishment of a Financial Centre in Malta.* London, Archive Folder: CO 926/1862.
— (1970) *Tax Havens and Tax Concessions in the West Indies.* London, Archive Folder: FCO 44/356.
— (1973) *Tax Havens in Cayman Islands.* London, Archive Folder: FCO 44/861.
— (1974) *Investment Industry in New Hebrides.* London, Archive Folder: FCO 32/1101.
United Nations, Department of Economic and Social Affairs, Population Division (2007). *World Population Prospects: The 2006 Revision, Highlights,* Working Paper No. ESA/P/WP.202. New York, United Nations.
United Nations Security Council (2005) *Resolution 1617 (2005).* S/RES/1614 (2005), last revised 29 July.
Van Der Bruggen, E. (2001) State Responsibility under Customary International Law in Matters of Taxation and Tax Competition. *Intertax,* 29, no. 4: 115–139.
Van Fossen, A. (1999) Globalization, Stateless Capitalism, and the International Political Economy of Tonga's Satellite Venture. *Pacific Studies,* 22, no. 2: 1–26.

—— (2002) Norfolk Island and Its Tax Haven. *Australian Journal of Politics and History,* 48, no. 2: 210–225.
Vanistendael, F. (1997) Judicial Interpretation and the Role of Anti-Abuse Provisions in Tax Law. In Cooper, G. S. (ed.) *Tax Avoidance and the Rule of Law.* Amsterdam, IBFD Publications BV in co-operation with the Australian Tax Research Foundation.
Vlcek, W. (2004) The OECD and Offshore Financial Centres: Rearguard Action Against Globalisation? *Global Change, Peace and Security,* 16, no. 3: 227–242.
—— (2007) Surveillance to Combat Terrorist Financing in Europe: Whose Liberty, Whose Security? *European Security,* 16, no. 1: 99–119.
—— (2008) Development vs. Terrorism: Money Transfers and EU Financial Regulations in the UK. *British Journal of Politics and International Relations,* 10.
—— (forthcoming) A Leviathan Rejuvenated: Surveillance, Money Laundering, and the War on Terror. *International Journal of Politics, Culture and Society.*
Waincymer, J. (1997) The Australian Tax Avoidance Experience and Responses: A Critical Review. In Cooper, G. S. (ed.) *Tax Avoidance and the Rule of Law.* Amsterdam, IBFD Publications BV in co-operation with the Australian Tax Research Foundation.
Walker, E. (2002) Proposed U.S. legislation may close Bermuda loophole. *The Miami Herald* 1 July. sec. Business.
Walker, J. (1999) How Big is Global Money Laundering? *Journal of Money Laundering Control,* 3, no. 1: 25–37.
Walker, R. B. J. (2004) Conclusion: Sovereignties, Exceptions, Worlds. In Edkins, J., Pin-Fat, V. & Shapiro, M. J. (eds) *Sovereign Lives: Power in Global Politics.* New York and London, Routledge.
Walter, I. (1989) *Secret Money: The Shadowy World of Tax Evasion, Capital Flight and Fraud.* 2nd ed. London, Unwin Hyman Ltd.
Warn, K. (2003) Go-ahead for plan to crack down on tax evasion. *The Financial Times* (London) 16 October. sec. Asia and International Economy: 6.
Webb, M. C. (2004) Defining the boundaries of legitimate state practice: norms, transnational actors and the OECD's project on harmful tax competition. *Review of International Political Economy,* 11, no. 4: 787–827.
Wechsler, W. F. (2001) Follow the Money. *Foreign Affairs,* 80, no. 4: 40–57.
Weil, J. (2005) How Big Banks Played Key Role in Tax Shelters. *The Wall Street Journal Europe* (Brussels) 19 August. A1, 3.
Wight, M. (1977) *Systems of States.* London, Leicester University Press.
Wilson, J. D. (1991) Tax competition with interregional differences in factor endowments. *Regional Science and Urban Economics,* 21, no. 3: 423–451.
—— (1999) Theories of Tax Competition. *National Tax Journal,* LII: 269–304.
Witherell, D. W. (2002) 'Strengthening the Offshore Defences against Economic Crime and Abuse.' Paper presented at the 20th Cambridge International Symposium on Economic Crime, Jesus College, Cambridge, 10 September.
Woodward, R. (2004) Global Monitor – The Organisation for Economic Cooperation and Development. *New Political Economy,* 9, no. 1: 113–127.

World Bank (2003) *GNI per capita 2002, Atlas method and PPP*. World Development Indicators database ed., World Bank, 2003, last revised July, available at <http://www.worldbank.org/data/databytopic/GNIPC.pdf>.

Zagaris, B. (2004) OECD Issues Progress Report on Harmful Tax Practices and Outlines 'Defensive Actions'. *International Enforcement Law Reporter,* 20, no. 5.

Zuckerman, G. (2005) Hedge-Fund Firms Prepare For Costs of More Regulation. *The Wall Street Journal Europe* (Brussels) 9 June. sec. Money & Investing: M1, M5.

Index

Page numbers in **bold** indicate that the reference is to a table or figure.